C000144984

Investigating Farscape

Investigating Cult TV

Series Editor: Stacey Abbott

The **Investigating Cult TV** series is a fresh forum for discussion and debate about the changing nature of cult television. It sets out to reconsider cult television and its intricate networks of fandom by inviting authors to rethink how cult TV is conceived, produced, programmed and consumed. It will also challenge traditional distinctions between cult and quality television.

Offering an accessible path through the intricacies and pleasures of cult TV, the books in this series will interest scholars, students and fans alike. They will include close studies of individual contemporary television shows. They will also reconsider genres at the heart of cult programming, such as science fiction, horror and fantasy, as well as genres like teen TV, animation and reality TV when these have strong claims to cult status. Books will also examine themes or trends that are key to the past, present and future of cult television.

The first books in **Investigating Cult TV** series:

Investigating **Alias**, edited by Stacey Abbott and Simon Brown
Investigating **Charmed**, edited by Stan Beeler and Karin Beeler
Investigating **Farscape**, by Jes Battis

Ideas and submissions for **Investigating Cult TV** to
s.abbott@roehampton.ac.uk
p.brewster@blueyonder.co.uk

Investigating FARSCAPE

Uncharted Territories
of Sex and Science Fiction

Jes Battis

I.B. TAURIS

LONDON · NEW YORK

Published in 2007 by I.B.Tauris & Co Ltd
6 Salem Road, London W2 4BU
175 Fifth Avenue, New York NY 10010
www.ibtauris.com

In the United States of America and Canada
distributed by Palgrave Macmillan, a division of St Martin's Press
175 Fifth Avenue, New York NY 10010

Copyright © Jes Batis, 2007

The right of Jes Battis to be identified as the author of this work has been
asserted by the author in accordance with the Copyright, Designs and Patent Act 1988.

All rights reserved. Except for brief quotations in a review, this book, or any
part thereof, may not be reproduced, stored in or introduced into a retrieval
system, or transmitted, in any form or by any means, electronic, mechanical,
photocopying, recording or otherwise, without the prior written permission
of the publisher.

Investigating Cult TV Series
Hbk ISBN 978 1 84511 341 4
Pbk ISBN 978 1 84511 342 1

A full CIP record for this book is available from the British Library
A full CIP record is available from the Library of Congress

Library of Congress Catalog Card Number: available

Typeset in Palatino by JCS Publishing Services
Printed and bound in Great Britain by TJ International Ltd, Cornwall

Contents

List of Illustrations

Acknowledgments

This book would not have been possible without the help of colleagues, friends, and fans of the show. Thanks to Noah Porter, Sean Zwagerman, and Matthew Rohweder, who were some of the first people to read the early manuscript and offer suggestions; thanks to Angela Ndalianis at the University of Melbourne for publishing a version of Chapter 2 in *Refractory*; thanks to online fan communities like *Farscape-1* and *Frell Me Dead* for offering suggestions (and critiques) of the manuscript as it developed; thanks to Adam Garcia and everyone else behind the *Farscape Encyclopedia Project* who graciously agreed to have their work reprinted; thanks to Philippa Brewster, my editor at I.B.Tauris, who first took an interest in the project and was incredibly supportive from the earliest stages of the proposal to its eventual completion (she was also great at answering anxious emails from a neurotic author); thanks to Jessica Cuthbert-Smith, my intrepid copy-editor, who patiently helped me to revise the proofs and didn't even yell at me when whole pieces of the manuscript vanished into a wormhole; thanks to others who offered support and encouragement along the way: Rhonda Wilcox, David Lavery, Lorna Jowett, and Michele Byers; finally, thanks to all of my friends and colleagues at Simon Fraser University for providing me with such a nurturing and supportive environment to undertake yet *another* book project before defending my dissertation (special thanks to my supervisor, Peter Dickinson, for not killing me when I announced the project).

And thanks to the *Farscape* crew: Brian Henson, David Kemper, Ben Browder, Claudia Black, and everyone else who gave us four years of pure magic.

I hope you frelling love this book.

To Matt—because he lived to read this.

Introduction: Nightmares and Wonders

A Critical Introduction to *Farscape*

Once upon a time, there was a boy named John. One day, when John was doing astronaut things, a big blue wormhole gobbled him up, and spat him out at the far end of the universe.

—John Crichton (*Farscape: The Peacekeeper Wars*, Pt. I)

During its fourth and final season, *Farscape*—showcasing the imaginative power of the Jim Henson Creature Workshop, and helmed by Brian Henson—was the Sci-Fi Channel's highest-rated original series.[1] It created, and continues to create, a fiercely dedicated fanbase whose female component (48%) remains unusually high for an SF television program (Martin 1999). It was cancelled on September 6, 2002; by September 7 the fan-led campaign Save Farscape was already being organized (Porter 2005: 5). Those same fans would have to wait two years until Sci-Fi aired a miniseries, *Farscape: The Peacekeeper Wars* (*PKW*), in response to their criticism of the show's cancellation. But a four-hour miniseries couldn't possibly serve as closure[2] for an epic story like *Farscape*, and there were still a great deal of unanswered questions and plot imaginings, as well as concentrated fan discussion around the future of the show. Would there be a movie next? A second miniseries? A spin-off? And why had the show—nominated for an Emmy at the time of its cancellation (Sainsbury 2002)—been pulled when it was arguably doing so well? What did *Farscape* do wrong?

This book is about the opposite: what *Farscape* did right. Well, not entirely. It is not an uncritical celebration of the show; but, as the first book of its kind, it does bear a certain responsibility in terms of introducing the various social, imaginative, and fantastic engagements that make *Farscape* a natural target for scholarly analysis. I am not particularly interested in arguing over why the show was cancelled, but rather in discussing what made it such a fascinating and infinitely viewable text to begin with. There is a reason, after all, why *Farscape* fans are so enormously dedicated. Like fans of other prematurely cancelled series, such as Joss Whedon's *Firefly*, or Winnie Holzman's *My So Called Life*, they recognize when a show achieves a level of narrative complexity and emotional resonance that makes it 'special.' They know what was taken from them, and want it back. And they question the financial justifications, operating within a universe of marketing pragmatism rather than imaginative possibility and creative merit, that necessitate such a cancellation.

As one of these fans, I realize that it is impossible to separate my commitment to scholarly critique from my emotional engagement with the show. Impossible, and inadvisable; because critical acumen needs to emerge from a space of emotional connection and personal investment. It does no good to 'shut off' one's love for an object of analysis, because the result is a critique that makes no sense. Therefore, I am writing this book as an academic-fan. I love *Farscape*, but I also have no compunctions about criticizing it—and there are elements of the show that very much need to be criticized, just as there are elements that need to be celebrated. This book will attempt to do both, utilizing the broad discursive and material forces of gender, sexuality, and language as its primary framework for analyzing the show. Moya, as a living starship, has multiple layers to be uncovered, just as *Farscape*'s narrative has multiple social, sexual, and political investments as a televised text. *Farscape* remains genrebending, but it also builds upon and retains canonical elements of traditional science fiction—such as technology, alien encounters, and interstellar warfare—and those elements are what arguably make it coherent as a program to begin with.

The quote that I opened this introduction with provides a sort of macro-retelling of *Farscape*'s story. Crichton is relating his story here to yet another group of aliens, and it sounds like a fairy tale—to him, it probably feels like a fairy tale as well. In this sense, *Farscape*'s preoccupation with epic themes, symbolic archetypes, and dream visions places it firmly within the realm of the fairy tale, and, as Jack Zipes reminds (or cautions) us by reconfiguring Freud's definition of the 'uncanny,' 'the very act of reading a fairy tale is an uncanny experience in that it separates the reader from the restrictions of reality from the onset, and makes the repressed unfamiliar familiar once again' (1991: 55; 174). Crichton's obsession with wormholes, borders, space/time, is a mirror of the fairytale obsession with bodies, sexuality, and death. This builds upon Brooks Landon's assumption that 'while much of science fiction is not set in outer space, most science fiction rests on carefully articulated and demarcated spaces, or zones of possibility and impossibility' (Landon 1997: 17). The two preoccupations, spatial and organic, theoretical and physical, are linked. In this sense, the show truly is about a 'boy named John' and his dreams of adulthood, as much as it is about a man named John Crichton. Thanks to some time-hopping storylines, the audience actually gets to view both man and boy.

Crichton, an American astronaut played by Ben Browder, is indeed 'gobbled up' by a wormhole and then 'spat out' into far end of the universe:[3] the Uncharted Territories. In the beginning, his primary concern is simply to return home. But over time his emotional attachments, as well as his political and ethical commitments, branch out considerably. He learns to question just who the 'aliens' are in this story, and, by extension, to question and explore the multiple versions of humanity available to him. Crichton is the opposite of the Martian character Valentine in Heinlein's classic *Stranger in a Strange Land*—he is a human transplanted into an unfamiliar universe, and he quickly finds that certain 'human' characteristics are able to save his life, while others appear ridiculous, even offensive, to the aliens with whom he makes contact. Having grown up as a traditional 'SF geek,' Crichton's extensive knowledge of Earth pop culture allies him with *Farscape*'s own viewing audiences. Rockne O'Bannon, the show's creator, along with Browder, has stated in several interviews[4] that Crichton *is* the audience—that he represents their point of view within the *Farscape* universe. This is a point that I will discuss and problematize later—the notion that Crichton, an able, middle-class, heterosexual white male, is able to 'stand in' for every audience member.

John begins *Farscape* as the quintessential symbol of American idealism and expansion—the astronaut—and changes, through multiple circumstances and realizations, into a much less stable site where all kinds of interesting questions about technology, masculinity, and nationhood are able to converge. Browder, also in interview,[5] has pointed out that the show itself gestures towards the dissolution of a coherent American ethos, reconfiguring America as an 'alien universe' comparable to *Farscape*'s Uncharted Territories. Conceptions and critiques of nationhood are thus one of the organizing principles behind the show's narrative, even if they often occur subtly, or are eclipsed by the show's reputation as 'edgy' or 'sexy' rather than political. If anything, fantasy and SF genres are always over- rather than under-politicized; they always possess a surplus of political imagination and national prefiguring, given that they are so often occupied with explorer narratives and moments of first (alien) contact. *Farscape* is as much a show about cultural convergence, racial tension, and colonial expansion, as it is a show about astronauts, wormholes, and impressive explosions.

In fact, explosions—if they occur at all—tend to occupy only a minute or two of each episode (a very expensive minute), while rich and evocative dialogue occupies the remaining forty minutes. Part of what makes *Farscape* unique as an SF text is that it is often successful in combining character development with action, in ways that range from affecting to ridiculous.[5] An excellent example of this occurs in the episode 'Family Ties' (1.22), when Crichton and D'Argo are about to launch a last-ditch assault on a heavily fortified command-carrier—a maneuver that will most likely cost them their lives. Crichton asks D'Argo how he's feeling, and D'Argo's reply, 'I have to pee,' is perhaps the perfect response. Keep in mind that D'Argo is a seven-foot tall alien, called a Luxan, who sports tentacles and carries a massive sword which can also fire laser blasts. What is more improbable here? That he is a Luxan with tentacles and a laser-sword, or that, at the eleventh hour, as the episode reaches its climax—he has to pee? *Farscape* continually mixes the imaginative with the absurd in this way, poking fun at its own adoption of SF conventions even as it attempts to challenge and subvert them.

With every episode, the show offers a broad arena for social analysis, textual critique, and language-play. Literary theorists should pay attention to its simultaneous use and disruption of familiar SF generic codes (the space opera, the planetary romance, the modified frontier myth, and others) as well as its unique status as an SF text that concentrates more on interpersonal relationships than it does on scientific speculation. Language theorists should pay attention to the crucial role of alien vocabularies and communicative acts within the show, to its narrative reliance on speech and emotional expression; Camille Bacon-Smith is perhaps right in suggesting that 'it's the science fiction community that creates and popularizes the language with which we name the future' (2000: 1). Gender theorists should pay attention to its complex feminist commitments, its empowering—but not uncritical—depictions of female characters, and its various deconstructions of the type of heroic masculinity that normally drives fantasy narratives. Postcolonial and Critical Race theorists should pay attention to its nuanced treatment of global—indeed, intergalactic—expansion, as well as the multiple racial and cultural interactions that allow its story to take place. Finally, academics interested in Television Studies should pay attention to *Farscape*'s deft manipulation of the serial genre in order to create a fascinating televisual hybrid: an epic space opera[6] fused with a sprawling romance.

Like *Buffy the Vampire Slayer*, *Farscape* is one of those shows that often remains a guilty but unvoiced pleasure among academics. Whether 'SF geeks' or not, they are drawn to the tension between narrative complexity and total irreverence that makes the show so watchable. *Buffy* has, within the last two to three years, attained a certain level of cultural currency within academic studies. Thanks to the pioneering efforts of scholars like David Lavery and Rhonda Wilcox—arguably the founders of Buffy Studies—as well as innumerable graduate students who have passionately written articles and conference papers on the show, *Buffy* has invaded multiple academic spaces and transformed itself into a vibrant and interdisciplinary site of analysis. Given how dedicated, expressive, and imaginative *Farscape* fans have proved themselves to be, I suspect that they will whole-heartedly participate in academic discussions of *Farscape*, once the forum is established. And if academics continue to re-read, critique, and popularize the show through their analyses, then they will build upon what the fans have already begun by helping *Farscape* to survive, even grow, in spite of its cancellation.

This book has a lot of ground to cover, but I have organized it around the interconnected markers (something like socio-textual axes) of language, gender, and power within the show. *Farscape* is often cited as being a 'sexy' show, and there is, indeed, a lot of sex going on, most of it exotic and inter-species. The show's formative and narrative-driving relationship, between John Crichton and Aeryn Sun, is an inter-species pairing[7] whose undeniable sexiness often serves to mask the racial and cultural boundaries that are constantly at work within it. In this sense, citing *Farscape* as a 'sexy' program tends to belie its visible commitment to exploring links between race and sexuality, as well as its various deconstructions of gender. In this book, I will primarily be discussing the ways in which the characters' own unique 'performances' of gender and sexuality are defined within (and delimited by) structures of language and power. Language is perhaps *the* overarching force within *Farscape*, and it is only through the mastery and manipulation of various speech-acts, as well as multiple alien languages, that the show's characters are able to create themselves as social and sexual beings.

In the beginning, these characters are heavily embodied by symbolic titles that have been conferred upon them by others. D'Argo is a *warrior*; Chiana is a *tralk*, which translates loosely as 'slut'; Zhaan is a *priest*; Rygel is a *dominar*, an emperor only three feet tall; Aeryn is a *soldier*; and Crichton, of course, is a *human*. Throughout the show's progression, these terms fracture and become unmoored from their wider social contexts, as the individuals to which they belong learn to cite themselves differently. When John first boards the starship Moya, he discovers that his language is useless. No one understands what he's saying—even after they learn to translate— just as he doesn't understand most of what they're talking about. Gradually, he begins to adapt to their lexicon. He stops saying 'minute' and starts saying 'microt'; he stops saying 'hour' and starts saying 'arn.' Crichton's linguistic adaptation is a point of colonial interest, especially when he learns to use—and use well—what is arguably the most important word in the *Farscape* universe: *frell*. I will explain this in more detail later.

Much of what makes *Farscape* engaging as a program is its fascination with sexuality and gender. All of its characters traverse multiple gender stereotypes, often moving fluidly from one identity to the next, changing from episode to episode. Chiana is infinitely more than a *tralk*, although she does, in large part, help to explode the category itself by providing innovative and unique performances of it. Her sexual desire and commitment to pleasure, often read as excessive by the other characters within the show, opens up a vast terrain of analysis around the female body, sexual expression, and the fusion of language with sexuality—for, if any character on *Farscape* has mastered the act of 'talking sex,' it is undoubtedly Chiana. She expresses her desire as much through speech as through physicality, and the unique body movements—perfected by the actress Gigi Edgley—that are a necessary accompaniment to her speech patterns make Chiana's language all the more corporeal. Edgley's training as a dancer no doubt contributes to this, just as

Veronica Hey's background in avant-garde theater makes her comfortable with Zhaan's careless nudity. Chiana's stereotype as a seductress is not unproblematic, and I would argue that *Farscape* often misses the mark with her character, reinscribing masculine constraints around her even as they attempt to make her transgressive. But the show's very willingness to deconstruct this stereotype, to render Chiana as unapologetically sexual and then to explore what that might *mean*, is a critical gesture that deserves further attention.

Similarly, the pairing of Crichton and Aeryn provides multiple reconfigurations of the gender relations normally in place within science fiction and fantasy texts. On this issue—which I will discuss throughout the book—Vivian Sobchack insists that 'biological sexuality and women are often absent from science fiction narratives, and when they do turn up they tend to be disaffiliated from each other, stripped of their cultural significance as a semiotic relation' (1990: 103). Aeryn Sun represents several fascinating reversals of this criticism, which has emerged from multiple feminist quarters. When they first meet, Aeryn easily overpowers Crichton, pinning him to the ground and demanding to know his 'name, rank, and regiment' ('Premiere,' 1.01). Her physical superiority over him becomes commonplace within the show, in part defining their relationship, despite the fact that Crichton himself rarely seems uncomfortable with it. Aeryn is presented as functionally the opposite of Crichton—she is logical where he is emotional, she is strategic where he is impulsive, and she is disciplined where he is untrained. Crichton's own emotional expressiveness, his ability to empathize, remains something that continually baffles Aeryn.

It is safe to say that no other SF 'action hero' breaks down as much as Crichton does, despite his joking admission in *The Peacekeeper Wars* that 'Crichtons don't cry . . . often' (*PKW*, Pt. 2). His masculinity encodes a vulnerability that makes him unique within the SF genre, and this is due not simply to *Farscape*'s innovative writing, but to the willingness—indeed, eagerness—of Ben Browder as an actor to present himself as emotionally raw and physically violable, as opposed to the assumed inviolability of SF icons like Captain Kirk and Buck Rogers.[8] Crichton specifically and self-consciously distances himself from these figures, saying 'I am not Kirk, Spock, Luke, Buck, Flash or Arthur frelling Dent' ('Unrealized Reality,' 4.11). So who is Crichton? He answers the question provocatively: 'I am Dorothy Gale from Kansas.' Given that—at various points in the show—Crichton switches bodies with a woman, dons drag in order to infiltrate a proto-feminist alien movement, and is physically (as well as sexually) overpowered by several female characters, we may have to take him at his word. His own sense of masculinity appears to be as flexible as his evolving understanding of what it means to be human.

Science fiction as a genre continues to be under-represented within academic studies of gender and sexuality. Although edited collections on the generic construction and history of SF are numerous, similar discussions on sexuality within SF writing are limited—and discussions of queer sexuality are rarer still. The works of Lucie Armitt (1999), Brian Attebery (2002), Robin Roberts (1993), and Annette Kuhn (1990) are all relatively recent, and only a few queer academics (myself included) have evinced any sort of interest in writing on fantasy/SF literatures and cultures. In fact, most of the innovative scholarly writing on fantasy and gender to emerge within the past few years has been focused on *Buffy the Vampire Slayer*, whose genre-crossing elements make it a likely target for interdisciplinary analysis. Critics have, since the 1970s, written sporadically on gender and SF, concentrating mostly on the work of canonical 'gender utopia/dystopia' authors like Ursula K. Le Guin, Samuel Delany, and Octavia Butler. In terms of what Darko Suvin (1979) calls science-fantasy, fantasy-fiction, and other 'hybrid' genres, there has been very little scholarly material composed on gender relations—such as within the writing of J.R.R. Tolkien—largely, I suspect, because of his work's iconic impermeability. *The Lord of the Rings* is supposed to be a text about epic adventure and humanizing themes, not a text about sexually ambiguous hobbits and female marginalization.

But *Farscape* offers a unique vehicle by which to explore the various social and political investments that are always present in SF/fantasy writing, and which arguably define it as a genre that has emerged from earlier utopian literatures, as well as the *voyage extraordinaire* tales of H. Rider Haggard. Central characters within these types of narratives, because they are often humans that have invaded, or been invaded by, a secondary fantastic world (like John Crichton), bear a heavy symbolic weight in terms of transmitting both national and sexual values. Sometimes they act as Columbus figures who adopt imperialist attitudes, attempting to educate fantastic characters through the use of evangelical nationalism—but, at the same time, they are always transmitting a specific set of values around gender and sexual orientation as well, embodying not just the ideal normative citizen, but also the ideal hetero-human subject.

Even when a fantasy text's central character is not human, s/he still often stands in as a legible human subject who demonstrates the discursive categories that have historically made literary characters 'normative': whiteness, economic stability, heterosexuality, and clearly identifiable gender. But the supernatural worlds within SF narratives also operate as destabilizing forces, troubling these categories along with the very subjectivity of the characters who try to uphold them. In this sense, fantasy literature produces defiant spaces within which gender and sexuality can be split, troubled, and re-written along spectrums of plurality and variance. Characters in fantasy texts often 'get away with' peculiar gender performances, or blurrings of gender boundaries, because they are forced to negotiate these radically alien spaces.

SF literatures have long been criticized for their subordination of female characters, as well as their exclusion of racial and sexual minorities, and Rosemary Jackson's oft-quoted statement that 'fantasy traces the unseen and unsaid of culture' (1981: 4) does little to challenge or explain these absences. But characters like Chiana, Aeryn Sun, and even the coldly opportunistic Commandant Grayza on *Farscape*, all serve to trouble this idea of generic subordination. Rather than expressing, as they often do in fairy tales, what Lucie Armitt defines as 'the object which is lacking (conventionally the princess), but also the source of the lack itself' (Armitt 1996), women in *Farscape* are powerful, dynamic, sexual, and communicative. They aren't doing 'astro chores' and tending to the home fires like the women in *Lost In Space*; Aeryn, Chiana, and Grayza are all characters that drive *Farscape*'s narrative, often choosing to act while male characters like Crichton and D'Argo remain passive. Compared with *Star Trek*'s female character Seven-of-Nine—who spends most of her time in a skin-tight body suit for no discernible reason—or the sexless Captain Janeway, for that matter, or *Star Wars*' passive Queen Amidala in her ornate costumes, *Farscape*'s women are a great deal more interesting.

As Noah Porter points out in his article '*Farscape*: Gendered Viewer Interpretations in Virtual Community,' an analysis of the scholarly and popular material available on *Farscape*—specifically an analysis of fan discussion—reveals that 'the case could be (and has been) made for the gender roles on the show being either extremely progressive or rather misogynistic' (Porter 2006: 30). What remains clear is that *Farscape* fans discuss gender and sexuality on the show with the same critical interest as academics, and a quick survey of most *Farscape* message boards will reveal questions like 'how is Chiana being configured as a female character' rather than 'what is Ben Browder wearing in that episode?' *Farscape* fans are willing to critique the show, and part of its enduring power, I think, lies in its ability to critique itself—in the show's ability to irreverently send up its own conventions, as well as to thoroughly interrogate the ideal constructions of race, sexuality, and gender which remain the organizing principles behind most SF television. Exegesis before explosions.

Over seven chapters, this book will attempt to draw various links between gender, language, and power as they define *Farscape*'s multiple narrative threads. Why is communication so important to these characters? How do they empower themselves, or gain power over each other, through creative manipulations of language, and how do overlapping languages in turn attempt to define and control them? In what ways do they talk about sex, and in what ways does sex talk about them? Does *Farscape* offer radical and dynamic performances of gender—performances that break with the tradition of most SF narratives—or does it merely play with conventions while ultimately adhering to traditional gender roles on television? I can think of no other program that portrays an 'all-American' male astronaut who finds himself on board a living, female, *pregnant* starship named Moya. Crichton is, in fact, implicated in several birthing scenarios, and his involvement with female (and inter-species) reproduction is just one more fascinating articulation of his evolving masculinity.

Chapter 1 serves as a critical overview of *Farscape*'s main and recurring characters. It is divided into six subsections, treating Crichton, Aeryn, Zahn, D'Argo, Chiana, and Rygel, respectively. The characters of Pilot and Moya will be treated in Chapter 6. My goal with this preliminary discussion is to sketch out the world of *Farscape* for those who have never watched it, and to introduce the character interactions and tensions that will become material for analysis throughout the rest of the book. What is a Hyneirian Dominar? Who are the Peacekeepers? Why is John Crichton so obsessed with wormholes, and what is his intimate—and at times, I would argue, tensely homosocial—connection with a reptilian and cadaverous alien called Scorpius? Who are these escaped prisoners fleeing from, and what are they fleeing towards? How do they transition from a distrustful band of aliens to what Zhan and others term as a family?

Chapter 2 will discuss Moya, the living starship known as a Leviathan that serves as a moving 'home' for *Farscape*'s characters, along with her symbiotic relationship with the alien Pilot. Carlen Lavigne presents the crew of Moya as a familial structure, suggesting that 'if Moya is the mother, Pilot is the father, and both are completely subject to the whims of their children' (Lavigne: 2005). Moya is arguably the most crucial female presence on *Farscape*—literally keeping her crew alive—despite the fact that she has no definitive voice of her own, and is constantly being overridden by other characters. Her pregnancy in the first season is an inaugural moment that brings *Farscape*'s characters closer together, as well as an event that produces a 'hybrid' ship, half-Peacekeeper and half-Leviathan, called Talyn. This chapter will address several of the critical questions that Moya's presence in the show raises, including the invasion of her female body by aliens, the surveillance and appropriation of her reproductive abilities—by the Peacekeepers—in order to produce a weapon, and the broader implications of a 'biomechanoid' starship that thinks, feels, and loves.

Chapter 3 will deal specifically with the relationship between Crichton and D'Argo, and more broadly with alternative and evolving conceptions of masculinity that operate within *Farscape*. Crichton and D'Argo's interactions, I would contend, are far more complex and extensive than the standard socialization between two male characters on an SF program. In order to read the various masculinities at work within *Farscape*, most of them innovative and flexible, we need to look at the inventive and entertaining ways in which Crichton and D'Argo communicate, as well as the ways in which they configure their friendship as one based on mutual admiration, respect, and love. D'Argo is at first characterized as an 'alpha-male' character, a warrior, a general, and it is his aggressive masculinity that is most often in conflict with Crichton's. But what, precisely, does it mean for an alien to be masculine? How might masculinities translate between human and alien cultures, and how do Crichton's and D'Argo's own performances of masculinity actually complement each other?

1. Crichton and D'Argo floating in space

Chapter 4 will analyze the unique roles of Aeryn and Chiana as feminine counterpoints within the show. Aeryn's own sense of discipline, her rigorously controlled sexuality, and what Zhan calls her 'selflessness,' are all constructed in opposition to Chiana's capriciousness, her vocal sexual desire, and her alleged selfishness. But Aeryn is no more a 'soldier' than Chiana is a '*tralk*,' and both of these women spend most of their time reconfiguring such stereotypes and carving out new identities. Still, given that *Farscape* occurs from Crichton's point of view, there remains a great deal of investment in trying to 'figure out' these women, to 'chart' them through many of the same techniques that the Peacekeepers have used to map the Uncharted Territories. In some ways, the female bodies and minds in *Farscape* remain a final frontier, a realm off the map for intrepid explores like Crichton. Does the show thus attempt to colonize its female characters in this way, trying to mold them normatively through masculine effort into mothers, wives, and daughters? Or is their relationship to the show's narrative a good deal more complex than that?

Chapter 5 will address one of the concepts that, I think, makes *Farscape* such an original SF text—bodies and bodily functions. More than any other program on television—aside from forensic shows like *CSI*—*Farscape* keeps the audience's attention on bodily matters, and explores bodies as microcosms for more extensive social relations. The aliens in this show frequently possess bizarre and unfamiliar bodies; they bleed, cry, spit, vomit, urinate, defecate (often in front of each other), and lose control of their bodies in ways that make them increasingly vulnerable. Herein I will discuss various examples of this bodily permeability, as well as the relationship between body borders—what Julia Kristeva (1980) would call 'abject' substances—and spatial/temporal borders that can be penetrated via wormholes. In a show so consumed by borders and boundaries, it is impossible to discuss the penetration of space/time without discussing the penetration of its characters' bodies and minds. It also remains ironic that Rygel, the center of most disturbing bodily activity on *Farscape*, is the show's tiniest character. His stature may be small, but his body is impressively vocal, gesturing to all kinds of bodily speech practices that exist beneath (or are extensions of) the linguistic level.

Chapter 6 will deal primarily with language-power and language-play in *Farscape*. Although Crichton is injected with 'translator microbes'[9] in the series premier, which allow him to understand most alien languages, there is still a great deal of speech material that he doesn't comprehend. In the beginning, it is often a question of Crichton's language against competing alien languages, and thus a battle between familiar pop-culture knowledge and exotic alien concepts. But as Crichton adapts to the *Farscape* universe, he also modifies and expands his own language practices in ways that allow him not just to communicate with his friends, but to survive as well. This chapter's focus on language extends to *Farscape*'s emphasis on interpersonal (and inter-alien) communication, and will discuss the show's privileging of evocative dialogue over action sequences. Plus, it will answer burning questions, such as: what are *mivonks*? Who aboard Moya is *magra-fahrbot*, and just what the *frell* is going on in this show.

Finally, Chapter 7 will take up questions of nationhood, technology, and colonial expansion within the show. Crichton, we must remember, is not merely figured as a 'human'—he is always and continually defined as an American astronaut, an emissary of the

United States, and thus a symbolic reservoir of uniquely American ideologies and practices. Crichton's main adversaries are the Scarrans and the Sebacean Peacekeepers—the latter genetically linked to humans—whose enthusiastic commitment to a project of interstellar mapping and conquest renders them as coherent reflections of human civilization. My goal with this chapter is to discuss the various colonizing techniques of these aliens, as well as Crichton's own questioning of what it means to be 'American' when America is on the other side of a wormhole. How do Crichton's own ideals of nationhood influence his character, and how does he, in turn, deconstruct and challenge those ideals as he comes in contact with alien cultures?

This book attempts to be as interdisciplinary and flexible as possible, while using language, gender, and sexuality as social templates by which to analyze *Farscape* as a text. I recognize that simply gesturing towards articulations of gender and sexuality within a text—like points on a map—does not represent responsible analysis, and thus I intend to look at *Farscape* structurally as well, analyzing the literary, visual, and economic forces that make it viewable. It is not 'simply' a story about gender relations, just as it is not 'simply' a story about wormholes, astronauts, and pulse rifles. *Farscape* contains and plays with the properties of several literary/ media genres, including the space opera, the soap opera, the action film, the comedy, the horror, and something more disassociated that we might call 'postmodern,' non-linear, dreamlike, poetic. It is about a boy named John, an astronaut named John Crichton, and a little piece of knowledge stuck inside a human's brain that all sorts of alien races would kill to possess. It is about a girl named Aeryn, and a soldier named Aeryn Sun, and the journey that she makes as a result of meeting Crichton. It is about a ship named Moya, a caretaker named Pilot, and the various attempts of these characters to define their daily lives against the exotic forces that are constantly invading and threatening them. And it is about home: where it is, how you lose it, where you rediscover it, and how people seem to create it wherever they go.

The title of this introduction, 'Nightmares and Wonders,' references John Crichton's address to the audience at the beginning of every *Farscape* episode. 'My name is John Crichton, an astronaut,' he begins, and proceeds to relate the story of the show. This address changes from Seasons 1–4, and the version that I have chosen is from

Season 3, because I think that it most clearly voices the tensions in *Farscape* between wonder and fear, innocence and suspicion, tolerance and rejection, community and exile. 'Earth is unprepared for the nightmares I've seen,' Crichton says, referring to the countless alien forces that have threatened his life. And thus he poses the question that will drive his character throughout the show's narrative. Addressing Earth itself, he asks: 'should I stay . . . and not show them you exist? But then you'll never know the wonders I've seen' (*Farscape*, Seasons 1–4, Credits). Crichton is continually torn between protecting Earth from 'nightmares,' and protecting alien cultures from Earth. Often, he can't discern the nightmares from the wonders. But he tries.

There are countless things that I won't be able to talk about in this book, but I am confident that other scholars will pick up where it leaves off, utilizing it, expanding upon it, and critiquing it where necessary. Other books might be written specifically on *Farscape*'s use of theoretical science; its racial and cultural relations; its costumes, prosthetics, and effects; its vast alien anthropologies and histories; and its critical relationships to other SF benchmarks like *Star Trek* and *Star Wars*. I have chosen to address, primarily, sex and gender because it is what makes *Farscape* most interesting to me. It is, I think, what makes the show transgressive within its own genre, producing radical versions of masculinity and femininity that break with SF conventions, and offer a sort of living space for alternative genders. As a queer theorist and scholar of gender studies, I first connected with *Farscape* because it depicted characters whose sexuality was interesting, and whose experiences of gender remained fluid, ambivalent, and challenging. I would contend that female and queer viewers are drawn to *Farscape* for the same reason, and thus the show presents something rare: an SF text, within a genre supposedly designed for straight white men, that women and queer viewers can emotionally identify with.

There is also the simple fact that I love the show, and that I want others—academics and non-academics alike—to watch it and appreciate it. I want, in that sense, to talk about the 'wonders I've seen' on the show, as well as the potential 'nightmares' that ought to be dealt with and criticized. In the interest of reaching a broad audience, I have tried to make my analysis scholarly but accessible, rigorous but anecdotal at the same time. I am not interested in merely fostering a small audience of academic *Farscape* writers, but in tackling in as critical a way as possible the questions and issues that the fans themselves have raised. I hope that, by the end of this book, you too will fall just a little bit in love with these characters; that you too will daydream about living starships, Luxan warriors, and tiny Dominars. Dreaming is what *Farscape* is all about, after all—dreaming the human, dreaming the nation, dreaming cultures, and dreaming, ultimately, of home.

So read a little. Dream a little *Farscape* with me.

Prisoners and Friends
The People of *Farscape*

The strangeness of the Other, [its] irreducibility to the I, to my thoughts and my possessions, is precisely accomplished as a calling into question of my spontaneity, as *ethics* . . . as the ethics that accomplishes the critical essence of knowledge.

—Emmanuel Lévinas (1969: 33; 43)[1]

Close Encounters my ass.

—John Crichton ('Premiere,' 1.01)

Farscape is big. Like Moya, it overwhelms us. It presents us with vast worlds, complex alien cultures, impenetrable mysticism and super-natural events, and a large cast of characters with their own unique narratives and histories. There are no disposable ensigns on *Moya*, and no throwaway aliens—everyone *matters*, and every piece of crazy and delightful intertext eventually returns to haunt (or please) the viewer. When I first sat down to write this introductory chapter, I was surprised at how erratically it took form, how many fits and starts were necessary to produce something that finally made sense. Having watched every episode of *Farscape*, including the *Peacekeeper Wars* miniseries, and having already plotted out each chapter of this book, it seemed as if writing this particular chapter—merely an introduction to *Farscape*'s narrative themes and character interactions—should prove easy.

After all—there was certainly no lack of material to discuss. *Farscape* is officially 'over' as a program (but not yet over as a text, given John Fiske's assertion that 'a program becomes a text at the moment of reading, that is, when its interaction with one of its many audiences activates some of the meanings/pleasures that it is capable of provoking' [1978: 14]), yet it continues to intrigue, affect, and trouble both academics and fans, including academic-fans like me.

There remain many episodes that I can watch over and over again, still engrossed (or traumatized) by them, despite the fact that I know the dialogue by heart, that there are no surprises left. Most, but not all, of these episodes are among the show's saddest: Zhaan's death in 'Wait for the Wheel' (3.04), especially the moment when she names Crichton 'innocent'; Chiana's desolation and loneliness on the royal cemetery planet, which is also a moment of fierce defiance for her, as she tells Crichton that 'I'm only your *tralk* in your dreams' ('Taking the Stone,' 2.03); and, of course, the Season 4 finale, wherein Aeryn's last words—'you and your timing,' in an episode aptly named 'Bad Timing' (4.22)—are a sublime send-off to four years' worth of chaotic events, bizarre surprises, and highly creative validations of Heisenberg's Uncertainty Principle as it applies to both cosmological phenomena and televisual narratives. And you will have to pardon my layman's use of cosmological vocabulary throughout this book, but it seems, given *Farscape*'s bridging of 'hard' SF with serial drama, an appropriate framing device.

In spite of all this theorizing, I have had a lot of trouble beginning this chapter, and still more finishing it. Part of this is the pressure that I feel in writing critically about a show that hasn't yet received a great deal of scholarly treatment. Another part stems from *Farscape*'s generic indeterminacy, or its location as what Darko Suvin (1979) calls a 'science-fantasy' text, which is a sort of hybrid SF/fantasy genre that requires analytical double-duty. But I believe that the bulk of this anxiety, this hesitancy, emerges from a sense of honor and loyalty that I feel, both to *Farscape*'s characters and to its creators. I want to make the show as accessible as possible; I want to make it as psychologically engaging and socially troubling as possible; and I want to introduce it to a range of new audiences, both popular and academic. But I also need to point to its gaps, its problems, its various exclusions as an SF program that still has to follow traditional generic constraints, and thus misses the mark in terms of cultural representation nearly as often as it succeeds.

And perhaps I'm merely being self-important and neurotic here, especially considering that this is only one book about one show that was cancelled over two years ago. *Farscape*, however, has never been just 'one show'—it has always occupied, within both the psychological landscapes and textual (re)productions of its fans, multiple terrains of imaginative possibility and cultural exploration. The show has, in spite of the external forces marshaled against it—such as network pressure, production costs, and conservative critics looking for *90210 In Space*—always presented itself within an epic, self-important register, which is what makes it such a classic SF narrative; but it also remains a thoroughly neurotic and fractured text, which is what gives it the ability to critique SF as a genre while still hovering (somewhat like Rygel's floating throne) around its discursive edges.

One of the primary elements that separates *Farscape* from more traditional SF shows like *Star Trek* is its positioning of John Crichton, the human character, as an alien other, rather than as the standard human anthropologist/captain who studies alien cultures with keen fascination. In the Uncharted Territories, Crichton himself is the alien, and the crew of Moya find him to be confusing, inscrutable, even primitive. He is an alternative version of what Gayatri Spivak (1999) calls the 'native informant,' providing a window into human cultural interactions and social performances, while retaining the privilege and 'western' currency—at least among the show's audiences—that traditional native subjects are crucially denied as they perform their own stories and histories for white western spectators.

'What is *wrong* with you people?'[2] John demands in the premiere episode of the show, just before he is knocked unconscious by an alien with a venomous tongue. That alien is D'Argo, a tentacled, tattooed, ill-tempered Luxan warrior, who—eventually—becomes John's closest friend. But before this friendship emerges, and before Moya's mismatched crew of prisoners and political exiles begin to bond with each other, John's question remains quite appropriate. What *is* wrong with these people? Where do they come from, why do they act the way they do, and why is John so often bewildered, frightened, and—at times—repulsed by them? Clearly, his human (and North American) perspective needs a bit of broadening in order to take in the variety of alien cultures and languages that proliferate aboard Moya. But it is also a question of ethical positioning. Crichton, through his American moral and ideological frameworks, presupposes a discrete set of rules for social interaction that should be operational everywhere—even halfway across the universe. These aliens—'my friends,' as he later calls them—help to convince John over time that his perspectives are just one model among many that exist in the Uncharted Territories, like one of the many potential realities[3] that exist on the other side of an unstable wormhole.

When Crichton exclaims that 'humans are superior!' in the episode 'Crackers Don't Matter' (2.04), with his face covered in alien goo, wearing oversized goggles and a superhero-style cape, and carrying what looks suspiciously like a manhole cover as a shield, the show's playful deconstruction of human evolutionary prowess also encodes a more critical subversive edge. Human superiority—within social, political, and technological arenas—is a point that *Farscape* continually debates; and, although this debate is echoed in pseudo-anthropological concepts like *Star Trek*'s 'prime directive,' I would contend that more traditional SF programs eventually come around to establishing human ethical superiority, whereas riskier shows like *Farscape* are willing to challenge this assumption from multiple angles.

The goal of this chapter is to introduce the principal characters of the show, and, in so doing, to expand its deceptively simple premise—a human astronaut gets sucked into a wormhole—by gesturing towards the multiple ways in which these characters challenge and complicate that original premise. Ultimately, *Farscape* is a rich and powerful text that narrates the lives of enduring characters, and—despite its incorporation of alien technologies, space combat, and fast-paced action sequences—without the idiosyncratic and lovable material of these characters' lives, the story itself would have no real currency. Viewers care intensely about Captain Kirk and Buck Rogers, but rarely do they get to see these generic (and masculine) icons in positions of emotional distress, physical and psychic vulnerability, or familial intimacy. With *Farscape*, there is rarely a time in which the viewer *doesn't* see Crichton, D'Argo, Zhaan, or Chiana in a position fraught with psychological trauma. These characters are in a constant state of low-grade emotional turmoil and life-threatening danger, always on the move, always running (often from each other), and continually having to re-address and challenge their own trusted ideological and emotional perspectives.

At first glance, the show's inaugural storyline seems to align with traditional SF epic narratives around interstellar conflict, competing alien races, and technological innovation—what Farah Mendlesohn calls 'global' narratives, in that they 'are too large to be encompassed within much mainstream fiction or . . . would reduce such fiction to rhetoric' (2002: 124). John Crichton, an American astronaut, accidentally falls through an unstable wormhole while testing out his IASA spacecraft, *Farscape-1*. He is then inadvertently pulled aboard Moya, a living spaceship called a Leviathan, who is attempting—with her crew of prisoners—to escape[4] from a race of military-oriented and expansionist aliens called the Sebacean Peacekeepers. Crichton plays a part in the escape, and thus the show's narrative comes to revolve around this unlikely group of aliens, thrown together against their will, as they attempt to outdistance the Peacekeeper forces pursuing them. Unlike the crew of the *USS Enterprise*, who are on a mission of peaceful contact and scientific (as well as cultural) discovery (read: colonization), the crew of Moya are constructed as refugees and escaped inmates, desperately trying to evade the powers that seek to re-incarcerate them.

Despite what may seem to be, as I've outlined it above, a fairly organized theoretical framework for analyzing the show, it still feels like an impulsive endeavor, emerging from spectatorial passion and emotional engagement as much as it might be said to emerge from abstract scholarly interest and objective theorizing. I must admit that the impetus for writing this book struck me completely by surprise. I had avoided watching *Farscape* for years, on the sensible grounds that, every time I *did* happen to catch an episode, it always seemed confusing and irredeemably silly. I would frequently come upon an episode that was halfway through, and, no matter how diligently I applied myself to figuring out just what was going on, I always failed. This originally struck me as a narrative flaw within the show; but, as I got to know *Farscape* better, I realized that it was actually one of the show's most innovative storytelling techniques. I now attribute this spectatorial confusion—a standard element of *Farscape* plotlines—to what I like to call the 'what the *frell*' effect.

In nearly every episode of the show, there occurs a moment, or several moments, within which a familiar narrative line gets crossed, a familiar character says something that makes no sense (given their established patterns of dialogue up until this point), or a familiar situation gets, well, a bit *frelled* up. *Farscape*'s flexible spaces of narrative and narration—that is, both how the story unfolds, and which multiple points of view it unfolds from—actually encourage these moments of cognitive dissonance (an intratextual version of Suvin's 'cognitive estrangement,' which he identifies as the foremost characteristic of SF as a genre). I will discuss Suvin's work in more detail later, but, for now, he defines 'traditional' SF as a literature that combines aspects of *estrangement*—that is, fantastic elements that fall somewhere between the uncanny and the marvelous—with aspects of *cognition*: that is, the ways in which SF forces the reader to consider her own empirical environment, and the scientific rationalization in which SF grounds its fantasies (Suvin 1979: 7–8). *Farscape*'s 'what the *frell*' moments occur partly due to the show's willingness to alienate, as well as tease, its core audience, and partly due to the televisual version of the uncertainty principle that I mentioned earlier. These characters are so fraught to begin with, plotted along such crazy lines of narrative collision and social interaction, that disjunctive moments are bound to occur as they bounce wildly off one another. If they didn't occur, then the show would be in denial of the exotic and complex universe within which it operates.

The moment that first drew me into *Farscape* was, predictably, a bizarre one. I had tuned in for about the last fifteen minutes of the episode 'Family Ties' (1.22), the finale to Season 1. The image on the screen was one that would grow extremely familiar to most viewers, since, after the second season, it became embedded within the show's opening credits[5]—that is, the image of Crichton and D'Argo floating, hand in hand, above the ruined planet that once served as Scorpius' 'Gammak'[6] base. I was intrigued by the rich texture of the image, as well as its varied representational codes and symbolic possibilities: two men—one human, the other alien—holding hands, both physically and psychically vulnerable to the enormity of space, simply hovering, their figures impossibly small against a cosmic background.

In the final moments of the episode, Crichton addresses Moya directly, saying 'thanks for everything. Now do what you have to do,' insisting that she escape with her newly born baby (the as-yet-unnamed Talyn). This not only left me brimming with questions—such as, what exactly is a 'Moya,' and how can she give birth in outer space?—it also made me a lot more interested in the character of John Crichton. Here was the typical SF hero, the hetero human male versus the rest of the universe, yet he was surprisingly vulnerable, even pleading with some kind of living starship. He wasn't sacrificing himself for the sake of an interstellar experiment, or for the sake of the all-important 'fate of the galaxy'; he was, in fact, sacrificing himself for the sake of his friends. It was an inversion of one of the primary rules applied to 'hard' SF, which is that characters should always be secondary to the cognitive development of the environment and its various technologies. As a structural principle of the genre, this privileging of technological over human conflict is outlined, and extended to its highest level of character instrumentality, by Gwyneth Jones' assertion that 'a typical science fiction novel has little space for deep and studied characterization . . . because in the final analysis the characters are not people, they are pieces of equipment' (1999: 5).

If anything, even what appear to be 'pieces of equipment' within *Farscape's* universe—such as the Leviathan starships, Moya and Talyn, the DRDs ('Diagnostic Repair Drones'[7]) with their own unique personalities, and even Crichton's favorite firearm (which he affectionately names Winona[8])—turn out to be characters with nuanced historical backgrounds. Nothing can be taken for granted in the Uncharted Territories, which echoes Ursula Le Guin's wry observation about SF writing in general: 'the reader can't take much for granted in a fiction where the scenery can eat the characters' (1993: Intro).

That said, let us move on to an exploration of these characters. I will be treating here only the 'primary' protagonist characters in the show, which include John Crichton, Aeryn Sun, Rygel, Zhaan, D'Argo, and Chiana. I will discuss recurring characters, such as Stark, as well as the ambivalent 'villains'—Scorpius and Bialar Crais—throughout the rest of the book. I will also treat Moya and Pilot specifically in Chapter 3, which concentrates on Leviathans.

He Claims to be a Human . . . From a Planet Called Erp: John Crichton

Both the show's creator, Rockne O'Bannon, and the actor who plays Crichton—Ben Browder—have said in interview that Crichton is designed, as a character, to be the audience's point of view. In this case, 'audience' refers not only to the broad extradiegetic audiences that consume *Farscape*, but more specifically to the SF fans who share Crichton's knowledge of western pop culture. Crichton is, in many ways, a hyper-competent and finessed version of the typical SF fan. He has extensive knowledge about *Star Trek* reruns, *Star Wars* plotlines, and James Bond gadgetry, but that connotative and 'cultural' knowledge is balanced out by his academic background in theoretical physics and astronomy—he is, after all, an astronaut with a PhD.

This deliberately distances him from *Star Trek* characters like Captain Kirk and Captain Picard, whose knowledge is coded as military, and even from Captain Janeway, who describes herself as a scientist but also works within the paramilitary framework of the United Federation of Planets. Crichton is a scientist with no combat training whatsoever—a point made clear when Aeryn, trained since childhood as a Peacekeeper soldier, easily overpowers him in the premiere episode.

2. Crichton's image is overlaid with messages

But this attempt at fan mimesis, I would argue, is continually disrupted by Crichton's physical appearance: he is in top physical condition, and probably one of the most attractive astronauts ever to supervise an EVA[9] mission. This is a familiar moment of televisual disjuncture, in which a program attempts to make a connection to its audiences while simultaneously adhering to irrational North American standards of hyper-beauty. Characters like Angela Chase on *My So Called Life*, and Dana Scully on *The X-Files*, are supposed to be read as 'plain' and socially awkward by audiences—hence, 'just like them'—when in fact the actors who portray these characters are conspicuously attractive (Byers 1998: 715). They are also white, heterosexual, able-bodied, and economically comfortable, which are all epistemic categories that audiences are expected to conform to. Crichton is no different, in that his 'geekiness' as an SF fan remains entirely subsumed by his hyper-competency as an attractive male in top physical condition.[10] He demonstrates both extensive academic knowledge of theoretical science (though not always cool powers of analytical observation), and empathic skills generally not found among male SF protagonists.

Crichton is, in this sense, a hybrid character: a fusion of the 'typical' SF fan (if that typical fan happened to grow up with an astronaut for a father) with the archetypal SF scientist/hero, and then modified along flexible feminist guidelines in order to become a leader capable of empathy, compassion, even mothering techniques, as well as physical and psychic vulnerability. He is thus the bionicizing or hyper-finessing of the traditional SF hero, the hero made 'better, stronger, faster,' but also 'more sensitive, more vulnerable, more compassionate.' If Lee Majors and Lindsay Wagner were cybernetically fused into the Six-Million-Dollar/Bionic Man-Woman, Crichton might possibly be the result.

This makes him incredibly durable and attractive as a character— to female and queer audiences,[11] especially—but it also places him at a considerable performative and material remove from those audiences, who are not all (and not even by majority) male, white, heterosexual, hyper-competent, or free of all economic concerns. Any attempts, by either the actors or the creators of the show, to suggest that Crichton is an unproblematic point of view for *Farscape*'s multiple audiences remains an irresponsible and inaccurate collapse of those audiences into the coherent, male, middle-class subject that networks and advertisers are speaking to directly (as well as courting financially). He is certainly not an accurate representation of every SF fan. But neither is he a faithful simulation of all the SF protagonists who have come before him.

What actually ties Crichton to *Farscape*'s audience is a shared sense of shock and bewilderment towards the Uncharted Territories in general. Like the viewers, John often has no idea what to make of the aliens with whom he is interacting. He (sometimes) uses deductive reasoning, but generally acts impulsively, using the intuition and stubborn indefatigability that, according to the show, is supposed to characterize humans in general—that is, an illogical resilience in the face of seemingly hopeless odds. John has no specific classification, such as *soldier*, *priest*, or *monarch*, but is rather what Nestor Canclini might call a 'multi-national assemblage, a flexible articulation of parts' (2001: 18). He is referring, here, to transnational 'culture' in the context of audiovisual globalization, but, given Crichton's fluid American ideological positions, as well as his emblematic status as the sole human in the Uncharted Territories (which, in light of Canclini's quote, we can read as the Third World), I think the comparison works.

Although Crichton has many memorable moments that span across four years of *Farscape*'s (and his character's) textual evolution, I thought I would, for brevity's sake, mention only one which I find to be critically representative of him. It occurs in 'Family Ties' (1.22), an episode I have already cited above. After Rygel admits that he was going to betray Moya's crew to the Peacekeepers, and that he reneged on the deal only when it seemed apparent that the Peacekeepers would betray *him* as well, the Dominar attempts to defend his behavior. 'I know I can be selfish, but, given the chance, I can usually—' But Crichton cuts him off here. 'Do what? Do the right thing? Rygel, I figure the right thing begins at the beginning of the day, not after you've been caught.' This may seem like a *Trek*-esque bit of moralizing, in which the colonizing character patronizingly teaches the alien all about what's right and wrong. But Crichton does not end the conversation this way.

Instead, as Rygel turns, demoralized, to float away on his 'throne'—which suddenly seems smaller and more disingenuous than it ever has been—Crichton bends down and gently kisses Rygel on the top of the head. The motion is swift, just as a parent might quickly, almost sneakily, embrace a child before they had the chance to squirm away and run off. This moment seems to typify much of Crichton's presentation as a character on the show, as well as exemplify—through ambiguous social interaction, rather than 'hard' SF technological intervention or 'soft' SF intellectualizing and theorizing—his nuanced methods for dealing with conflict. Instead of upbraiding Rygel for behavior that is obviously natural for him, given his predilection for deceit, theft, and self-preservation (which, as Jonathan Hardy, the actor who voices Rygel, has pointed out, makes Hyneirians probably the closest alien race to Humans), Crichton responds with precisely the opposite of what Rygel is accustomed to—tenderness.

Not only is John kissing a tiny alien (puppet)[12] here, but he is kissing a tiny alien who closely resembles a slug, and who first greeted him (in the premiere episode) by spitting in his face. And, although John is physically affectionate towards all of Moya's crew—which inscribes him as a kind of mothering presence—he is, I think, at his most compassionate when dealing with Rygel, who so rarely reacts positively to his entreaties.

I will further discuss both Crichton's paternal and maternal roles, as well as his ambiguous masculinity, in Chapter 3.

I Am Irreversibly Contaminated:[13] Officer Aeryn Sun, Special Peacekeeper Commando, Ikarion Company, Pleisar Regiment.

Aeryn states repeatedly, over the course of four seasons of *Farscape*, that 'I am a Peacekeeper soldier.' This military title and affiliation comes to signify her as a character above and beyond any other, despite Crichton's assurance in the premiere episode that 'you can be more.' And this assertion remains problematic, given that it is made by a human male who considers himself—though he would never admit it—a 'civilizing' influence on Aeryn. As Lavigne notes in her article on *Farscape*'s female characters, 'Crichton repeatedly tries to rectify the soldier-like Aeryn he knows with any role she might play as his wife on Earth' (2005). It's often difficult to determine just how Crichton is attempting to socialize Aeryn—whether he is trying to invoke a sort of 'latent' humanity within her, or trying to reformulate her own sense of femininity into something more recognizable as 'normative' domestic femininity. Probably, it's a little bit of both; this means that *Farscape*, despite its presentation of provocative and dynamic female characters, is not entirely innocent of attempting to establish a traditional SF female role almost symptomatically as a result of the Crichton/Aeryn romance. In order for that romance to be legible to audiences, Aeryn needs, however subtly, to bear at least a resemblance to some normative (and exclusive) definition of femininity.

As a Peacekeeper soldier, Aeryn has grown up on a space station, completely isolated from her parents (who, we discover later, broke strict social conventions by conceiving her and were severely punished for it). If we use *Star Trek* as a kind of metatext against which to enact comparisons of *Farscape*'s aliens, then Aeryn would be a peculiar hybrid of Vulcan and Klingon cultural traditions. She is extremely analytical, and eschews emotional responses—especially expressions of vulnerability—in favor of cool deductive reasoning and pragmatics. When Crichton attempts to explain 'human' compassion to her (which can be read as either an interesting moment of cultural difference, or a patronizing moment of western evangelicalism), she replies simply: 'I know this feeling. I hate it' ('Premiere,' 1.01).

Yet, unlike the relatively peaceable and insular Vulcans, the Sebaceans appear to have a Human colonial and expansionist flair. We learn later, in *The Peacekeeper Wars*, that Sebaceans probably originated as an ancient species of Humans that were 'imported' from prehistoric Earth by another alien race. Originally serving as the protectors of that race—a police presence of sorts—they evolved over time into an expansionist power, and their 'Peacekeeper' moniker came to represent a cruel irony as they invaded other solar systems and subjugated alien races. The metaphorical comparisons here to America as an expansionist nation practically scream to be made, although *Farscape*, dependent as it is on the idealistic national portrayal that most networks disseminate and exploit, needs to tacitly suggest these comparisons while simultaneously insisting that audiences *not* make them—*these aliens are us, but they are aliens, but they are us*. The fantastic element of the show's 'science-fantasy' genre helps to restrict such literal interpretations, while the speculative element opens up a space of irony, if not of prognostication, given that both speculative and extrapolative SF (what Carl Malmgren calls the "if this goes on' variety' vs. the "what if?' variety' [1991: 12]) are not the literatures of the *impossible*, but of the 'not yet possible'[14] (Landon 1997: 17).

Zhaan calls Aeryn 'selfless' ('Wait for the Wheel,' 3.04), and, indeed, she does often think in terms of collective utility—or in terms of a depersonalized military pragmatics—rather than what she, Aeryn, as a living subject, wants or desires. I read this definition of 'selfless' as having a double-connotation as well (which, given the multiple connotations that produce *Farscape* as a text, as well as its inventive and modular uses of language, shouldn't be too far-fetched), in that it refers also to Aeryn's self, her subject, which has been subsumed by the rigorous ordering and surveillance techniques of the Peacekeepers. These tactics for controlling and restricting the subject, as well as for creating an internal policing system within each 'citizen,' closely resemble the governmental interventions of the nineteenth century that worked through 'the instrumentalization of the micro-fascisms of everyday life—of the band, the gang, the sect, the family' (Rose 1999: 26); the statist regulations of psychology, sexuality, education, and commerce, engendering a sense of 'freedom' within its citizens that remained entirely compatible with the current government's fiduciary and political concerns.

By encouraging unswerving loyalty, and reducing sexuality to 'recreation' that remains strictly monitored by the state apparatus, the Peacekeeper 'High Command' has produced all of the conditions necessary for Foucault's panopticon to operate; and the Peacekeepers themselves have individually created and maintained Foucault's 'inspecting gaze, a gaze which each individual will end by interiorizing to the point that he is his own overseer, each individual thus exercising this surveillance over, and against, himself' (1995: 155). And with this comparison I am not trying to sketch out an easy, automatic-pilot, deconstructive exercise by aligning this alien culture with a tidy bit of western poststructuralist thought, and thus validating my own claims about *Farscape's* academic appeal.

But, although it probably violates the anthropic principle—which states that, if the universe were even slightly different than it is now, we wouldn't exist, nor be able to ask *what if the universe was different?*—I would contend that, given the physiological and cultural similarities between Humans and Sebaceans, it seems likely that a theory similar to Foucault's panopticism would be present, but suppressed, within Sebacean intellectual culture. I am not suggesting, then, that only a human—like John Crichton—could possibly be enlightened enough to figure out this psychological bind. Aeryn figures it out quite splendidly on her own, and she makes this knowledge public—and damning—when she tells Bialar Crais: 'you will never order me again' ('The Hidden Memory,' 1.20).

I will discuss Aeryn Sun in further detail—specifically as part of a feminine subjective and physical duality on *Farscape*—in Chapter 4.

I Am Nobody's Puppet: Dominar Rygel XVI

Rygel is a Hyneirian, a quasi-amphibious alien race characterized by their enthusiastic commitment to capitalist expansion, as well as their Machiavellian web of political alliances, trade agreements, and treaties that are, most likely, revocable. He was once the Dominar of 600 billion subjects (if we are to believe him); but, after falling victim to a military coup staged by his treacherous cousin, Rygel was deposed and taken prisoner by the Peacekeepers. Although his behavior is generally self-serving, and his loyalties can be gossamer-thin, we should not forget that Rygel was imprisoned and tortured by the Peacekeepers for 300 cycles, which adds up to roughly 288 solar years.[15] After such an incalculable period of incarceration, psychological (as well as physical) assault, and sheer loneliness, Rygel's post-traumatic stress disorder would be formidable. It's actually somewhat surprising that he manages to get through each day at all, let alone engage in regular social interactions with Moya's crew.

It is true that Rygel demands more than any other character on the show—more food, more money, more comfortable quarters, and

3. Dominar Rygel XVI

more respect—but, having made the transition from a confident monarch to a traumatized refugee and prisoner, he has also lost more than any other character. This fact is, I realize, debatable. Aeryn, after all, lost her entire culture and worldview; Crichton lost a loving family; D'Argo lost his son, as well as his wife. But none of them lost 600 billion subjects, nor 288 years of their life. Rygel, purely in terms of social positioning and psychological assurance, has made the most violent and radical transition of any character on *Farscape*—precisely because he has come so far from where he started.

Zhaan calls Rygel 'wise' ('Wait for the Wheel,' 3.04),[16] and she is correct—Rygel is probably the most intelligent character on board Moya. He often says what nobody else is willing to, and his logic is geodesic—cosmologically speaking—in that it often finds the shortest (and most brutal) distance between two points. Rygel is the only character who ever seriously thinks about money, and, although he's generally thinking about getting money for himself, he also manages to aid and abet schemes that enrich the rest of the crew as well. One such scheme—robbing a 'shadow depository,' which is basically a bank for intergalactic thieves—goes bad when the 'money' that they steal (in the form of gold ingots) is replaced by ravenous spider-mechanoids that infest Moya's hull and begin to literally eat her from the inside. The metatextual moral here—money devours—is, though cleverly executed, a bit heavy handed. But Rygel refuses to stoop to any sort of metaphoric level ('Dominars do *not* travel in reverse' ['Through the Looking Glass,' 1.17]), and retains his mercantile perspective faithfully. When Chiana, panicking, insists that 'our money's alive . . . it's eating the ship!', Rygel's reply is sedate, and firmly in context: 'Yes—but we're *poor*.'

Later, while traveling in *Farscape-1* with John—shortly before Zhaan's death, although he has no way of knowing this—Rygel describes the unique living-situation of Moya's crew with his trademark acerbic probity: 'What friends? We were thrown together against our will, and we're all just trying to make the best of it until we get the chance to screw the others and get what we want' ('Could'a, Would'a, Should'a,' 3.03). The show places Rygel at his most selfish here in order to give him a redemptive moment in the next episode, made possible by his reaction to Zhaan's death. His farewell to her remains, I think, one of the Dominar's greatest quotations, and also serves as the title for Zhaan's sub-section in this chapter. Everyone reacts to this moment with bare emotion—although not with the hyper-pathos that would characterize a 'disease-of-the-week' television movie.

Chiana's simple 'we love you, Zhaan,' breaks me every time I hear it; D'Argo closes his eyes; Pilot makes a soft, mewing sound as he cries; Stark's insane mumblings—'decompression, decompression, where to go, where to go?'—are more prescient than he realizes: for Zhaan's departure from their lives *is* a kind of explosive decompression, leaving them scattered, directionless, and more vulnerable than they've ever been. Even Aeryn crumbles at this moment, lunging forward, trying to stop Zhaan and spitting out an ineffectual *no* as Crichton restrains her. And Crichton has no pop-culture reference for this, no words at all with which to say goodbye to this alien, this strange woman with whom he has shared spiritual unity, and who has saved his life on more than one occasion. Only Rygel is able to speak, and his send-off to Zhaan is both a requiem and an expression of love—which is something that Dominars don't feel easily. 'Goodbye,' he says, 'you big, beautiful, blue bitch.' And with that, she vanishes into a blur of light, then flame, then inscrutable nothing—just the blankness (but not emptiness, we know) of space.

We should also remember that Rygel is the only one capable of literally 'reassembling' Aeryn and Crichton after they are 'crystallized' by the Eidolons, and the method by which he accomplishes this brings him, in a very material sense, closer to those two characters than anyone else. It also allows him to make another one of his most memorable declamations, this time to Jool in *The Peacekeeper Wars*: 'Get your own fantasy, dreadlocks—they're having *my* baby' (*PKW*, Pt. 1).

I can think of no better sentiment with which to conclude Rygel's introduction.

I'm Only Your *Tralk* in Your Dreams: Chiana

The word *tralk* translates generally as 'slut,' although it can also be used more specifically to refer to a woman engaged (or who appears to be engaged) in prostitution. Although it appears to be neuter in terms of grammatical gender, it is always used in *Farscape* to refer to women, which may be a bit of dodgy politicization on the part of the show's writers. On the one hand, it suggests that human prejudices regarding women's sexuality tend to persist throughout the universe, which creates a denaturalizing space within which such prejudices might be critiqued—when aliens exhibit human behavior, then the behavior itself becomes alien, external, and therefore analyzable. On the other hand, this limiting of *tralk* creates yet another universe, however alien, wherein women are considered sexually commodifiable, whereas men are not.

Much of Chiana's epistemic work as a character on *Farscape*, I think, is focused on dismantling and unpacking this idea of the *tralk*, the slut, the sexually available (and commercially viable) woman. This is not a recuperative analysis; I am not offering the facile and potentially insulting suggestion that Chiana is, by virtue of her sex and gender play, a visible advocate for the rights of women—let alone for the rights of women in the sex trade. As far as we know, Chiana never has to contend with any of the threats that real, survival-sex-trade workers (that is, women working at bare subsistence-level) face daily, including physical/psychological abuse, drug addiction, hunger, homelessness, and lack of basic social assistance. Chiana operates on the pleasure principle, and, although she often uses sex as a way to escape potentially threatening situations, she rarely seems to be in any grave danger. In this sense, her character provides a safely ludic and psycho-erotic outlet for audiences: she allows them to 'experience' certain non-threatening aspects of sexual commodification and visibly erotic sensuality, while shielding them from the spectrum of violence that such a lived reality would invite extradiegetically, beyond the safety of Moya.

Chiana is Nebari—a humanoid race distinguishable from Sebaceans only by the fact that they are monochromatic; that is, gray-skinned, with white hair. The Nebari resemble, in many not-so-subtle ways, stereotypical depictions of Russian communists within 1950s SF cinema. Booker argues that movies like *Invasion of the Body Snatchers* (1956), with its threat of 'emotionless robot replacements' overrunning human civilization, showcases an alien threat 'who look the same as everyone else, but feel no emotion and have no individuality ... directly echoing the era's most prevalent stereotypes about communists' (2001: 127). During the long 1950s— the period between 1946 and 1964, which Booker describes as 'the great period of American Cold War hysteria' (2001: 3)—most SF cinema made lumbering on-screen conflations between alien/

communist invasion, and any film dealing with an outer-space threat attempting to devour the American populace—such as *The Blob* (1958)—necessarily had to be read as a spectacular representation of communist ideology, a malevolent communist life form with a voracious appetite, sucking up rugged individualism.

Given how the Nebari are constructed as a ruthlessly conformist society ('A Clockwork Nebari,' 2.18), rejecting any kind of spontaneous sexual expression or variant gender, especially intersexuality ('Fractures,' 3.18), it's possible to see *Farscape* as a complicit actor within this brand of traditional stereotyping. But, as mentioned above, through the defamiliarizing techniques of science-fantasy as a genre the spectator is also given a chance to see this human behavior as alien, external, a part of the Other. By decoupling certain stereotypes from public discourse, we can place them at an angle, a sort of cosmic relief, thereby viewing them as something that *we* create contingently rather than as a transparent facet of human discourse. This same 'alienating' effect occurs with masculinity and femininity, which I will discuss in Chapters 3 and 4; although I should also state that defamiliarization through fantastic genres does not always create a space of resistance, nor uncritically dissolve the overwhelming discourses of marginalization that control most popular texts.

When Chiana fears that her brother, Nerri, has died, she escapes to a royal cemetery planet ('Taking the Stone,' 2.03) in order to grieve for him, as well as to experience a kind of self-annihilation. Aeryn later does exactly the same thing, seeking solace on the planet of Valldon in order to grieve for Crichton ('The Choice,' 3.17), and her process of psychological exploration—like Chiana's—is dealt with flexibly and non-critically by the show. This is a defining event for Chiana, because it allows her to stake out her own subject, separating herself from the two paternal figures in her life: Nerri and Crichton. When Crichton tries to convince her not to participate in a suicide ritual, she rebukes him, and, although she is on her knees, the gesture is entirely discursive, and Chiana maintains both physical and dialogic superiority as she speaks. 'Why I'm here,' she says, 'it's not about you. In case you haven't noticed, I'm not your kid, I'm not your sister, and I'm only your *tralk* in your dreams' ('Taking the Stone,' 2.03).

I will discuss Chiana's relationship with Aeryn, as well as the representational and ideological codes (Fiske 1978: 5) that define her as a sexualized female character, in greater detail in Chapter 4.

You Are a Real Pain in the Eema!: Ka D'Argo

The 'Ka' in D'Argo's name means 'general,' although he is not actually a general—a fact that he doesn't explain until later in the show. Despite his fearlessness and obvious battle prowess, D'Argo maintains a quiet sense of hesitancy, even inadequacy, in terms of his identity as a warrior. In the premiere episode, upon learning that he is thirty cycles (twenty-eight solar years) old, Zhaan proclaims: 'you're but a boy!' When D'Argo protests that he has seen two battle campaigns in his lifetime, Zhaan merely smiles, replying archly: 'only *two*?' These two characters are initially coded as opposites of each other—the pacifist priest and the violent warrior—but *Farscape* works to deconstruct this binary carefully, revealing Zhaan's violent and anarchic past, as well as D'Argo's inherent kindness and psychological struggles with his own anger. This genetic trait, called 'hyper-rage,' becomes a fetish site for D'Argo, a psychic surface upon which he can displace all his feelings of exile, loneliness, and grief, just as Zhaan's quest for spiritual enlightenment serves to deflect her own fears of mortality, abandonment, and emotional detachment.

D'Argo is a Luxan—a martial and militaristic race, highly reminiscent of *Star Trek*'s Klingons. They are so reminiscent, in fact, right down to the same warrior culture and religious codes of conduct, that it seems at first as if *Farscape* has borrowed this alien trope wholesale from the earlier series. Subtle differences do emerge. Luxans, for instance, have tentacles and venomous tongues—very long tongues, which they can basically use as appendages—whereas Klingons merely have ridges on their foreheads. Both races use a ritualistic blade in battle, which becomes the mark of a male warrior. The Klingon *bat'leth* blade is a kind of double-edged sickle; the Luxan *qualta* blade is a gun/sword hybrid that also fires laser blasts.

I repeat that these differences are subtle. Despite *Farscape*'s commitment to create visually exotic aliens, made possible by the alchemy of the Jim Henson Creature Workshop, the only quantifiable difference between Luxans and Klingons is that . . . Luxans have tentacles. And long tongues. I'm not going to defend *Farscape* in this instance, nor situate D'Argo as a kind of evolution of the archetypal *Star Trek* Klingon, because he isn't—he is, rather, a convenient modification of this SF archetype, ascribed the visual and cultural markers that code him as a 'warrior' alien; and, since the inception of *Star Trek* in 1966, that archetype has been synonymous with Klingons. The convenient thing about archetypes, however, is their adaptive capacity.

Like Tolkien's Elves and Dwarves, or Le Guin's college of wizards (*Harry Potter*, anyone?), *Star Trek*'s Klingons have penetrated the cultural fabric of SF to the extent that they are traditional generic benchmarks rather than exclusive, individual characters. Not borrowing from *Star Trek*'s considerable repertoire of alien cultural mythology would be almost impossible for a show like *Farscape*, which bases itself upon human encounters with exotic extraterrestrial life. SF, like fantasy genres, depends upon the adaptation and innovation of its historic imaginaries and canonical texts. So, D'Argo may closely resemble a Klingon in appearance, but Vulcans also resemble Tolkien's Elves (in terms of their emotional detachment, psycho-mystical abilities, and physical appearance), and those Elves resemble their medieval counterparts, the Sidhe, in Celtic mythological cycles like the *Mabinogion*. These sorts of comparisons can grow infinitely recursive.

When D'Argo first meets John, as I described earlier in this chapter, he knocks him unconscious with a tongue K.O. Later in that same episode, he pins Crichton against a wall, telling him that 'if you threaten my freedom, I'll kill you' ('Premiere,' 1.01). Aeryn, still unsure where her loyalties lie at this point, tries to sympathize with Crichton. 'They're a brutal race,' she says of Luxans, 'indiscriminate in their deployment of violence.' This 'non-discriminatory' or aimless violence is in direct opposition to the 'discriminating' violence of the Peacekeepers, which Aeryn codes here as, in fact, a civilizing violence. We learn, over the course of the show, that D'Argo is actually quite discriminating in his use of violence, and, as he himself states in the episode 'Mental as Anything' (4.15), 'I am violent . . . when I choose to be.' His blustering anger and over-confidence can indeed be 'a real pain in the *eema*,' although he continually proves his loyalty and devotion to Moya's crew by defending them in nearly every episode.

I will discuss D'Argo's relationship with John, as well as the ways in which spectators can recognize a sort of recombinant masculinity within him—a human version of masculinity deferred onto an alien body—in Chapter 3.

You Big, Beautiful, Blue Bitch: Pa'u Zotoh Zhaan

What to say about Zhaan? When we first encounter her character, she is with D'Argo on Moya's main bridge, trying to engineer an escape from the Peacekeepers. Like D'Argo, she eyes Crichton—the human newcomer—skeptically, and has no compunctions about tying him up or knocking him unconscious. In fact, Zhaan's own personal ethics are more than a little mysterious. She values life, and, ashamed of her past, observes that 'the instant I committed murder, I sacrificed the right to exist' ('Family Ties,' 1.22). Yet, in an earlier episode, she—along with D'Argo and Rygel—are able to cut off one of Pilot's many arms (against his will, obviously), in order to pay off a morally bankrupt scientist, and in turn buy themselves technology that would allow them to return to their original home-worlds ('DNA Mad Scientist,' 1.09). Zhaan admits in the premiere episode that she was 'the leading anarchist' on her world, and thus her claims of peace and spiritual enlightenment—sought through intense meditation and other reflective techniques—are necessarily a reflection (and subvention) of her violent past.

Zhaan is a Delvian, a species that evolved from plantlife—her genetic history gives her certain regenerative powers, although it's unclear exactly how the Delvians manifested psychic (and, I would argue, mystical) abilities. As a pa'u, or priestess, Zhaan has a number of psychic talents, including the ability to share 'unity' with the mind of another. This all seems very Vulcan at first, but unity is quite explicitly coded as a pan-sexual experience—Crichton describes it as being similar to an acid trip—whereas the classic Vulcan mind-meld holds only a suggestive eroticism. Zhaan can also attack someone else's mind, which she does (twice, reluctantly) in order to defend her companions from the 'psychic vampire' Maldis. It is Zhaan's body, I would argue, rather than her mind, that becomes a site of conflictual expression and performance within the show. As an alien who is blue from head to toe, and who frequently meditates naked, Zhaan represents a freely sensual (though not necessarily sexual) presence on board Moya. She, like Chiana, is entirely comfortable with her body, although Chiana expresses that comfort through overt eroticism, whereas Zhaan expresses it through physical intimacy.

Zhaan is the primary maternal presence on *Farscape*. She guides Crichton through his shaky transition period immediately after he appears on Moya; she is quietly patient with Aeryn, despite the Peacekeeper's initially hostile reactions to this kindness (which, in Aeryn's mind, is weakness); she rightly calls D'Argo 'sensitive' ('Wait for the Wheel,' 3.04), and is one of the only characters truly to recognize the Luxan's deeply buried sense of emotional dependency, as well as his tenderness; she becomes Moya's de facto medical officer, tending to minor wounds and, in the process, teaching Aeryn more about the sciences that she eventually admits to finding fascinating. Finally, after protecting Moya from being 'de-commissioned' by her creators, she becomes the ship's official protector, and remains the only one—aside from Pilot—who ever hears Moya speak ('I Do, I Think,' 2.12). The ship's words, 'Moya . . . fulfilled,' remain an enigmatic mystery. Is it the love of her crew that has fulfilled her? The love of Pilot? Like Zhaan herself, it seems that Moya doesn't fear death, precisely because she has experienced love— existing in a symbiotic relationship with both Pilot and her crew, she has known what it is to need and be needed, to sustain and be sustained. Moya is at peace with the idea of death, just as Zhaan, when the moment comes, is equally at peace.

'My children,' she names them, 'my teachers, my loves' ('Wait for the Wheel,' 3.04). Her citation of them all is a recuperation, a transformation of their original 'citations' which were external and limiting. The soldier becomes 'selfless Aeryn'; the outsider becomes 'innocent Crichton'; the warrior becomes 'sensitive D'Argo'; the *tralk* becomes 'exuberant Chiana'; and the two-foot-tall Dominar, on his floating throne, becomes 'wise Rygel.' These new names also have their limitations, but they are meant to be exceeded, to be adapted and built upon. In *Bodies that Matter*, Butler proposes that 'I can only say 'I' to the extent that I have first been addressed, and that address has mobilized my place in speech' (1993: 225). In this sense, these characters labored beneath a previous address—they carried the baggage of an external 'I,' an 'I' that they were continually in the process of deconstructing. Zhaan's final gift to them is a new naming, a new address that provides living space, that actually hopes to be exceeded. Just as Crichton told Aeryn that she could 'be more' than a Peacekeeper soldier, so Zhaan tells 'her children, her teachers,' that they can be more than their social epithets; more, even, than the new addresses that she has given them; existing within language, as a condition of language, must also be a continual mediation of that language, a continual renovation and rearticulation of the terms that define our subject.

Zhaan's death, however, is certainly not more important, or more affecting, than her life on board Moya. Although some might argue that her ultimate recuperative act is the resurrection of Aeryn, it is her daily expressions of compassion and empathy, her daily interventions into the lives of these characters, that ultimately make the most impact on them. When Aeryn, hovering in a sort of preconscious limbo, asks why she is to be saved, Zhaan replies simply: 'Because I love you. More importantly, Crichton loves you' ('Season of Death,' 3.01). This conviction of love's necessity—the realization that Aeryn and Crichton need each other, and that their subjects, which she herself has helped to foster and shore up against the various forces that sought to tear them down, are now interlaced—is something that Zhaan arrives at instinctively. Through her various intimacies with these characters, she also manages to pass on some of this instinct, which, oddly enough, seems both human and alien at once.

Other Characters

Farscape presents us with a large and flexible 'family' of alien characters, and I don't have the space (this could be a pun) to discuss all of them in detail. Jool, for instance, is a humanoid alien who comes from an aristocratic social class—John nicknames her 'princess,' and she begins her tenure on the show as a bit of a spoiled diva, only to sacrifice herself in *The Peacekeeper Wars*. Jool is brilliant, speaking several languages and possessing various technical and medical aptitudes, but these skills don't do her much good on Moya, and she has to start improvising quite quickly. As a character, she never seems to 'fit,' and her early departure to the world of the Eidolons seems to signal that lack of integration.

Noranti, an ancient and prototypical 'witch-woman,' enters the cast at the end of Season 3, and lasts until *The Peacekeeper Wars*.

Although her first act on the show is to inform a very surprised Crichton that Aeryn is pregnant, she quickly devolves into a position of comic relief. The pleasure of Noranti's character, however, comes from a bit of subversion on the show's part, for what other SF program features an old alien character who actually appears and acts her age? Noranti is perhaps the first middle-aged alien to occupy a recurring role on an SF show, and she does attempt to fill the mothering role that Zhaan left behind (with mixed results — proving, in *Farscape* fashion, that categories such as 'mother' and 'wise woman' aren't universal).

Sikozu crashes the party quite literally — she is shipwrecked aboard Moya, and quickly learns that her various talents — speaking multiple languages, being categorically brilliant and ruthlessly logical, having the unusual ability to walk on ceilings — won't do her any good unless she learns to communicate with the rest of the crew. John nicknames her 'Sputnik,' which refers not just to her spiky hair (resembling the Russian spacecraft), but to her inevitable Cold War-style betrayal of Moya and her crew. Sikozu begins a romantic (and very physical) relationship with Scorpius, which demonstrates a surprising level of tenderness and intimacy, further queering the SF model of the dominating villain.

Now that I have introduced *Farscape*'s principal characters, I can move on to the argumentative streams of this book, which focus on the interactions of language, gender, and power within the show. The next chapter will treat 'language power and language play,' exploring *Farscape*'s unique linguistic modalities, its alien vernaculars and lexicons, its bizarre slang — as well as its characters' dependence upon language in order to negotiate a hostile intergalactic environment. This discussion will also look at Crichton's linguistic adaptiveness, his 'surrender,' in a sense, to alien languages, as a colonial narrative of sorts.

These character introductions were meant to be more intriguing than deconstructive, although I have attempted to foreground some of the major connections, as well as the major conflicts, that typify these characters and link them together. I hope that you are already beginning to speculate about them; that you are already having trouble getting them out of your head.

They are worth the attention. So let us proceed.

2 Moya
Births, Biomechanoids, and Companion Species

The machinic is internal to the organic and vice versa in irreversible ways.
—Donna Haraway (2004: 302)

Do you remember when you first came aboard Moya? Velorek stroked your cheek like this to calm you. Back then, I couldn't fathom why he would do a thing like that. . . and now, I couldn't fathom not doing it.
—Aeryn (to Pilot) ('The Way We Weren't,' 2.05)

Moya . . . fulfilled. Willing. Yes.
—Moya ('I Do, I Think,' 2.12)

Moya is the living 'biomechanoid' starship upon which most of the action in *Farscape* takes place, and, arguably, the show's central character—although she has no voice of her own with which to communicate. Pilot, the alien who exists in symbiosis with Moya, speaks for her. But it remains difficult to tell where Moya ends and Pilot begins. Lavigne notes in her article on gender within *Farscape* that 'Pilot's sentences frequently begin [with] 'Moya and I,'' which suggests that he is a 'passive' character who is symbiotically linked to the ship (2005). Yet it is no easy task to determine who is speaking through whom, and whose desires are being served when Pilot 'speaks for' Moya. The bond that they share is, I think, less symbiotic in the strictest sense, and closer to Donna Haraway's description of 'companion species'—that is, a 'co-constitutive [relationship] in which none of the partners pre-exist the relating, and the relating is never done once and for all' (2004: 300).[1]

Both Moya and Pilot are cyborgs, in that their biological functioning is dependent upon an interface between organic and machinic parts; and Moya's crew are, in a sense, cyborgs as well, since they are equally dependent on Moya for their own life support—for her technological regulations of temperature, gravity, atmosphere, and other elements whose equilibrium ensures their survival. But what does it mean, precisely, to call Moya a cyborg—specifically given her distinctive feminine embodiment, as well as her maternal connection with reproduction of all kinds (human, alien, and cyborg) within the show? If we are to situate Moya's presence within Haraway's notion of 'cyborg consciousness'—which continually walks a fine line between technist informatics and feminist political acumen—then where does a living, biomechanoid starship 'fit?' How is Moya's pregnancy, and Aeryn Sun's later pregnancy, indicative of biological reproduction within SF genres, and how do they simultaneously break away from those conventions?

The goal of this chapter is to address these questions by linking recent discourses on women's reproductive rights and new reproductive technologies (NRT) with parallel discourses on feminine embodiment and the role of the cyborg. Along the way, we will focus on the Moya/Pilot relationship as one that both echoes Haraway's theories around companion species and poses a bit of a quandary for cyborg studies. What kind of cyborg, after all, emerges from the interface between a pacifist male alien who speaks a heteroglossic language (see Chapter 6), and a living female starship who depends upon her crew (as they depend upon her) for survival? The female cyborg is often granted a liberatory and even recuperative sexuality within cyborg studies, but do Pilot and Moya actually *have* sexualities, erotic investments, physical desires?[2] *Farscape* seems to continually emphasize their bodies while simultaneously stripping them of sexual desire, which is precisely the opposite of what it does with all of its other characters. I will try, throughout this chapter, to offer explanations for this, but I suspect that it has something to do with a conflict around mothering, as well as a containment of bodily permeability and physiological dependency.

When Crichton first sees Moya in the 'Premiere' episode, his eyes go very wide, and he says: 'That's big. That's really big' (1.01). Even from the very beginning, Moya, as an embodied presence within the show, is conceived as being just on the boundary of the monstrous. As Crichton's module (his only means of protection) is pulled inexorably into the organic mouth of the ship's maintenance bay, spectators get the sense of an intergalactic Moby Dick stretching wide its jaws, preparing to swallow the tiny and supremely vulnerable spaceman. Later in the episode, Crichton delicately touches Moya's hull, admitting that 'this ship is amazing'; but the previous image, Moya as a devouring force, is still fresh in our minds. Although she lacks weapons or adequate defenses of any kind, Moya's sheer size makes her threatening and powerful—as demonstrated when the dying female Pilot crashes her own bonded Leviathan, Elack, into the surface of a planet, decimating two Peacekeeper ships and facilitating Crichton's escape in a later episode ('What Was Lost II', 4.03).

I want to focus this discussion primarily on Moya's pregnancy, and its relation to topological pregnancies within SF genres (and in general media). Moya becomes pregnant halfway through the first season, and her pregnancy, like Aeryn's, is a public event[3] that requires complex monitoring and regulation. It is actually D'Argo who initiates Moya's pregnancy when, while searching for harmful Peacekeeper technology, he accidentally breaks an electronic 'seal' and begins the ship's gestation process ('They've Got a Secret', 1.10). We do not learn until after Moya's offspring, Talyn, is born, that Moya's pregnancy is an unusual one—she was experimented on by the Peacekeepers in order to produce a hybrid child. Whereas most Leviathans seem to be fitted with only the minimum of Peacekeeper tech—life support systems and the like—Talyn is a true cyborg, a blending of sophisticated weapons technology and Leviathan organic materials.

He is a 'gunship,' and thus capable of wiping out lesser ships with his impressive array of weaponry. His cannon, in particular, becomes almost synonymous with violent phallic power[4] in the show; when Rygel asks Pilot if Talyn has 'grown bigger since we last saw him,' it is, of course, Chiana who replies anxiously that 'his cannon sure looks bigger' ('The Ugly Truth', 2.17). Talyn's monstrous birth seems, at first, to be recuperable, but he eventually takes his own life in order to prevent himself from doing harm to others. The circumstances of his death, like those of his birth, are rife with medical and psychological intervention. Unlike Moya, whose ethical considerations are usually compatible with the rest of the crew, Talyn is coded from the start as a headstrong adolescent being who doesn't have the experience to make his own decisions. He more than once fires upon another ship without provocation, or because he is frightened, as in the previously mentioned episode.

Crais calls Talyn's sacrifice a 'hero's death' ('Into the Lion's Den II', 3.21) but it is clear that, like Crais himself, Talyn's actions have placed him beyond the show's understanding of ethical rehabilitation. What makes this all the more disturbing is Talyn's evolving characterization as a failed experiment, a Peacekeeper intervention, and a monstrous hybrid. He dies not simply in the service of the narrative, but in the service of a broader sense of biological normativity that *Farscape* itself feels it must preserve. In some sense, the birth of D'Argo Crichton, John and Aeryn's son, is an eminently natural reproduction meant to ameliorate (or erase) Talyn's more upsetting birth; but it is also a triumphant re-staging of normalcy within the show, a mythical closure that reaffirms healthy, human reproduction while trying to avoid the more threatening alien pregnancy that preceded it. Little D'Argo's sheer ordinariness, his five pudgy fingers and toes, are an ironic contrast to the extraterrestrial circumstances of his birth. But D'Argo is, we must remember, half-Sebacean, which leaves a lot of unanswered questions about his hybrid physiology. Will he have a paraphoral nerve, like Aeryn, for filtering out toxins? Will he suffer from the same Sebacean 'heat delirium' that Aeryn is vulnerable to? Or—as I rather suspect—will his human genes overpower Sebacean genetic 'problems' and thus allow him to possess the best of both worlds? Only time, and perhaps another miniseries, will tell.

Alien pregnancy is a common trope (in the Classical Greek sense of a 'turn') within SF, and it generally does not end well. In some way, the very conditions of confinement within a starship, of being surrounded on all sides by terrifying black space, resemble amniotic preconsciousness and the fetal 'experience.' Vivian Sobchack notes that 'the emotions generated by the narrative and the visual imagery [in SF] in regard to being, for example, in a spaceship are those of confinement, of discomfort, of dependence . . . [they] emerge from repressed representation of human biology and its process . . . the infantile intimations of original being and not-being' (1990: 112). Being on board a starship, then, is very much like being *in utero*, entirely dependent upon a life support system beyond your control, vulnerable to invasion and intervention from all manner of sources. This human anxiety often gets projected onto alien pregnancies, especially those involving human/alien miscegenation.

We need look no further than the four *Alien* movies, which begin with an astronaut whose body is invaded by a gestating alien. The central antagonist within this film is a mother herself, the alien queen, whom Barbara Creed[5] calls 'the archaic mother . . . [she has] total dedication to the generative, procreative principle. She is outside morality and the law' (1990: 135). Like Moya, who can sometimes harm the crew in order to protect her offspring (or herself), the signification of motherhood within *Alien* is always double-edged. There is the monstrous mother, the queen, whose 'total dedication' to fecundity and reproduction makes her amoral; and there is the unreliable mother, the betraying mother, in the form of the ship itself (called the *Nostromo*). The ship's computer, itself called 'Mother,' is a fickle matron who cannot protect her crew from suffocation, explosive decompression, or various other forms of interstellar demise. Her cold metallic voice, ringing throughout the halls of the ship, announces all manner of deadly situations with complete dispassion—including the imminent self-destruction of the *Nostromo* itself.

Moya never intentionally tries to kill her crew, but she does remain an unstable presence within the show. There is a reason why the Peacekeepers normally try to prevent Leviathans from reproducing. Leviathan pregnancy is pathologized by the Peacekeepers because it differs in every way from regulated Sebacean reproduction, clean and sterile, within interstellar laboratories. It is messy and unpredictable, and in this instance, it results in a dangerous hybrid (Talyn), who is capable of inflicting indiscriminate violence. Crais sees Talyn as morally malfunctioning—he lacks the ethical reasoning necessary to tell right from wrong, friend from enemy. But Crais himself has, up until this point, been coded as sociopathic. He kills his own first officer ('The Hidden Memory', 1.20), pursues Crichton across the galaxy because he believes him to be his brother's murderer, and judges Aeryn Sun to be 'irreversibly contaminated' through her contact with other alien beings.

Thus, it is all the more disturbing when Crais convinces Talyn to kill himself (and Crais with him) by initiating starburst within the confined space of Scorpius' command carrier (producing an explosion that will slowly consume the ship, and everyone on board). Unlike Zhaan, who sacrifices herself with a clear conscience, knowing that 'my goddess will embrace me' ('Wait for the Wheel,' 3.03), Talyn dies in part because he has been convinced—by Crais, by the rest of the crew, even by Moya—that *he* is 'irreversibly contaminated,' that he is somehow fundamentally wrong, deficient, and void of ethical understanding. Talyn's fiery starburst consumes two of the show's most problematic and morally ambiguous characters, and in doing so expresses what I think is a familiar conservatism within SF traditions. When the smoke clears, only the incontrovertibly 'good' aliens are allowed to survive, because survival is generally a *human* agency within SF, a trait ascribed ethically to humans in particular (as the stubborn survivalists and rugged individualists of the universe). But where does this leave Moya—the mother who authorizes Talyn's death? Is this not emblematic of the monstrous mother: the parent who stands by and allows her own child to perish, and to believe that he *deserves* to perish?[6]

In fact, this autonomy on Moya's part is in direct opposition to the medical discourses that normally construct mothers as unreliable caretakers, or as simply biological vessels for the crucially important fetus. This embodiment of the fetus—through imaging technologies like ultrasound, as well as the rhetorical strategies of pregnancy manuals—renders the fetus as a threatened life form that 'must be protected from the faulty functionings and decisions of the uninformed woman' (Lay et al. 2000: 19) In her collection *Body Talk: Rhetoric, Technology, Reproduction*, Mary Lay describes this embodiment of the fetus as just one of the tactics by which 'the knowledge systems of high-tech medicine often devalue women's experiential and embodied knowledge . . . their knowledge of their own bodies' signs and needs' (2000: 6). The woman's body becomes an unreliable monitor of fetal health, which necessitates the intervention of technological (rather than organic) monitors in order to make up for the 'faulty functionings' of the mother herself.

Over the last several decades, a spectrum of technological devices designed for fetal monitoring have come to dominate the practice of obstetrics, fusing the maternal body with an array of bewildering mechanical tools designed to compensate for the putative flaws of that body. These tools include: intrauterine catheters that measure contractions, subcutaneous electrodes that monitor the blood pH levels of the fetus, and ultrasound technologies that measure the fetus' respiration and movement (Balsamo 1996: 90). While ostensibly making childbirth safer and more 'efficient' (with the labor-language often applied to obstetrics not lost on feminist critics), these technologies have simultaneously devalued the bodily agency and caretaking abilities of the mother.

Anne Balsamo notes that 'reproductive technologies provide the means for exercising power relations on the flesh of the female body. These power relations are in turn institutionalized' (1996: 89). With obstetricians serving as the final arbiters and interpreters of the data that these technologies produce, mothers themselves are rendered nearly obsolete as 'the fetus ... [becomes] the primary obstetrics patient' (1996: 90). This is not to say that the cyborgian process of childbirth is entirely an ominous one, or that it does not significantly decrease the risk of infant (and mother) mortality. But these technologies remain risky. Amniocentesis, for instance, has been known to 'increase the risk of miscarriage, and routine ultrasound screening has been shown on major studies in three continents to carry increased risk of intrauterine growth retardation' (Davis-Floyd and Dumit 1998: 3). These monitoring techniques often do little to improve the outcome of a pregnancy radically, but do add significantly to the cost of prenatal care (Davis-Floyd and Dumit 1998: 3).

Robbie Davis-Floyd and Joseph Dumit, in their book *Cyborg Babies: From Techno-Sex to Techno-Tots*, point out that 'biomedicine mutilates the natural rhythms of birth by multiple interventions in every phase' (1998: 10). This results in a literal tug-of-war between organics—the maternal body—and what Haraway calls the 'articulata' of technoscience, wherein obstetric technologies seek to block organic drives at every turn. Pain-relief drugs (which slow labor) are followed by more drugs which quicken labor; women are not allowed to eat or drink, then given IVs which administer the fluids that they were denied in the first place (Davis-Floyd and Dumit 1998: 10). When technological intervention places stress on the maternal body, more technological intervention is then applied in order to alleviate the effects of the first wave and produce a satisfactory set of 'readings,' until it is impossible to tell where the laboring woman's body ends and the array of facilitative instruments begins.

This is what Anne Balsamo refers to when she says that 'a pregnant woman is divested of ownership of her body [and] becomes a biological spectacle' (1996: 80). The mother thus becomes a 'birthing machine' attended to by technicians, and her relationship with the fetus is seen not as crucially symbiotic, but as unreliable and threatening—she is container, and the fetus itself is her precious cargo, which must be technologically protected from her pathological body at every stage of its development.

This differentiation of the fetus from the maternal body—both through technological intervention and through the cultural rhetoric of pregnancy manuals, seems to have a lot to do with masculine identity formation, which is not a big surprise to psychoanalysts. Sarah Franklin notes that 'the powerful drive to constitute fetal personhood . . . must also be located in relation to these characteristic psychic requirements of 'successful' masculine individuation' (1991: 190). Countless cultural productions not limited to SF/fantasy genres tell us, in wildly creative ways, that the pre-consciousness of the infant is something to be feared. The warm, directionless dark of amniotic symbiosis must be intervened against, not simply because it represents a breakdown of masculine signification, but because it is a level of existence founded on bodily permeability and maternal dependency.

Julia Kristeva describes this state as the semiotic, which must be ruptured by language, by self/other differentiation, and by a rejection of reliance on the female body, in order for the process of signification to occur. Language becomes the 'thetic,' the breakdown (or break-in) of the semiotic state of being, which produces the conditions necessary for both psychological development and patriarchy. This is where Kristeva's notion of abjection emerges, for abjection is the unconditional (if forever partial, deferred, and frustrated) disavowal of anything relating to the maternal body, but specifically those bodily functions and fluids that render the body violable and dependent—an open text rather than a closed system. In truth, the fetus is an immunological outsider, an extra-bodily presence whose own foreign antigens produce a reaction in the pregnant woman's body; but it is a reaction of 'tolerance' rather than rejection (Martin 1998: 131). Pregnancy thus challenges self/other binaries by placing the immune system within a philosophical bind, forcing it to blend self *with* other.

As a result, in Emily Martin's words, 'the pregnant woman becomes a kind of paradigm case of boundary transgression, as well as the forbidden mixing of kinds' (1998: 126). Her body becomes a site of risky identity-formation, of organic blending (a shift from the empirically knowable immune 'system' to an inscrutable *chora* of physiological and energetic drives) whose *tolerance* is a challenge to masculine linear signification and psychological individuation; a challenge to the stable you/me boundaries that are supposed to occur within the bodily interface. Obstetrics technologies can 'understand' the fetus—they can monitor it, image it, map it, read its vital signs—but they cannot fully understand the maternal body itself, nor its methods of non-technological childbirth, which is what makes the relationship between women and new reproductive technologies such an anxious one. As the sonogram fixes and locates the fetus, making its heartbeat and respiration and movements 'real,' the concomitant hope is that such an imaging technique might also map the pregnant woman's body in an effort to make it empirically and informatically readable (like a genetic text), and thus technologically malleable.[7]

I have provided this (brief) context on obstetrics and NRP in order to situate Moya on *Farscape* as a special case of 'boundary transgression'; she is, in some sense, a mediatory site between reproductive and cybernetic discourses that manages to upset both traditions, because she is a pregnant cyborg. Moya is intervened upon by reproductive technologies, yet ultimately retains control over the lives of her crew members. She is biologically bound to Pilot, but their link as 'companion species' is one of mutual benefit rather than servitude or exploitation. She is denied a speaking voice, yet still has the capacity to decide where her crew will go and what they will do. She needs help in order to deliver Talyn (and it is Chiana, the 'least maternal' character, who comes through in the end), yet she is also willing to harm her crew members in order to facilitate the birth. And she spends two seasons protecting Talyn from harm, only to ultimately (and impossibly) decide that he must die for some greater ethical purpose that the show never manages to explain to anyone's satisfaction, aside from the inescapable fact that the narrative demands it.

Moya thus experiences a curious sort of agency through many of the forces that would normally constrain her (such as medical intervention), and is held back by many of the cyborgian elements that should theoretically liberate her (such as the cyborg's 'differential consciousness' and its lack of bodily boundaries). She gives birth, yet she is never sexualized within the show. Given that there are both male and female Leviathans, we must consider that Leviathans engage in the same sexual relations as other sentient beings; Moya's pregnancy, however, becomes a combination of immaculate conception (D'Argo breaking the mysterious seal) and technological intervention (the Peacekeepers inseminating her, or altering the DNA of her fetus in some way to produce a hybrid gunship). Whatever the case, it is the very 'unnaturalness' of Moya's pregnancy, I would argue, that necessitates the death of her offspring followed by the recuperative birth of D'Argo Crichton. Talyn's hybridity, his body inscribed with dangerous technology, his body as a site for the blending of mysterious organic drives (Leviathan) with murderous agency (Peacekeeper weapons), marks him as a monstrous offspring within the show. Little D'Argo is then born from his ashes as the ultimate humanizing force, the supremely normal baby who emerges from an inter-species pairing. And his normalcy is a direct result of Crichton's civilizing genes—his 'human influence' on Aeryn.

We cannot understand Moya without understanding Pilot, because the two are bonded physiologically and psychologically. Although Pilot speaks 'for' Moya (parsing her thoughts into a communicable language), the ship also speaks 'through' Pilot by registering her own emotions—specifically her anxieties—upon his captive body. Just as Rygel's small stature belies an effusive and powerful person-ality, Pilot's massive size (he is easily eight feet tall) conceals what is actually a timid and fundamentally peaceful alien. His four arms—each ending in a large claw—could effortlessly overpower the crew, but instead they flicker across Moya's control panels, regulating the ship's vital systems. Like Moya, Pilot is a vast non-presence within the show, a background life form who nonetheless controls almost every aspect of life on board the ship. He demonstrates, on more than one occasion—but specifically in the episode 'The Way We Weren't' (2.05)—that without his careful administration, Moya's crew would never survive.

Farscape reveals very little about the origins and living conditions of Pilots before they are bonded with Leviathans—in fact, we don't even have a 'native' name[8] for the Pilot species. They are known uni-versally by the practical moniker that we assume the Peacekeepers gave them, since the Peacekeepers appear to have more or less enslaved them (along with the Leviathans). It is unclear, though, whether the Peacekeepers initiated the bonding process between Pilot and Leviathan as a mutually carceral relationship, or whether that process has been facilitated more peacefully by other races. The Relgarians, for instance, seem to know a great deal about the Levia-than/Pilot bond (Pilot calls it a 'covenant'), and appear to co-exist peacefully with both species ('Into the Lion's Den II,' 3.21).[9] We have also seen Pilots and Leviathans existing beyond the control of the Peacekeepers, such as the dying female Pilot who is bonded with Elack (as well as the pathologized Leviathan—without a Pilot—who tries to kill Moya when she enters the sacred Leviathan burial grounds ['Dog with Two Bones,' 3.22]). As with the Banik slave race, it is difficult to determine precisely what the conditions of Peacekeeper servitude are for Pilots, and how they came under the Peacekeepers' control to begin with.

What remains crucial about the Pilot/Leviathan covenant is that their physiological bonding is beneficial, but not wholly necessary, for the survival of both species. Leviathans are born, live, and die without the intervention of Pilots, and do not require Pilots in order to survive; Pilots too are fully autonomous beings with their own homeworld, appearing to exist perfectly well without being bonded to a Leviathan. Both species, we must assume, developed separately from each other, and were introduced to their current 'co-constitutive' relationship by a cultural intermediary—the Peacekeepers, the Relgarians, the Builders who purport to have created Leviathans, or some other third party. Moya's original Pilot, who is horrifically gunned down by Peacekeeper soldiers when she refuses to allow Moya to be experimented on, says to the officer Velorek that 'you have no understanding of the covenant between Leviathan and Pilot' ('The Way We Weren't,' 2.05). Although the Peacekeepers themselves have produced the coerced *relationship* between Leviathan and Pilot, they have not produced the *covenant*—the bond that emerges from their linked consciousness. In this sense, an autonomy rises out of a forced partnership, and a peculiar unity—like some unexpected peptide chain folding itself to create DNA—rises out of an oppressive system. The Peacekeepers have created the conditions necessary for Pilot/Leviathan enslavement, but they have no power to regulate the startling new identity that results from this coercion.

Pilots can live for thousands of cycles, and the Pilot/Leviathan bond normally lasts for 300 cycles, which is the life-span of the average Leviathan ('My Three Crichtons,' 2.10). Although Pilots and Leviathans don't always agree on everything, for the most part their bond appears to be harmonious and mutually satisfying. Leviathans allow Pilots to explore the galaxy—to 'see the stars,' as Pilot himself says wistfully—and Pilots allow Leviathans to sustain a crew, whose presence in turn provides an emotional sustenance and fulfillment for them ('The Way We Weren't,' 2.05). As Moya herself states, when she is finally given a voice by the Builder Kahaynu, 'Moya ... fulfilled' ('I Do, I Think,' 2.12). She even bids Zhaan to 'sing,' which means that Moya is not simply a regulatory force within the lives of her crew, but an intimate companion who shares their feelings and takes solace in their presence. This solace remains something that the Peacekeepers cannot understand, and also something that they could never have anticipated. They can only react in colonial bewilderment as, despite all their best efforts, an unforeseen joy arises from the oppressive bond that they created purely to further their own intergalactic expansion.

Haraway calls the genus of the companion-species a 'queer family' within which cyborgs are merely 'junior siblings' (2004: 300). But what constitutes a cyborg? Not an easy question to answer, given the prolixity of cyborg theories that have been developing since the late 1970s—building from the Macey Conferences on Cybernetics held from 1943 to 1954 (Hayles 1999: 7)—and not a question that this chapter intends to answer. In her crazily cited (and I will add one more citation to the humanities pile) essay 'The Cyborg Manifesto,' Haraway describes the cyborg teasingly as 'a hybrid of machine and organism, a creature of social reality as well as a creature of fiction' (Haraway 2004: 149). In this sense, she is embedding a failsafe mechanism within her own concrete/theoretical paradigm, because the cyborg will always be overinvested with meanings that exceed its corporeal realizations—it will always have a fictive element, and thus never be entirely locatable through the *techné* of empirical validation and technoscientific construction. Like Butler's excessively remediated notion of performativity,[10] the cyborg is an articulation that exceeds the parameters of its own expression by individual humans, a metaphysical hinge linking 'bodiless' informatics with enfleshed organics, linking amoral cyberspace with deeply concerned political investments and tactics for living within the world. As such, it is not reducible to a single methodology, but necessitates what Haraway herself describes as 'a multi-species and multi-expertise way doing/thinking worlds and ways of life' (2004: 308).

And, as Katherine Hayles reminds us in what is another eminently citable book, *How We Became Posthuman* (1999), the division between information technologies and malleable bodies, between the blinking cursor and the breath, is a largely artificial one that has been forcibly laid over decades of ambiguity and anxiousness around the permeable body and the embodied/'embodiable' possibilities of biotechnology, informatics, and cyberspace. Hayles sees our posthuman bodies not as vessels whose materiality is being erased by cybernetic enhancement, but as an always-mediated relationship between flesh and technology wherein neither element 'pre-relates' (in Haraway's words) the other—'the posthuman view thinks of the body as the original prosthesis that we all learn to manipulate' (Hayles 1999: 3). Just as 'prosthesis' originally referred to the distending and deformation of the human body by technologies of premodern torture, so is the body prosthetic in itself because of its capacity for material transformation and adaptability. A term that originally denoted torture has now come to signify a broad spectrum of rehabilitative and ameliorative technologies, new limbs and cybernetic peripherals that extend the body's senses rather than punishing human transgression. At the risk of sounding glib, it is a case of life imitating art/art imitating life—on *Farscape*, joy emerges from the 'punishment' of the Leviathan/Peacekeeper bond, and in 'the real,' new articulations emerge from an idea that once signified colonial oppression and physical breakdown.

When Haraway originally described the cyborg as 'a creature in a post-gender world' (2004: 150) in 1985, it is doubtful that she could have anticipated the explosion of what we now tenuously call 'gender theory' during the early 1990s, along with the near-mythological implications of Judith Butler's work on sexuality and bodily performativity (as well as the pioneering work of Eve Sedgwick that Butler built her research on). The crux of Haraway's cyborg is that it is ostensibly 'post-gender,' while simultaneously committed to an emancipatory feminist consciousness and evolving political discourses on women's rights. The open-text/open-body tactics of the cyborg are not a recent innovation that has emerged parallel to the development of biotechnology, but actually a much older and much more politically specific living strategy. Chela Sandoval insists that 'colonized peoples of the Americas have already developed the cyborg skills required for survival under techno-human conditions as a requisite for survival under domination for the last three-hundred years' (1999: 248).

For Sandoval—and for Haraway as well—the crucial value of the cyborg is not some manner of de-sexed and transcendent peripherality, but 'the technological embodiment of a particular and specific form of oppositional consciousness ... [linked with] U.S. third world feminism' (1999: 248). Feminist activists have been 'doing' cyborg theory for a lot longer than academics within the humanities and social sciences, and if the reality of the cyborg is to matter on a geopolitical level, it must matter because of its deep commitments to species interdependence and bodily interface—not because it is a sexy 'concept' that has been leapt on by poststructuralists (and videogame-loving teenage boys) who desire a new way of dreaming about cyberspace. The cyborg thus stands at the boundary between reproductive technology and the emancipation and internal sustainability of women's bodies. It is not simply a way of 'plugging in' to something larger than individual human beings, but a vital articulation for the blending of informational technologies, mechanical infrastructures, and organic/machinic relations that 'modern' human reproduction has become—with women's bodies, as usual, in the heart of the maelstrom.

The problem with a great deal of cyber theory is that it elides the feminist political possibilities[11] of the cyborg's shared consciousness, while reinscribing the cyborg's technological accoutrements as de-gendered technoscience (and de-gendered almost always means masculine). If cyborgs proliferate within most SF narratives, then SF becomes a crucial site for the continual re-politicization of technological advancement and organic transformation. For, although many SF texts deal with the 'consequences' of genetic modification, cloning, and other reproductive/biotechnological tactics, their conjecture tends to become apocalyptic rather than specifically critical. It is certainly not enough to claim that genetic modification is threatening some stable, knowable notion of 'humankind' without acknowledging that women's bodies are most often the terrain upon which genetic inscription and intervention takes place. With the character of Moya, *Farscape* is not the first SF text to depict a living starship (see Anne McCaffrey)—but it is the first 'mainstream' televised SF narrative to juxtapose a starship's unique feminine embodiment against a backdrop of colonial expansion and interstellar warfare. Moya becomes the body upon which the Peacekeepers wish to carve out their own colonial fantasies, and thus the body that her crew must protect at all costs, for as they ensure Moya's physical autonomy they are also ensuring their own. The inter-species connection here should not be lost on us.

Haraway stipulates that the cyborg must always contain an element of the fictive, and it is important to recognize (this may seem obvious, but it is not) that Pilot and Moya are not 'real' in the strictest sense. Not only are they not real, but their unreality is dual-layered, much like the dual-layered DVDs that contain the audio and visual information (in separate streams) of the *Farscape* series. They are not real in the sense that they are, like Moya's entire crew, characters on a television show—but they are also not real because they are technological productions. Moya is a combination of impressive CGI effects and elaborately built sets, and Pilot is a massive, animatronic puppet orchestrated by multiple puppeteers. All of Pilot's complex expressions are controlled by human movements, and all of Moya's organic majesty is coded by human programmers and set-builders. Yet these characters have a lived reality. Their 'artificial' emotions become legible to spectators, and the willing suspension of disbelief that gives them life is not always so simple, nor so willing, because the spectatorial pleasure (and pain) that emerges from fantasy is just as often a loss of control, a dissolving of real/fantasy boundaries, and the acknowledgment of an emotional violability and psychological interface with the text itself.

Pilot and Moya definitely have a life of their own, but—as with the 'is Moya a cyborg?' question—we must ask what it means,

4. Is Pilot real?

precisely, to call their existence a 'life.' When Pilot laughs, or frowns, or looks worried; when Moya careens out of control through space, or is struck by a laser blast—what are we 'seeing?' What are we feeling? How is their life conditional upon the same emancipatory elements of cyborg consciousness that produce social change, and how does accepting these characters as being 'alive' necessarily expand the allowable permutations and interconnectivities of both human and alien bodies? To take a closer look at Moya and Pilot as living beings in a companion-species relationship with each other, we can examine two powerful episodes: 'The Way We Weren't' (2.05) and 'DNA Mad Scientist' (1.09), within which their unique bond gets explored.

In 'The Way We Weren't,' specifically, Pilot's complex physiological and emotional connection to Moya becomes narratively aligned with Aeryn's growing romantic relationship with Velorek, thus linking their development as characters. We see that Aeryn's gradual acknowledgment of her ability to love—and her admission of her own vulnerabilities—emerges not from her relationship with Crichton, but from her first interactions with Velorek and Pilot. In fact, it is through watching Velorek communicate with Pilot, through his tenderness and physical intimacy with an alien being, that Aeryn begins to map her own understanding of compassion and inter-species dependence. As she explains in the quote that begins this chapter, a physical move that she once 'couldn't fathom' doing becomes, in time, something that she 'couldn't fathom *not* doing' ('The Way We Weren't,' 2.05). And, to some extent, there are elements of physical connection which remain unfathomable, unknowable, within *Farscape*. The unexpected touch, like the loving address, can take us unawares, can remain an inscrutable space of human compassion, an irresistible orbit around which humans (and aliens) pivot but which they can never ultimately control. But, as the show continually demonstrates, it is the cipher of human connection, and loving compassion, that itself remains worthy of vigilant guardianship—with its secret intact—rather than the dismantling of that secret.

'The Way We Weren't' begins with a murder—the murder of Moya's original female Pilot, who refuses to submit to the Peacekeeper medical intervention which will eventually produce their hybrid gunship, Talyn. The episode moves back and forward through time, starting with what we learn is a digital recording of events that took place aboard Moya long before her current crew had met each other. Velorek tries to convince the Pilot to relinquish control of Moya, and then threatens to replace her with another Pilot—who turns out to be the Pilot that we've come to know. Up until this point, none of Moya's crew realized that their beloved Pilot had a predecessor, or that the bond between Moya and Pilot was actually a tenuous one, even artificial. But now we realize that Moya was already bonded before she even met Pilot—*he* is the interloper, and the old Pilot is the being with which she originally shared symbiosis. Velorek is in the midst of arguing with this Pilot when Crais storms into the chamber, and demands her execution. Crais, as usual, will not stoop to converse with a colonized species. His discourse comes from the barrel of a pulse rifle.

The scene that follows is horrific. It is a murder, and it does not happen outside of the frame, or off to the side of the screen, but directly beneath the gaze of the camera. Half a dozen Peacekeeper soldiers open fire on the Pilot, and bolts of energy rip through her body as she screams, and screams. Her scream is unbearable. It shatters all attempts at textual interpretation, and cuts through the celluloid of the film like a scalpel cutting through astonished flesh. It mutates and distends, becoming animal, unspeakable, unhearable, until it is grotesque vibration that surges through the body of the spectator. As the Pilot's body is penetrated and mutilated by pulse-rifle blasts, as her dying agony is captured from multiple angles—including an extreme close-up that obscures most of her face, leaving just her mouth, gaping and locked in that terrible cry—we understand, we have to understand, that we are watching somebody die. This is not an animatronic puppet getting hit with a laser blast, and not a faceless Peacekeeper soldier, but a living, peaceful, recognizable being who is dying before our eyes. What we are watching is the closest thing to a snuff film that SF can manage, and we are able to watch it, we are given access to it, because it purports to *not be real*.

It is, however, very real for me. This Pilot is real. She is *real*. She is real, and she dies before our eyes, and this has to be a moment of inexpressible shock and untranslatable grief. What we are watching is a cobbled-together articulation of CGI animation, animatronics, camera angles, sound effects, and scripted movements, yet what they produce is a moment of incredible fracture. This is similar to the experience of abjection created by horror films, wherein

[the] film does not constantly work to suture the spectator into the viewing process. Instead ... the suturing process is momentarily undone while the horrific image on the screen challenges the viewer to run the risk of continuing to look ... the spectator is constructed in the place of horror, the place where the sight/site can no longer be endured (Creed 1990: 137).

I defy any spectator to watch this scene without wanting, needing, to look away. It is, as Barbara Creed describes, both a 'sight' and a 'site,' both a visual representation of horror—deferred from language, since horror is, at its core, extra-linguistic, inexpressible save through bodily gesture—and a uniquely horrifying *place*, a site where the horror itself is allowed to occur, where the viewer's own experience becomes unsafe and un-sutured to the comfortingly linear narrative of the film. We are returned to the narrative only when one of the soldiers removes her helmet, and we see, with astonishment, that it is Aeryn Sun. This all takes place before she met Crichton and the rest of the crew, before she met Pilot, when she was still a Peacekeeper soldier—and she was just following orders.

It is only fitting that I cannot adequately describe the emotions that this scene produces through academic language, since the death of the Pilot is not an event that submits easily, or cleanly, to a close reading. What this episode comes to focus on is not some banal moral exemplum, not a 'let's learn from our mistakes' axiom, but the very contours of grief, of grievability. Not all lives are grievable, or at least not grievable within the limits of (but we're not hegemonic) western pluralism. Butler asks, in *Precarious Life*, 'what counts as a livable life and a grievable death?' (2004: xv), and the answer is far from simple. Those who cannot be grieved—that is, deaths occurring 'beyond' the discursive and geographic boundaries of the first world—become, for Butler, 'unreal,' and thus 'neither alive nor dead but interminably spectral' (2004: 33–4). This same sense of de-realization applies to aliens within SF narratives, and this is not a shifty lateral gesture of interpretation on my part, but an acknowledgment of the clear connections between racialized aliens in SF and people of color throughout the world. Aliens are not stand-ins for people of color within SF narratives, but they do become science-fictional representations of racial difference, and their race is often inscribed as inhumanity, as an insurmountable gap between the liberal human subject and the culturally-caricaturized alien (i.e., Klingons are wholly warlike, Vulcans are wholly pacifist, but humans are always innovative cultural pluralists).

When an alien dies in an SF text, are we supposed to grieve that death?[12] Do we have the language with which to grieve it? Butler insists that 'I am as much constituted by those I do grieve for as by those whose deaths I disavow' (2004: 46), and if we side with her (which I do, although you don't have to, necessarily), then our inability—or unwillingness—to grieve alien deaths, to be horrified by alien slaughter, says something about our social realities as spectators. Part of this might have to do with the mysterious nature of grief itself, which remains as much about the subject who lives as it is about the subject who dies. Grief is always a thunderclap, always a blindsided strike. It blasts through your body like decompression, and takes something with it along the way. In Butler's words, it is a loss within a loss: 'if I lose you, under these conditions, then I not only mourn the loss, but I become inscrutable to myself. Who "am" I, without you?' (2004: 22). Grief leaves the subject open to radical fracture, and thus, to make something grievable is to give it power over you, to say *I'm open. You can take something from me.* To extend this vulnerability, this fragility, to alien lives—to make them grievable—would be to admit an affinity with them, and thus to admit a shared violability as *living* (rather than human/alien) subjects.

In 'The Way We Weren't,' Aeryn is the subject who becomes de-realized, who becomes alien, while both Pilots (the living and the dead) become subjects to be grieved. Aeryn's remorse is total as she is seen attacking a punching bag, trying to channel her own guilt, striking out again and again (as the laser blasts struck the Pilot, again and again) until, her hands bloodied, she collapses on the floor and begins to weep inconsolably. Crichton, ever the nurturer, tries to comfort Aeryn, but his physicality only seems to make her feel worse. 'I deserve to die,' she says, standing before Pilot. But we soon learn that Pilot was also complicit in the old Pilot's death. He was handpicked by Velorek to replace her, and, although his home-world's elders deemed him too young to be bonded with a Leviathan, he accepted Velorek's offer anyway ('The Way We Weren't,' 2.05). We also learn that Pilot was not allowed to bond naturally with Moya, but was rather 'grafted' onto her body, forced into her systems, an interloper whose presence was never fully accepted. The grafting causes Pilot chronic pain, and that pain is also an amplification of his own grief for what he did, for the deal between himself and Velorek, which was partially responsible for the old Pilot's death. In flashbacks, we see the process of this grafting, and it is a violent one, with Pilot's own viscera being stretched and distended, his body being sewn and sutured (without anesthetic) into Moya's organic and cybernetic infrastructure.

The episode culminates in Pilot 'disconnecting' himself from Moya, and thereby disconnecting the ship's life support system—what he describes searingly as 'your precious life support' to Aeryn and Crichton. Only as a result of Aeryn's attempts at reconciliation, her willingness to lay herself emotionally bare, does Pilot finally agree to be reconnected to Moya—but this time through a *natural* bonding process, the bond that he should have had in the first place, and which D'Argo says that he 'deserves to have' ('The Way We Weren't,' 2.05). Moya's crew are almost completely dependent on Moya and Pilot for their survival, and yet, up until this moment, they had no idea that Pilot was in constant pain due to his faulty connection with the Leviathan. It is the scientific intervention of the Peacekeepers, done in the name of military advancement, that produces this imperfect kinship, and only Pilot himself—with the crew's cooperation—can re-render this bond into the 'covenant' that it is supposed to be, the natural companion-species link that, in Haraway's words, 'brings together the human and non-human, the organic and technological, carbon and silicon, freedom and structure' (2004: 297). This bond extends past mutual dependency between two sentient beings, and includes 'such organic beings as rice, bees, tulips, and intestinal flora, all of whom make life for humans what it is' (Haraway 2004: 302); relationships whose syncretism makes biological life possible.

The distinction within the show between 'graft' and 'covenant' is also a distinction between 'intervention' and 'inter-species cooperation,' and thus between technoscience and organic interdependency. There are two distinct ways to create a cyborg relationship like the one that Pilot shares with Moya, and the Peacekeeper method for doing this is brutal and interventionist. The alternative is to let both species bond with each other naturally, which ends up producing a true companion-species relationship that is harmonious and mutually beneficial to both Moya and Pilot, who get to share each other's company (and bodies, and feelings) for 300 cycles. It is, as Aeryn calls it, a 'journey,' and a journey that she, as part of Moya's crew, wishes to take with Pilot. Characterizing the cyborg experience as a journey remains fitting, since the process itself should be one that is constantly evolving, never satisfied with a current shape or form, always, as Haraway says, 'committed to partiality, irony, intimacy, and perversity' (2004: 151). The cyborg's own refusal to acknowledge one community, one kind of person-hood, one way of being within the world, is what makes it such a flexible and powerful political device.

In the episode 'DNA Mad Scientist' (1.09), the crew discovers that they can secure the coordinates of their respective homeworlds—for a price. That price turns out to be one of Pilot's arms, since the 'mad scientist' in question with the homeworld information also collects genetic samples from 'rare' aliens, and Pilot's species is among the rarest. One of the things that separates *Farscape* from other SF pro-grams is its willingness to go to dark, ambivalent places, to vilify its own characters while retaining within them a curious core of lova-bility, and so it is not entirely surprising when the crew members actually *do* cut off one of Pilot's arms in order to get their precious coordinates. Aeryn and Crichton—significantly, the two most 'human' characters—are the only ones who abstain from this act, and both of them are horrified when they realize what has hap-pened. Crichton asks Pilot: 'how can you not be angry . . . insanely angry?' But Pilot's reply, as usual, is sedate. 'When one of my spe-cies is bonded to a Leviathan, we give our lives to the service of others,' he says. 'I consider it a perfectly equitable arrangement' ('DNA Mad Scientist,' 1.09). The brutality of the act is softened, somewhat, by the realization that Pilot's arm will grow back. But his sacrificial attitude is still a bit of a mystery to Crichton, who has no idea what it feels like to 'give [his life] to the service of others.' At least not yet.

During the course of this episode, Aeryn is injected with some of Pilot's DNA, and thus begins to transform into a hybrid being, a hybrid of Pilot and Sebacean. Surveying the high-tech lab of Nam-tar, the alien scientist who alters Aeryn's DNA, we get the impression that his techniques of genetic modification are a bit more sophisticated than those of human geneticists. He doesn't need to use electrophoresis (an electrical process that separates DNA strands), or tissue cultures, or bacterial manipulation. He simply inserts a long needle directly into Aeryn's eyeball. Given what we know about Pilot's physical complexity, it seems doubtful that his DNA would comply nicely with Aeryn's own. Human DNA is basi-cally a double-stranded helix made of nucleotides (essentially, sugar molecules with nitrogen bases) that bind together to form cyborg substances, industrious little sugar/phosphate/base hybrids called deoxyribonucleotides (Hill 2000: 39). They become two complimentary strands that can then be used to replicate each other, and which even include special enzymes that 'proofread' each strand for genetic errors (Hill 2000: 44). But Pilot's DNA would probably be a lot more complex—maybe it would have three strands, or it would look like a cube, or an octagon.

The point here is that this DNA combination, in fact, doesn't 'work', and produces an indescribable being who is part-Pilot and part-Aeryn. She begins to hear Moya as Pilot hears her, to feel her systems and experience what it is like to be bonded with the Leviathan. Eventually, Crichton manages to reverse the process of metamorphosis, and Aeryn becomes herself again. But that knowledge, that experience of symbiosis and interconnection, remains with her. Aeryn reminds Pilot of this when she is defending herself in 'The Way We Weren't' (2.05), saying that ' we are closer than any two others on this ship. I still carry remnants of your DNA inside of me.' Aeryn, the Peacekeeper soldier whose experience of 'individuality' has always been contingent upon her placement within a 'platoon, a rank, a regiment,' now experiences a unique reversal of this commitment to community. Rather than the erasure of her own self, which has always been the price of finding community among the Peacekeepers, Aeryn now understands that a different sort of connection exists: a connection—like the Pilot/Leviathan bond—that does entail sacrifice, but that expands the self rather than annihilating it. This is the closest that any crew member, other than Zhaan, comes to understanding the precise 'covenant' between Leviathan and Pilot.

'DNA Mad Scientist' ends with an unlikely scene—a scene between D'Argo and Pilot, which rarely occurs in the show. Pilot says, not coldly, but simply logically, that 'Luxans are not given to apology,' and in this moment it seems that, as species, both Luxans and Pilots understand each other quite well. Pilot knows that, if D'Argo were to apologize, it would be a violation of his own cultural precepts, just as D'Argo understands that it is in Pilot's nature to make sacrifices in order to help Moya and her crew. When D'Argo withdraws a curious device, called a *shilquen*, Pilot asks 'what manner of weapon is it?' But then D'Argo begins to play the *shilquen*, and we understand that it is not a weapon—and that this serenade is for Pilot alone. It is not an apology, or a repayment, but rather an iteration of tenderness; a response to D'Argo's own violence, and Pilot's pain, without trying to disavow either. In this sense, D'Argo implies that violence and beauty, pain and solace, simply *are*. They occur often side by side, emerging from each other, binding with each other like the long, sinuous peptide chains that bind to form DNA. Nobody other than Moya, we presume, hears this response to what is essentially the mad and provocative disorder of the universe.

It takes a cyborg to live within such a universe. But, if we trust our instincts, then we are probably, as Haraway says, already cyborgs, which means that we're at least on the right track. Moya, as an embodied female cyborg who is also bonded with a male alien, presents us with an array of cyborg identities rather than a single way of living within the mediation of organics and technology. In this chapter, I have tried to use Moya as a living artifact for linking parallel (and sometimes oppositional) discourses together—that is, discussions of women's reproductive rights with discussions of cyborg studies in general. In this, I am not suggesting that Moya is some fantastic alternative to the gaps within both of these discourses, but rather that she stands as a fascinating example of how the cyborg remains unfixable, and how pregnant bodies within SF narratives (as well as within mass media) can be rendered as spectacle even as they are infused with suspect cultural currency. Moya's own pregnancy is a fraught event, and her offspring's death is a double-voiced event. Talyn can be read as either a bleak criticism of medical reproductive intervention—in that his 'inflicted' hybridity is what renders him monstrous—or as an ambiguous affirmation of women's biological knowledge, in that it is Moya, ultimately, who understands Talyn's nature, and understands that he (for whatever reason) cannot be allowed to live.

If anything, I have tried to suggest with this chapter that Moya is not a passive being, subject to constant outside invasion, just as Pilot is not a non-character who happens to be 'plugged in' to the Leviathan. Both are complex, enduring characters, and both exist in a 'co-constitutive' relationship with each other that ultimately expands and benefits both of them. Unlike the uneasy cyborg relationships that proliferate in many contemporary SF narratives (as examples, see *Star Trek*'s colonizing Borg, *The Terminator*, *Robocop*, and so on), the relationship between Pilot and Moya is a powerful covenant that allows them to experience things that they couldn't if they were both autonomous beings. It is not just a cybernetic model, but a model of consciousness, an open-ended and 'differential' way of envisioning the world, with its arrays of companion-species, that admits physical violability and mutual symbiosis. As Haraway reminds us, 'nature is made, but not entirely by humans; it is a co-construction among humans and non-humans' (2004: 317). We need to see it as a 'co-construction,' rather than as a field to be inscribed by science. We need to see biology as a conversation, and a conversation 'always in the middle of things' (2004: 306), rather than as a material to be studied and altered.

We can never be certain if Moya really is 'fulfilled' by her crew, if she really is 'willing' to do much of what they ask because she is sustained by their presence. But her crew is certainly sustained by her, and more than willing to defend her with their lives. Moya is, after all, not just their companion, but their home. She is the 'living ship' that Crichton can't help but call amazing, even when he is disoriented and frightened during the show's very first episode. They may all be cyborgs drifting through space, carried along by the energetic currents of Moya's starburst, guided by the complex mathematical vectors (along with the equally complex emotional mathematics) of Pilot's daily calculations, regulations, protections. If so, their fusion within the 'queer family' of Haraway's companion species is one that brings both love and risk, sustenance and pain, at every turn. But even Rygel, I think, would echo Pilot's calm assertion that it is 'a perfectly equitable arrangement'—which, in heteroglossic cyborg speech, in the fused language of skin and machine, of soft textures and glowing consoles (whose light can also be comforting), is tantamount to an admission of love.

3 Alien Masculinities, Alienated Desires
Crichton, D'Argo, and Scorpius

Precisely because virtually nobody fits the definitions of male and female, the categories gain power and currency from their impossibility.

—Judith Halberstam (1998: 27)

Something is lost within the recesses of the loss . . . if I lose you, under these conditions, then I not only mourn the loss, but I become inscrutable to myself. Who 'am' I, without you?

—Judith Butler (2004: 22)

Thanks for your memories, John.

—Scorpius (as Harvey), *The Peacekeeper Wars*, Pt. 1)

Farscape is committed to presenting us with fascinating and perverse models of masculinity (as well as femininity, which I will treat in the next chapter). This discussion will focus on the unusual relationship between the three characters who represent a sort of masculine triptych[1] on the show: Crichton, D'Argo, and Scorpius. Although Crichton and D'Argo obviously have a deep and enduring friendship, some fans would disagree that D'Argo and Scoripus are connected in any way—given that they share almost no scenes together, and seem mutually opposed to each other ethically, politically, and even spiritually.[2] But I would contend that D'Argo and Scorpius are linked through their shared connection to John Crichton, and that together they represent opposing poles of masculinity against which Crichton's own maleness can be measured and observed.

As Judith Halberstam notes in her book *Female Masculinity*, heterosexual white masculinity is generally taken for a normative category rather than a model that is fraught with contradictions, and as a result white masculinity 'becomes legible as masculinity [only] where and when it leaves the white male middle-class body' (1998: 2). Scorpius and D'Argo, both aliens (in the cultural as well as the physiological sense) thus present critical symbolic registers against which Crichton's own masculinity, and humanity, becomes legible in interesting and unpredictable ways. If you'll pardon the pun, the extraterrestrial body represents a largely 'uncharted territory' in terms of Gender Studies. If hetero-masculinity is to be unmoored from the white male body, then the alien body seems like an excellent mirror by which to reflect and refract the various contradictions that make up maleness, modernity, and humanity. It is precisely due to the subaltern qualities[3] of this body, its inability to speak—or its coercion to speak in a way that only reaffirms liberal humanism and western imperialism—that the extraterrestrial becomes a necessary register for analyzing human discourse.

Crichton aptly sums up his own model for masculinity in *The Peacekeeper Wars* when he tells his newborn son that 'Crichtons don't cry . . . often' (*PKW*, Pt. 2). The 'often' of course playfully refers to Crichton's own emotional vulnerability, as well as the numerous times over the course of the show that he has shed tears for one reason or another. Interestingly, most of Crichton's most intensely vulnerable moments seem to occur in the company of other men.[4] He cries while being comforted by Stark ('The Hidden Memory,' 1.20), and while explaining to Crais how terrifying it is to be constantly hunted by the Peacekeepers ('Family Ties,' 1.22). Crichton is also at his most volatile when in the company of either D'Argo or Scorpius, who both seem capable of bringing out the best and the worst in him (often simultaneously). It's also possible that, given Aeryn's masculine qualities and her own 'butch' persona (what Leslie Fenberg might call 'granite butch'[5]), Crichton's vulnerability in Aeryn's presence is an interesting form of man-to-man discourse. He is perhaps breaking down in front of Aeryn not because she embodies femininity, but because she projects a covert form of masculinity. I'll discuss this a bit more in the next chapter, which will focus on Aeryn, Chiana, and Zhaan.

As I mentioned in Chapter 1, John Crichton is supposed to represent an uncomplicated point of view for the audience. The viewers instinctively sympathize with Crichton because he is so disoriented by his alien surroundings, and this sympathy, we assume, allows *Farscsape*'s multiple viewing communities to overlook the fact that Ben Browder (who portrays Crichton) is a dishy hetero-dreamboat with a chiseled physique and flirtatious body language. If Crichton becomes the point of view for the audience, then the audience is reading *Farscape* as a text through the hegemonic histories and cultural inflections of straight white masculinity. And I am using *hegemonic* here in the ambiguous way that Antonio Gramsci originally conceptualized it—as the bi-directional power flow between the state and civil society, a relationship as necessary to political society as power itself, which produces normativity through a combination of coercion/consent.

Gramsci envisioned the formation of an ethical proletarian state, which, through a political 'war of position' as well as a 'war of movement' (basically, ideological and class warfare vs. revolutionary action) could create an *alternative hegemony* to replace the oppressive state (1995: 243–4). This alternative hegemony, however, could only emerge through the widespread expansion of political education and class consciousness. *Hegemony*, therefore, is a tripartite concept—referring to both rule by coercion and rule by consent, as well as to a uniquely ethical relationship between the ideal proletarian state and civil society. So, when I talk about 'hegemonic histories' or 'hegemonic maleness,' I am using hegemony as a plural concept, a power relation that involves, importantly, *consent* as well as coercion.

Domination always includes a covert (or even patent) participation by the subaltern classes (Gramsci's concept, originally, referring primarily to the proletariat), and entering—or being involuntarily positioned into—a hegemonic relationship with white masculinity always involves hidden gestures of voluntarism and concession, agreement and surrender. I will return to Gramsci's conception of political education, as well as the contradictions in classical Marxism that he was attempting to resolve, in Chapter 7—which focuses on *Farscape* and nationhood.

Given the complexity of the narrator/audience relationship, then, Crichton's 'hegemonic' position remains conflictual for the show's female fans (nearly 50% of the viewership, which is unprecedented for an SF show), as well as its queer and non-white fans,[6] who must strain to see events from his normative point of view. He is like them, but not like them; possibly, they want to resent him, but they also might want to emulate him. And there is always a bi-directional flow of power here, always an insubstantial line between sacrificing power and having it stolen from you. Crichton himself does much to upset that balance of normativity, and, as I will argue, it is precisely through his unstable masculinity—as well as his provocative connections with other male characters—that he becomes capable of reflecting multiple viewpoints and lived realities.

When D'Argo and Crichton first meet in the pilot episode, they immediately dislike each other. Well, D'Argo immediately dislikes Crichton, at any rate, while Crichton himself is still in shock about being on board an alien spacecraft—with *real aliens.* 'Close Encounters my ass,' he says into his tape recorder at the end of the episode, thereby poking fun at the Hollywood simulations of extraterrestrial life that proliferate in shows like *Star Trek.* These aliens don't just have a funny ridge painted between their eyes. D'Argo actually has tentacles, Zhaan is blue, and Rygel is . . . well . . . a floating slug, basically. None of John's pop-culture knowledge, couched as it is in scientific geekdom, has prepared him for dealing with the cultural Other that these aliens represent. And if, as Lévinas (1969) suggests, our deepest ethical experience occurs across the subjective divide, in the encounter between self and other, then Crichton is pretty much *frelled.*

D'Argo's first words to Crichton are unambiguous. 'I don't know who you are, where you're from, or what you want. But if you threaten my freedom, I'll kill you' ('Premiere,' 1.01). Crichton's last words to D'Argo, before the Luxan dies, are a complete ethical reversal of this first moment between them. 'You are my closest friend,' John says. When D'Argo jokingly replies, 'you could have done better,' John shakes his head. 'Nowhere in the universe' (*PKW*, Pt. 2).[7] Their journey from open hostility to enduring friendship might seem, at first, merely to recapitulate the imperialist mode in SF, whereby a human character educates a 'savage' alien, thereby helping them to become more human. But, if anything, it is D'Argo who humanizes Crichton by showing him the various contradictions and antinomies within his own, native conception of humanity. D'Argo and Crichton both educate each other, and the end result of their relationship together is a testament to *Farscape*'s unique status as a show that values dialogue, character growth, and textual ambiguity over pat storylines and easy endings.

However, just as Crichton is beginning to adjust to D'Argo and the rest of Moya's crew, just as he is beginning to piece together a new mode of discourse for communicating with these fantastic and unpredictable beings, a bizarre variable gets thrown into the mix.

That variable is Scorpius, the half-Sebacean, half-Scarran military commander who believes that John possesses crucial knowledge about harnessing wormhole technology. In terms of theoretical study, Scorpius is a Foucauldian's dream come true. He wears a leather body suit, locks men into a sadistic torture-chair in order to penetrate the darkest recesses of their psyches (*Discipline and Punish*, anyone?), and he has an intense fascination with mind/body and space/time boundaries. His obsession with wormholes, like Crichton's own cathexis around the interstellar phenomena, is also at heart an obsession with a kind of spatial orifice—a torn opening in the fabric of space/time that has the capacity to deform and destroy the body, even as it holds the tantalizing possibility of transporting one to new worlds.

Scorpius refers to Scarran interrogation methods as 'mind-raping' ('Prayer,' 4.18), but his own interrogative technology—ominously known as the Aurora Chair—is also an instrument of rape and torture. Crais, Stark, and John—all men, interestingly enough—are given their turn in the Aurora Chair, and the result seems to be a curious mixture of intense pain and covert sexual satisfaction. After a particularly intensive session ('The Hidden Memory,' 1.20), we find Crichton lying on the floor of the cell that he shares with Stark on Scorpius' Gammak base, panting and convulsing, as if he has just undergone an experience of either remarkable pain or singular *jouissance*. The obvious suggestion, and one that I certainly won't be the first to make, is that there remains a thin line between the two sensations. This is a bit like what Nietzsche means when he says, in *Thus Spake Zarathustra*, that joy is tragedy—which is the real tragedy.[8] We can't tell where the pain ends and the pleasure begins, because both sensitivities bear a relationship as close as sign/signifier, or life/death, and we can't pry them apart.

'The Hidden Memory' is actually a remarkable episode, not simply because it illustrates Crichton's vulnerability, but because of the fascinating connection that it establishes between Crichton and Stark. As I discuss in Chapter 6, Stark is a member of the Banik[9] slave race—an unhelpfully vague classification, since we don't know if there are other slave races, or how they became enslaved—and, because he is also a mystical being known as a Stykera, Stark has the unusual ability of guiding souls into the realm of death. Mysticism does have a place within SF, but that place is generally peripheral, or serves as an exercise in cultural anthropology (see *Star Trek*'s

Vulcans, or the theocratic Bajorans). Rarely does it present itself as an independent force that can't be fully recombined and rationalized by technological motivation, rather than, in the words of Landon Brooks, as 'an action or artifact that seems magical but can be 'explained' in rhetoric that makes the magic seem a plausible product of advanced science or technology' (1997: 20).

But Stark, as well as Zhaan and Noranti, seems to possess mystical abilities that defy scientific explanation. This is one of the areas where *Farscape* excels as a kind of postmodern synthesis of more conventional SF programming, since it remains willing to incorporate variables into its own technological narrative that might actually contradict, or even disarm, the familiar tropes and production codes that make SF recognizable as a genre. *Farscape* is, admittedly, 'soft-SF,' in that it privileges communication and philosophical debate over rigorous technical explanation and mathematical certainty. But the inclusion of such a random and interesting element as alien mysticism—an element never explained to anyone's satisfaction, nor properly marshaled to serve the plot in any crucial way—shows that *Farscape* as a text actually thrives on its own contradictions and dialectical perversions.[10]

In 'The Hidden Memory' (1.20), after Crichton returns from a difficult session in the Aurora Chair—which is really a sadomasochistic exercise, with Scorpius as the dominatus—he finds himself unable to deal with Stark's mounting insanity. It is a peculiar convention of both SF and fantasy narratives that characters are often given names which represent moral possibilities. This can even occur at the phonetic level. Just look at the brothers Edgar and Edmund in Shakespeare's *King Lear*. Many readers respond to the hard 'g' fricative sound in 'Edgar' as something that is ominous or evil, but it is Edmund, in fact, who turns out to be the pathological one (well, they probably both are). 'Scorpius' is an evil-sounding name, not simply because it is homophonic to *scorpion*, but because of its hard consonants and reptilian sound. 'D'Argo' has a guttural tone to it, like the Klingon 'Worf,' which symbolically denotes physical prowess and martial strength, as well as aggression and inhumanity. 'Chiana' sounds like a child's name, similar to Pollyanna (although Eleanor Porter probably wouldn't appreciate the comparison), and Chiana is indeed childlike in many ways.

But no character fully embodies the psychological potential of his own name more than Stark, who is also stark raving mad. Well, not completely. As I suggest in Chapter 6, Stark seems capable of lucid-ity—as well as many other feats of both mystical and supernatural power—when he so chooses. Stark represents another perverse model of masculinity on the show, which I am going to call psy-chotic masculinity, but he is also de-gendered. Since most of the characters on *Farscape* are sexually active, their gender becomes leg-ible when we see who they're having sex with, or with whom they're in close physical proximity. Stark, although he does ulti-mately have a romantic relationship with Zhaan, is possibly the least physically demonstrative of all the characters. I would argue that he shares more intimacy with Crichton (both Crichtons, actually) than he does with Zhaan. In this episode, after Crichton pushes him away, Stark does something very surprising.

In an unexpected display of strength and control, he grabs Crich-ton bodily and holds onto him. Whether this occurs because Crichton is in a weakened state, because Stark is actually a lot stronger than he looks, or because—more radically—it is simply the natural thing to do, remains a puzzle. Either way, Stark manages to wrestle Crichton into a strangely intimate position. John lies with his head in Stark's lap, while Stark gently strokes his hair. He undoes his mask, and we are shocked to see that half of Stark's face is made of pure light. He is a sort of impossible being, then, an alien who straddles the border between energy/matter and spiritual/techno-logical, and his mind, like unstable energy, seems to flicker between crazy and sane.

When the light hits John's face, and he asks, startled, 'what is that?', Stark replies simply that he has given him '[just] a few thoughts.' Just as the core of Stark's mind is a place 'deep inside [that] Peacekeepers will never see,' so are we, the audience, denied access to these hidden thoughts, these images. They are a secret commerce between Stark and Crichton alone. Although this scene is discussed fully in Chapter 6, I mention it now because I think it rep-resents a really fascinating instance of masculine fracture within the show's narrative, as well as an unusual moment of physical inti-macy between these two characters. Never again do we see Crichton and Stark so close, except when Crichton #2 (or is it #1? We can't tell) is close to death, and Stark eases his spirit across the hidden boundary.[11]

Crichton lies here in Stark's embrace—in the hands of Stark, of insanity, being comforted by madness itself—and rather than squirming away, he submits to the touch; for a moment, the two of them participate in a kind of queer embrace. Stark begins to tell Crichton a story, as if they are not in a prison cell—as if stories have the capacity to transcend the reality of physical suffering—which they probably do—and, speaking of his race, the Banik, he explains that 'outsiders think that we do not feel. But it's only that our feelings don't always show.' What could this mean? Why is it necessary to explain this to Crichton, who is thinking only about escaping from his next round of torture, not about alien emotional dynamics? How does it relate to the show's plot in any way?

The point of this scene, this whole conversation, is that it has no point at all. Given the carceral reality of the prison cell, as well as the impending and probable death of both Stark and Crichton, any words at all that they might exchange would sound equally ridiculous. Crichton could very well be talking about 'Betty,' his prized Ford pickup truck, or how cold and dark the cell is, or how much he misses Aeryn, or how frightened he is, or how difficult it is to hold things together when your only companion is half-crazy. Anything would make just as much sense. That Crichton and Stark manage to have a conversation at all, let alone a conversation that seems to be about their own feelings, is in itself an unexpected act of defiance against oppressive reality, as well as a demonstration of total absurdity.

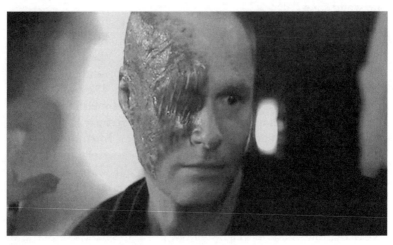

5. Stark finds his inner peace

Farscape is as equally committed to its absurdist moments as it is to delivering action-packed and suspenseful storylines, since the creators of the show (Rockne O'Bannon, David Kemper, and Brian Henson) understand that the most interesting fractures, contradictions, and unexpected resolutions occur along a spectrum of human (and alien) activity that is 10% action and 90% banality. Why should we care that Rygel has three stomachs, and loves to eat 'sork wings' and 'crispy grolack' (which actually sounds a lot like KFC)? Why does it matter that it took D'Argo cycles (years) to master the full use of his prehensile tongue, or that Zhaan is a tenth-level Pa'u rather than a ninth- or twelfth-level? It doesn't matter, and thus it matters because it doesn't matter. The ordinary ephemera of life, the stuff that goes on behind bathroom (rather than bedroom) doors, the marginal moments, don't traditionally 'matter' in action-driven narratives like SF. But it is precisely because they haven't traditionally mattered that these marginal events, histories, and desires need to be displayed and recuperated.

I want to return to this idea of the masculine triptych, which I introduced at the beginning of the chapter. Stark is a rogue masculine model within the show, a form of psychotic masculinity—that is, masculinity unmoored from any strictly ethical foundation, and thus a chaotic core *beneath* the masculine that any of the male (or female) characters might conceivably emulate—but the primary masculine figures within the show are still Crichton, D'Argo, and Scorpius. Why these three, and why haven't I included Crais? Firstly, because they are all present from the beginning to the end of the show (Crais is present from the very first episode, but he has an increasingly peripheral role as the show progresses). Secondly, because, although Crais does pursue and torment Crichton, he never has a close and physically intimate relationship with him, whereas Scorpius gets as close as possible—inside of his brain, in fact. Thirdly, because Crais chooses to sacrifice himself, thereby securing his own moral redemption. Scorpius sees no need for self-sacrifice, since he never admits that his motives are wrong. He is willing to die for his ideologies, but only because he's so convinced that they are ethically superior.[12]

The sacrifice of Crais and Talyn (who may have been coerced into giving up his life, depending upon how we read the event) remains an indecipherable part of *Farscape*'s narrative. Nietzsche reminds us that sacrifice is never selfless, since most human activity—even altruism—emerges from a primordial spirit of revenge. Martyrdom in general, and historical Christian martyrdom in particular, creates 'that ghastly paradox of a 'God on a cross,' the mystery of an unimaginable and ultimate cruelty' (Nietzsche 1919: 35). I am not suggesting that Crais' sacrifice is somehow 'ghastly,' but merely gesturing to the fact that we should resist decoding it conventionally, and admit that it is a sort of 'contrapuntal' event (in the way that Edward Said frequently uses the term, referring both to theoretical and musical plurality) with multiple meanings and contradictory values.

Either way, Crais vanishes at the end of Season 3, but Scorpius remains. He is John's original nemesis, standing by his side (and in his mind) just as D'Argo stands beside him from the very beginning. If D'Argo brings out the compassion, loyalty, and brotherhood in Crichton's personality (as well as his more infantile side), then Scorpius brings out his deepest fears, his oldest anxieties, and his most incommunicable and inexpressible desires. Crichton is the phallic core around which *Farscape* revolves, and Scorpius performs the original act of penetration when he implants a neural chip in Crichton's brain. The neural chip contains a second Scorpius, a copy of his personality, which Crichton nicknames 'Harvey' (after Jimmy Stewart's invisible, six-foot-tall rabbit in *Harvey*). Thus Crichton suffers a kind of double penetration—first bodily, when his skull is literally pierced by a wicked-looking probe that resembles a metal spike ('The Hidden Memory,' 1.20), and then psychologically, when Scorpius imposes his own mind over John's.

D'Argo seems to be everything that Scorpius is not. He is emotional and instinctive, while Scorpius favors deduction and control—in that sense Scorpius is an alien Stoic, mastering his own passions even as he attempts to master the perceived Scarran 'deficiencies' of his own body. John Carlberg suggests that Scorpius 'must constantly wear a special suit to cool his internal temperature, lest he be consumed by his own inner fire' (2005), and also alludes to the Christ/Satan dichotomy that Crichton and Scorpius seem to embody. Carlberg further points out that even Crichton's name is homophonic with Christ, and that his various deaths and resurrections (culminating with his death and rebirth in *The Peacekeeper Wars*, when he theoretically gives up his life in order to save the galaxy) all point to the reality of John being a Christ-figure. I don't believe that their relationship is quite that iconic, nor that functional—in terms of illustrating any sort of religious didacticism—but there is a spiritual element to it, just as there is a fascinating sexual element as well.

Scorpius becomes everything that Crichton disavows, while D'Argo becomes everything that Crichton either admires (loyalty, bravery, martial skill) or tries to regulate and balance (emotion, impulsivity, judgment). D'Argo is thus an equation in need of balance, while Scorpius remains a black hole of uncertainty—a nexus of seemingly negative qualities that John can only recoil from in horror, even as he shields himself from the reality that those qualities might be all too familiar. Here we have abjection in action: the foreclosure of elements of our own character, the disavowal of corporeal and psychological realities that seem too grotesque to fathom, even as they also seem to emerge from within rather than without. Julia Kristeva defines abjection as 'something that disgusts you ... an extremely strong feeling that is at once somatic and symbolic...a revolt against an external menace from which one wants to distance oneself, but of which one has the impression that it might menace us from the inside' (1996: 118).

When John insists that 'I don't care about what you care about the things you care about ... wormholes,' in the episode 'A Constellation of Doubt' (4.17), he isn't really telling the truth. He cares very much about wormholes—is obsessed with them, in fact, at least equally as obsessed as Scorpius—and all of his disavowals don't add up to a wholesale rejection of Scorpius or his interests and principles. Nor do they phase Scorpius, who, as always, just sits back and listens patiently to John, knowing that he will eventually reveal himself, that he will eventually crack, just as every skilled torturer understands the precise limits and breaking points of his subjects. How flesh separates, bleeds, breaks; how the mind falls apart like rotted cloth, or a spider web collapsing beneath the pressure of a single, careless breath. Scorpius understands John, because he is another *version* of John, just as Scorpius's neural clone is a second version of Scorpius himself, and John's neural clone (left behind in the fragments of the neural chip, once it has been removed from John's head) is yet another version, a version of a version. This is Baudrillard's simulacrum, which is the copy without the original, the reality without the Real.

Scorpius himself is hybrid—the child not just of mixed-race, but mixed-*species* parents—and so he understands what it is to walk boundaries, to defy classifications and racial taxonomies. Crichton does not, given that he emerges from a hegemonic tradition of entrenched white, middle-class masculinity, and so Scorpius is constantly attempting to instruct John, trying to show him his own deficiencies, but also his own hidden strengths. Crichton's masculinity would normally be transparent, invisible, but D'Argo (the virile warrior) and Scorpius (the sexualized villain) become a necessary symbolic backdrop, a sort of de-cloaking device (if you'll pardon the Klingon pun) for revealing Crichton's own process of being male.

In the episode 'Prayer' (4.18), Scorpius and John strike a pact—if Scorpius helps him recover information about where Aeryn has been imprisoned, John will give him the secret to harnessing wormholes. 'Every equation. Every formula. Everything.' Scorpius's reaction is both unexpected and perversely appropriate. He stops abruptly, and grabs John forcibly by the hand. Suddenly, the conversation has moved from equations to bodies, from abstraction to physicality, although Scorpius understands that the two ideas were never actually separate. Dialogue always contains bodies, as well as concepts, and science is as enfleshed, as embodied, as Crichton himself, with its own erotics, its own desires.

Scorpius cuts John's finger—he flinches, startled, but also obviously curious. He watches as Scorpius holds his finger above his mouth, letting a single drop of blood strike his tongue. Then he wraps his mouth around John's finger, licking it clean and sucking the blood. We are reminded of Gary Oldman in the contemporary film adaptation of *Dracula* (1992), who cuts his hand while in the presence of Jonathan Harker—played by Keanu Reeves—and then, surreptitiously, while Harker's attention is elsewhere, lovingly laps the blood from his own flesh like a hungry kitten (a comparison that Dracula himself makes to Mina Harker in Bram Stoker's original text). Scorpius calls this a 'Scarran Blood Vow,' but it is almost a kind of dark nuptial between them—a marriage vow that links them, blood to blood, in a silent and secret exchange of bodily fluids.

Scorpius cuts his own finger, and a clear fluid begins to drip from it. 'I will help,' he tells John slowly, 'if you taste.' The vampiric overtones here are practically overwhelming, but John doesn't actually seem repulsed as he holds out his tongue, allowing a single drop of blood to fall upon it. Both men have now tasted each other. If this isn't a sex scene, I don't know what is. The only more distinctly homoerotic moment in the show occurs in the episode 'Out of their Minds' (2.09), when Chiana takes over D'Argo's body and attempts to seduce Crichton (who is actually being 'inhabited' by Rygel). D'Argo puts his hand on Crichton's uncharted territories, and

6. *'I will go with you . . . if you taste'*

7. *Scorpius savors Crichton's blood*

although this occurs just out of the frame, it doesn't take much imagination to realize what's going on. I'll talk more about this scene in Chapter 5, which focuses on bodies and bodily politics.

What I'm trying to establish here is that Crichton and Scorpius are ethical and psychological opposites, but they also share certain covert bonds and desires. If Crichton comes from a privileged background—loving parents, middle-class suburbia, and the cultural flexibility necessary to do whatever he wants—then Scorpius represents the antithesis of that life. He reminds us in the episode 'Incubator' (3.11) that 'my first memory . . . was pain,' and goes on to describe how his experience growing up under Scarran oppression was a nightmare of physical and psychological torture.[13] The more pressure Scorpius puts on John, the closer he pursues him, the more he is forcing John to re-live his—Scorpius'—own terrifying adolescence. Thereby, he hopes effectively to write over John's life with his own, to replace John's memories, and to eventually *become* Crichton by transforming his entire worldview and replacing his own subjectivity with a malicious copy. Most villains feel the need to break down heroes, to brutally punish their bodies and destroy their spirits. But Scorpius is actually performing a kind of intimate torture here, a loving violation. He wants to become John, to replace John's psyche with his own, to make the human empathize with and understand the alien. It isn't just control that Scorpius is after, but a sort of cultural intimacy, which he is willing to create at the (reasonable) cost of John's body and soul.

D'Argo's philosophy is the inverse of Scorpius'—he wants to shore up Crichton's humanity, to expand his cultural awareness, while Scorpius wants to deconstruct and dissect it. Crichton doesn't necessarily 'learn' anything through D'Argo's friendship. *Farscape* isn't a fable, and it doesn't present us with easy moral exempla, or facile relationships that can be deconstructed in terms of their literary and cultural significance.

Wait.

Isn't that what this book is trying to do?

Well, yes and no. The discussions in this book center on culturally and psychologically significant elements within the show, but it isn't my purpose to 'explain' *Farscape*, to help you get it, to grant you postmodern secrets or an all-access-pass to the symbolism behind the episodes, the Real behind the real. I'm more concerned with exposing connections and establishing fractures, pointing to bizarre moments and wondering about the choices that both humans and aliens make.

Yes, I believe that Crichton's relationship with D'Argo is instructive in a number of ways, but it is also a friendship for the sake of a friendship. D'Argo and Crichton are drawn to each other because they are, in many ways, masculine opposites (even as they simultaneously share many qualities) but they also become friends because they like each other, and even, over the course of years, grow to love each other. Sometimes, all we need to learn from having friends is that having friends is all we need. I think. Maybe. If Kristeva can get away with saying 'love is the only thing that can save us' (1996: 121), then I don't feel so bad about claiming that all we need is love. And alienation. The two are intimates, and you can't have one without the other.

The problem with Crichton's white masculinity is that it tends to masquerade as the invisible visible, the ground upon which all figures play out their relations, rather than a subject that is actually figural or relational itself. Being a man, being white, being straight, are all not merely identities, but relations, ways of connecting and communicating, methodologies for living in a world that either oppresses or congratulates you (often both at the same time). Sally Robinson, in her book *Marked Men*, notes that 'white men, conflated with normativity in the American social lexicon, have not been understood as practicing identity politics because they are visible in political terms, even as they benefit from the invisibility ... [thus] what calls itself the normative in American culture has vested interests in *both* invisibility and visibility' (2000: 2–3).[14]

Crichton benefits from this invisibility until he finds himself aboard Moya, where he is suddenly quite *visible* as a bizarre subject, a creature to be studied. No longer a human, he becomes rather a *non-alien*, an object of curiosity. Everything that has given him cultural and symbolic currency, up until this point in his life, now completely reverses, becoming the very traits, oddities, and perceived deficiencies that make his 'humanity' so repugnant and fascinating at the same time to aliens of the Uncharted Territories. Whereas human cultural values usually trump alien 'traditions' (read: primitive animism and backwardness), in Crichton's case, what makes him human only serves to make him alien in this new world.

This is a pretty shocking reversal, and it understandably takes him a while to adjust to the fact that humans are, in fact, *not* superior. As Aeryn reminds her human interviewer in 'A Constellation of Doubt' (4.17), nobody even cares about the planet Earth. Humans aren't a threat to interstellar empires like the Scarrans or the Peace-keepers, and they don't even have the technology to be a potential ally. They don't rate at all, in fact. In 'Crackers Don't Matter' (2.04), when John ironically claims that 'humans are superior' (to whom?), the real critical thrust of the episode—and the subtextual jab behind its otherwise absurdist title—is that Humans Don't Matter. Being white, being heterosexual, being middle class, being attractive (by human standards), are all relations that no longer *relay* what they're supposed to, matters that don't 'matter,' or that matter in unex-pected ways.

If, as Judith Butler claims, all matter 'is founded through a set of violations' (1993: 29), and all bodies must foreclose or disavow cer-tain lived realities in order to have others 'matter' in the correct way (the western way), then Crichton is forced up against the radical materialization of this premise. He no longer matters in the way that he thought he did. This must mean, also, that he is no longer the man he thought he was, or the man that other people thought he was. Space transforms his masculinity, and John's relationship with both Scorpius and D'Argo, in exposing the transparent operations of that masculinity, also forces him down new paths, new premises, and new ways of embodying maleness. If D'Argo can be a different sort of 'man' to Crichton, just as Scorpius is a radically different 'man' to D'Argo, then 'man' as a discursive category, and as a sexed reality, becomes a much more flexible signifier to be shared among humans and aliens. These evolving relationships force us to ask, not simply what kind of 'man' D'Argo is, but what kind of Luxan John is, or what kind of human Scorpius is.

What does it mean to ask what kind of Luxan John is? It means the same thing as asking what kind of a man D'Argo is. Although 'male' and 'female' as gendered and sexed categories seem to trans-late well across alien cultures, we come to understand through D'Argo and Scorpius, as well as through Aeryn and Chiana, that gender is a local idea, a concept that emerges through cultural and physiological context rather than strictly through psychological individuation. D'Argo's conception of masculinity cannot be the same as Crichton's, since Crichton doesn't have tentacles, or a prehensile tongue, or a *qualta* blade. If Scorpius conceptualizes masculinity, it must be a curious mixture of his own genetic heritages, an uneasy combination of Scarran physical impregnability (since their skins are virtually impenetrable) and Peacekeeper military regimentation.

But Crichton did not grow up with a body suit designed to regulate his temperature, or cooling rods inserted into his skull, or Scorpius' unique ability to sense heat signatures from living beings. None of their masculine models can resemble each other, since alien contact proves, as so many other things do, that sex and gender are radically specific and contingent concepts. The extraterrestrial body unhinges normative gender, creating the opportunity for John to question his own masculinity, and the ethical encounter (in the sense of Lévinas and the self/other relation) necessary for him to realize that he is not the only male in the universe, nor the only human. Crichton isn't as brave or impulsive as D'Argo, nor is he as cunning and selfish as Scorpius. It is through adaptability, not cultural supremacy, that he manages to redesign a new masculine reality for himself, and thus the ability of the masculine sign to withstand cultural assaults—without crumbling—is once again demonstrated.

The primary difference in *Farscape* is that John's masculinity is represented as vulnerable and fractured from the very start, and thus its 'coherence' throughout the course of the show is actually just an interesting evolution and mutation of its own corrupt beginnings. No origin without corruption, and no starting point without an edge. John's maleness, his relational as well as his concrete understanding of being a man, always bears the Derridan trace of its own imperfection, the ghostly outlines and remembrances of everything that came before it, inchoate, and everything that will come after, insubstantial.[15] A masculinity as transparent and spectral as the various star charts that Crichton pores over, day after day (or should we say arn after arn?) as he searches for a way home. The triumph of *Farscape* as a deconstructive narrative, and the proof that Crichton is able to expand the limits of his own humanity, is that he eventually stops searching.

He becomes obsessed with wormholes, not merely because they represent a way home, but because they represent the dissolution of all boundaries, the disavowal of space/time itself. If the universe is founded on a set of violations, then the wormhole is the foreclosed matter, the matter that isn't supposed to matter, and the abjected substance of the cosmos. Crichton is thus searching for a home in the very heart of nothingness, trying to find reason and sense within the core of disunity and immateriality, the very border between life and death. If Scorpius can penetrate his mind, then Crichton can penetrate the very fabric of the universe—perhaps as the perfect embodiment of the Nietzschean spirit of revenge. But I don't think this is simply bad conscience in action. It seems as if Crichton, in trying to overcome his own bodily boundaries, is also trying to overcome the barriers and paraphysical systems that he sees in the material universe. His body becomes the unconscious surface of the Uncharted Territories; his maleness, his sexuality, his love for friends, for Aeryn, for home, becomes the permeable membrane of space.

This does make John a Christ-like figure of sorts, but if that is so, then he must be a sexed and gendered Christ. His reason is guided by his desires, and those desires are patently erotic. Crichton even eroticizes science, which isn't that hard to do, since it presents itself within the traditional positivist framework as *the* cipher for unlocking all human relations. What could be sexier than that? D'Argo, in turn, eroticizes violence, which he comes to understand as a necessary component of his body and soul rather than a trait to be mastered or overcome. In the episode 'Mental as Anything' (4.15), when confronting Macton—the brother of his wife Lo'Lan, who we learn actually killed his own sister in order to 'protect' her from D'Argo—he admits that 'I *am* violent . . . when I choose to be.' This may seem like a simplistic realization, but for D'Argo it is a moment of profound individuation. Just as John discovers that he can only survive through adaptability, D'Argo finally discovers that his violence is both a genetic and a psychological trait, an element of his persona that is both enforced and voluntary at the same time. He wants it and needs it, and in order to survive, he must accept it rather than dominate it.

Violence, for D'Argo, is the abjected component of his own masculinity, and in 'Mental as Anything' (taking place, fittingly enough, within the specular terrain of D'Argo's own mind), he must undo that act of abjection and reincorporate the violence back into his own lived reality. As Kristeva explains in *Powers of Horror*, abjection is not a singular act, but rather a daily process, like Nietzsche's law of eternal return, which must be undone day by day, moment by moment, like becoming aware of one's own breathing. Violence is D'Argo's fetish, but it is also the substance of his being Luxan, his phenomenological 'Luxan-ness,' and so he has to gather up all of that violence and slowly reincorporate it back into his daily routines, reinscribing it as a will to power, energy that is simultaneously creative and destructive, ordered and chaotic.

Crichton learns a very different lesson from this episode, and, appropriately enough, it is Scorpius who teaches it to him. When he fails the mental tasks set out for him by Katoya—the alien who runs a sort of mental training facility on a remote planet—John is stuck in 'remedial training,' which actually amounts to a small cage with a grate full of hot coals inside of it. In a moment of exquisite Zen instruction (or possibly Maoist torture), Katoya repeatedly drops a key through the bars of the cage, while John struggles to catch it. Each time, the key falls through the grate, and John burns his hands trying to retrieve it. The repetition grates on him, hour by hour, until he begins to lose his mind. Although, practically speaking, he probably left his mind—along with the majority of his cultural conceptions and political ideologies—back on Earth, where it belonged (and 'mattered').

As John's mind unravels, he does what he always does in these situations. He falls back on popular culture. If John's own vulnerability as a male (or perhaps, after all, his destructive capacity as a male) is what he abjects, then Earth pop culture remains his talisman, his symbol of individuation and human adaptability. There is no tense situation that John cannot defuse by mentioning Kraft Dinner, or *The Brady Bunch*, or football. This time, he begins to whistle the 'Colonel Bogey March' (made famous in the movie *Bridge Over the River Kwai* as symbol of masculine camaraderie), which neither Katoya nor Scorpius is able to recognize. His many attempts to shore up his own masculinity, and his own sanity, go largely unnoticed by the various aliens who either ignore or misread John's symbolic strategies. He is using a local language to fight against a global-galactic Other, who will devour him unless he agrees to meet it half-way, to encounter it ethically, to listen to the extraterrestrial rather than speaking for it.

When Scorpius insists that John learns how to focus his willpower (once again reinforcing the pedagogical and almost Platonic character of their relationship, with all of the interesting erotic potential that a 'Platonic' relationship actually implies within the Greek historical context), John replies with a bit of Seussical pop culture:

Scorpius: I cannot protect you from them [the Scarrans].
Crichton: *Little Cat A*—I don't want you to protect me because,
             Little Cat B—you haven't been doing such a bang up job
             of that in the first place, which brings us to *Little Cat C*—
             get me the hell out of here!

The 'Little Cats' are, of course, from Dr. Seuss' *The Cat in the Hat*, whose 'logic' Crichton now brings to bear in order refashion the situation, to recode it within the realm of popular culture, which is a realm that he can control. In *The Cat in the Hat*, the Cat produces several tiny versions of himself—the Little Cats—from underneath his hat in order to help clean up the mess (which he himself created). The cleaning effort begins with Little Cat A, but it isn't until Little Cat Z has made a final attempt, just before the children's parents return home, that the mess is at last tidied up to anyone's satisfaction. The Little Cats are a bit of perverse humor on John's part, a private joke that he knows Scorpius won't understand—even if Scorpius happens to be inside John's head. This proves, in a roundabout way, that Scorpius is incapable of 'reading' John's mind like a text, since the human (or alien) essence can't be converted into a legible datastream. Just as John first looks upon Moya, and says simply 'that's big,' without fully understanding her, so can Scorpius pore over John's brain like a singularly illegible star chart without actually understand what he's looking at. Hence, the Little Cats.

But there is also a bit of double entendre going on here (and don't we love academics for seriously pointing out the patently visible, and crucially explaining the obvious joke?) The Little Cats are also an incarnation of the neural clones that John and Scorpius share, the 'Little Cats,' or Little Johns and Little Harveys, that exist (or have existed at one time) inside both their brains. And, just as the Little Harvey is the simulacrum of Scorpius—who seems no more 'real' than his neural copy—the Little Cats are simulacra (and I'm very proud of this sentence) of the Big Cats, the Big John and Big Scorpius, who supposedly engineered them. The Little Cats have no original, which is what makes them simulacra rather than simulations or copies. This real/copy debate is taken up earlier in the show, with the creation of Crichton's duplicate, who goes on to live a parallel-yet-different life with Aeryn until he is unexpectedly killed. Who dies, in this sense? Who lives? The real, or the copy? Who is the clone, and who is the biological original?

Through this odd procession of clones and copies, Little Cats and Big Cats, holograms and projections, *Farscape* attempts to deconstruct the very notion of the human by surrounding it with copies that might also be originals, emanations that could just as easily be 'real.' Baudrillard suggests that 'the real is produced from miniaturized cells, matrices, and memory banks, models of control—and it can be reproduced an indefinite number of times from these' (1994: 2). Although this seems to exist in stark contrast to the Lacanian 'Real,' both concepts are actually quite similar, since Lacan saw the Real not as having anything to do with empirical reality, but as the opposite, unknowable sibling of the Symbolic—perhaps History—perhaps the body without organs (a concept lovingly shared, like an erotic body, by Marx, Deleuze, and Artaud). The result is the hyperreal, the refraction of the real into a spectrum of possibilities, reflections, shadow-worlds and simulatable functions.

In *Farscape*, the real is produced through microchips, through torture devices, through visualizing techniques and ultrasounds, through philosophical critique and relentless questioning. The real question that John should be asking Scorpius is not 'how do I get out of here?' but rather 'am I the Little Cat, or are you?' Of course, this question can't really have an answer; that question-answer makes about as much sense as any other potential reply to a question that can't really be answered from within western (or, evidently, even galactic) metaphysics.

How does this relate to Crichton's masculinity, his embodied maleness? It relates because his masculinity is being slowly and inexorably deconstructed, just as his humanity and sense of modernity is being deconstructed, by his multiple dialogues with aliens like Scorpius, D'Argo, and Katoya. This is extraterrestrial dialogism in action, or perhaps intergalactic heteroglossia.[16] One of the two. It should become clear by now that I enjoy queering Bakhtin's theories, just as I enjoy queering most erotic encounters within *Farscape*. I'm interested here not in somehow 'exposing' D'Argo and Crichton as queer, not in becoming an archeologist of the homosexual, or a genealogist of the bent (although I'd happily accept that term), but in queering the very notion of male friendship. All friendships emerge from an erotic potential, whether it is realized or foreclosed, and all human connections are limned and traced with the electric shadow of desire. Sexuality isn't queer, straight, or bi—it's sexuality, and represents in itself a spectrum of different positions, different politics, and different erotic possibilities.

My favorite queer moment between D'Argo and Crichton occurs when they are both floating in space. Anyone who ever said that desire doesn't occur in a vacuum, this scene proves you wrong. D'Argo and John are floating above the planet where Scorpius's mysterious Gammak base has just been destroyed. By what? By explosives, of course, since dynamite and nitroglycerin are the signifiers *par-excellence* of masculinity and patriarchal authority within SF narratives. In any other television show, D'Argo and Crichton would be zooming away safely in a shuttlecraft. *Star Trek* always presents us with a well-timed shuttle, an extension of the *Enterprise*'s own normalizing and paternalistic boundaries, appearing at the best possible moment. But there is no shuttle here. Both D'Argo and Crichton are simply floating, hand in hand, holding on to each other because they fear the reality of floating away. Because they fear the darkness, the cold, and the star-flecked night stretching out in all directions, the sheer impossibility and infinitude of deep space pressing against their flimsy subjectivities, like an entomologist pinning a moth to a card. And who wouldn't?

This moment is an extension of D'Argo's previous conversation with Crichton on the shuttle, just before launching the surprise attack against Scorpius, when he admits cagily that 'I have to pee' ('Family Ties,' 1.22). This is still possibly the greatest answer to a serious and epic question that I have ever heard, and it not only humanizes D'Argo, but 'Luxanizes' Crichton, rendering them both as 'men' who are feeling more than a little nervous and unmanly about their imminent role in this highly martial strike force. I like to think of the conversation that follows as a kind of masculine colloquy, a meeting of two masculine models that results in the refraction of both rather than the crystallization of one or the other:

> Crichton: Hey, D'Argo—how come I'm not afraid?
> D'Argo: Fear accompanies the possibility of death. Calm shepherds its certainty.
> Crichton: I love hanging with you, man.

Crichton then gives D'Argo his father's ring, claiming that it's a good luck charm, and D'Argo kisses the ring. All of the Lacanians are jumping for joy at the symbolic currency of this scene. John, his father, and D'Argo are all united in a secret masculine economy, a filial and necessarily erotic relationship, sealed by nothing less than a kiss. The ring here becomes the fetish for an evolving model of masculinity being shared by all three men—John's father, the 'old school' male imperialist, John himself, the male-in-progress, and D'Argo, the alien male, whose very claim to masculinity invalidates the entire category as a specifically human invention. What happens, Butler asks, when 'the one who represents what must be foreclosed for universality to take place . . . nevertheless speaks in its terms and makes the claim without prior legitimation?' (2001). D'Argo happens. Crichton happens. Masculinity is the ring that binds them together, and the flexible space that allows their various and inventive claims on gender to co-exist, sparkling like light on the surface of polished gold, light moving over the face of the waters, darkness outlining the surprise of the stars.

'I have to pee' could mean exactly what it is to 'be' a man, but so could 'I love hanging with you,' and so could Scorpius' equally provocative admission that 'my first memory . . . was pain.' The pain of being mattered, of being confined involuntarily to a gendered and sexed category, of being named and interpolated as 'male' within the language-universe and the symbolic economy of speech. Aeryn's repeated phrase, 'I am a Peacekeeper soldier,' remains just as convincing an affirmation of masculinity, as does Chiana's identity of *tralk*, or Zhaan's 'Delvian *seek*,' or Stark's psychotic masculinity. The ring that connects them is also a Möbius strip, an artifact that folds into itself, containing both sustenance and emptiness, matter and invisibility, absence and presence. It is worn, but it also wears the wearer, just as Bourdieu claims that 'taste classifies, and it classifies the classifier. Social subjects, classified by their classifications, distinguish themselves by the distinctions they make, between the beautiful and the ugly, the distinguished and the vulgar' (1984: 6).

Gender is not voluntary, but it is also not wholly oppressive, nor coercive, engineered. It is rather a remarkable surface upon which we inscribe a plurality of values and gravities, which themselves are not objective quantities or qualities but rather subjective utterances, unique to every era, enshrined in specific politico-economic realities (*à la* Marx) and *valueless* in and of themselves without the *idea* of absolute value to buttress them. 'I don't care about the things you care about, Scorpius.' Aliens don't care about what we care about— they don't see gender, or sexuality, on our terms, and they don't understand our values, our economic systems, our political imperiums. Gender can't exist in a vacuum. Desire can. As John holds

D'Argo's hand, he speaks directly to Moya, urging her to flee in order to protect her newborn offspring. 'Do what you have to do,' he tells her. And, as D'Argo slowly slips into unconsciousness, John finds himself all alone. He doesn't let go of D'Argo's hand. He holds on.

'I'm still here,' Aeryn says through his com-link, speaking from onboard her Prowler, 'but I can't get to you.' Her statement, which is also a kind of surrender, reminds me of the refrain that runs through a very different text—Nicole Brossard's *Mauve Desert* (1998), which revolves around queer relationship between four women, including the character Melanie, who is the daughter of two lesbian parents. 'There are ways of defiling words without digging into graves,' the book's shifting and omnipresent narrator says, 'I cannot get close to any you.' It is a habit of the reader to see this sentence as 'I cannot get close to any *of* you,' adding the possessive in order to inscribe the sentence with grammatical rationale, but the un-ciphered version—'any you'—remains much more densely powerful and disturbing. 'I can't get to you,' Aeryn pronounces. There is no 'you' to get. Part of Crichton is locked within D'Argo, and D'Argo has passed out. Possibly, he will die.

'It doesn't matter,' Crichton says, following Aeryn's statement. You can't get to me, but it doesn't matter, because there is, perhaps, no 'me' to get to. Here I can restate the quote by Judith Butler that this chapter begins with. 'Something is lost within the recesses of loss,' Butler says, speaking of mourning and the terms of grieveability, of the grieveable life, in her book *Precarious Life*. 'If I lose you, under these conditions, then I not only mourn the loss, but I become inscrutable to myself. Who 'am' I, without you?' (Butler 2004: 22). Who is Crichton without D'Argo, without Scorpius, without Aeryn? Can he even exist? Or is the remainder, the secret cipher left behind, just the black palette of space itself, an inscrutable chiaroscuro of luminance and utter dark, matter and energy, an absence where presence and certainty used to be? Does Crichton 'matter' without D'Argo? Does the universe matter without either of them? Or is the universe only worth saving because both of them occupy it, because loved people, their people, their aliens, occupy it, familiarizing and familializing it, softening it, until it becomes like the tender fluorescence of one of Moya's glowing panels?

I didn't intend, with this chapter, to sketch out a 'model' of masculinity for the show, but rather to explore how Crichton, D'Argo, and Scorpius all represent plural—or perverse—relations of masculinity that combine to create an unstable product. A type of maleness that is both alien and human, denatured like a split DNA helix, but also a kind of human alienation, a radical recombination of human and alien masculine traits that produces a new masculine text. Who is D'Argo without Scorpius to oppose him? Who is Crichton without D'Argo to comfort him? Who is Aeryn without the 'men' against which she measures her own female masculinity, her own masculine femininity, and her own embodied realness? What type of masculinity might Rygel embody, or Zhaan, or Moya, for that matter?

The next chapter isn't really a dialectical challenge to this one, but rather a supplement—a continuation of the same open-ended discussion, treating Aeryn, Chiana, and Zhaan as necessary feminine counterparts to the masculine 'models' that we've just discussed. These female characters project female masculinity, just as Crichton, D'Argo, and Scorpius project masculine femininity, and perhaps what we might call perverse maleness. It is just as possible that Aeryn and Zhaan define the parameters of masculinity in the show, while Crichton and Scorpius push the limits of femininity, as is the inverse proposition that men create masculinity and women create femininity.

In the Uncharted Territories, as in the violent plurality and chaotic tenderness of relational human existence, could anything be that simple?

4 *Tralks*, Teachers and Soldiers

Farscape and the Uncharted Territories of the Feminine

The protection of woman (today the 'third-world woman') becomes a signifier for the establishment of a *good* society . . . this group of women, unorganized landless female labor, is one of the targets of super-exploitation where local, national, and international capital intersect . . . by that route of super-exploitation these women are brought into capital logic.

—Gayatri Spivak (1999: 242; 288)

Jool (to Chiana): Wait for me!

Chiana: Not that way on Moya. You want to move faster, get better shoes.

Jool (affronted): Do you know how much these shoes cost, young whore?

Chiana: For me? Three sex acts. Probably double that for you.

—*Farscape* ('Wait for the Wheel,' 3.04)

When Aeryn Sun meets John Crichton for the first time, she immediately punches him in the face. She then kicks him, slams against a wall, and pins him to the ground, demanding: 'what is your rank and regiment? And why are you out of uniform? Rank and regiment, now!' ('Premiere,' 1.01). For Aeryn, rank and regiment hold the key to subjectivity and identity. She is *Officer Aeryn Sun, Special Peacekeeper Commando, Ikarion Company, Pleisar Regiment.*

But when she asks Crichton to identify himself, he has no such specific identity, no military chain of signifiers that might illustrate his character to Aeryn's satisfaction. He's just Crichton. And that's not nearly good enough for a Peacekeeper soldier. He needs a rank. He needs a regiment. He needs a purpose in life. Up until this point, Aeryn's embodiment, her own concept of herself as a female soldier, has been 'working' as such. It has worked for her. But this is the moment—her first contact with John Crichton, who, in Aeryn's words, 'claims to be a human ... from a planet called Erp' ('Premiere,' 1.01)—when her rank, regiment, company, and whole system of signification begins to come undone.

It's all Crichton's fault. Although, it's equally Moya's fault as well, and Chiana's, and Zhaan's. Everyone on *Farscape* seems to conspire in order to break and fracture Aeryn's identity. What remains to be seen is whether this break is necessary, whether it is good for Aeryn, and whether she needed transforming and 'evolving'[1] in the first place.

This chapter will focus on the central female characters in *Farscape*—Aeryn Sun, Chiana, and Pa'u Zotoh Zhaan. Although Zhaan dies at the beginning of Season 3, I would argue that her spirit lives on, both literally and figuratively, and that she continues to influence both Aeryn and Chiana with her peculiar model of mystical femininity. By looking at these three women as individuals, but also as contested ideals of what it means to be female in the Uncharted Territories, I want to trace the various and unique manifestations of feminine gender that are evident in *Farscape*. I also want to connect feminine politics within the show to ongoing theoretical conceptions of the female subaltern, drawing upon the work of Gayatri Spivak and Antonio Gramsci in order to map out the relationship between 'alien women' and 'third world women.' I recognize that this is a contentious claim, and so I will be treading very carefully here, being sure not to strip Third World Studies of its context, nor to imply that there is an easy metonymic slippage between the historical location of the female subaltern and the SF trope[2] of the female alien.

In the episode 'The Way We Weren't' (2.05), we learn that Aeryn has paid dearly for her rank and regiment—she betrays her lover, Velorek, in order to re-secure her position as a Prowler pilot. When Crichton tells Aeryn that 'you could be more' in the premiere episode, he is echoing Velorek's original statement. Even as he is being carried off by Peacekeeper soldiers—en route to be tortured and eventually executed—Velorek still endorses Aeryn's capacity for change. 'Congratulations, Aeryn,' he tells her. 'No ordinary Peacekeeper would have attempted this. I told you, you were special!'[3] Both Velorek and Crichton seem able to penetrate into the inner depths of Aeryn's psyche, showing her things about herself that she can't, or won't, see on her own. In this sense, Aeryn becomes the troubled analysand,[4] and the men in her life become the psycho-

8. *Aeryn stands over the alien cityscape of Valdon, which is reminiscent of the apocalyptic LA in Ridley Scott's* Blade Runner

analysts, revealing her 'inner potential' while chipping away at what they perceive to be the less savory aspects of her character. This recapitulates the original goal of Freudian psychoanalysis, which was to cure 'hysterical' female patients of their alleged neurotic disorders.[5]

It is a linguistic coincidence that Aeryn's name sounds a lot like 'error,' but I don't mind exploiting this coincidence. 'Aeryn' is also a unisex name, which makes it grammatically possible for her to inhabit both genders—and if, as Lacan suggests (2002), the unconscious is like a language, and we are all just subjects being interpolated within a linguistic field, then Aeryn's language as both a woman and a Peacekeeper is constantly being challenged by the men in her life. Crichton, Crais, and even Stark, all want her to be a certain kind of woman, a certain physical or cultural ideal that will satisfy their own desires. After Crichton dies (for the first time), when Aeryn absconds to the 'mystical' planet of Valdon in order to grieve his loss—an episode I will treat in more detail in Chapter 5, which focuses on bodies and bodily politics—she is pursued by

Stark and Crais. In disgust, she tells Stark that his advances are even worse than Crais', because 'you think you're so much better than him' ('The Choice,' 3.17). Similarly, when Crichton tries to re-initiate a romantic relationship with Aeryn, she flees from him rather than submitting to the pain of intimacy again. She wants to understand desire on her own terms, and constantly challenges the masculine dialectics that are imposed upon her—the scripts that tell her what type of woman, or what type of 'human', she is supposed to be.

9. Crichton vanishes, leaving Aeryn with her own reflection

Aeryn defines herself several times during the course of the show as a 'Peacekeeper soldier,' but what does this mean? How is it any more cognizant than Zhaan's definition of herself as a priest, or Chiana's submission to the identity of *tralk*, which others ascribe to her? As I mentioned in Chapter 1, all of the characters in *Farscape* are given tropological identities to inhabit—SF stereotypes—in the beginning, and part of their personal journeys involve deconstructing those stereotypes in order to find a living space inside of them. Aeryn needs to learn to live with what being a Peacekeeper soldier might mean to her, just as Crichton has to reconcile his love of science with his growing realization that technology can be harnessed in order to wreak massive destruction. His creative principle, his will to power as a scientist, and as a man, emerges from the same theoretical universe that produces nuclear weaponry, devices of torture like the Aurora Chair, and the ultimate embodiment of annihilation—wormhole weapons, which Crichton himself admits 'don't make peace. They don't even make war' (*PKW*, Pt. 2).

When Chiana first joins the crew of Moya midway through Season 1, she unites with Aeryn and Zhaan to form a mythological chain of feminine signification, moving from Zhaan (the eldest) to Chiana herself (the youngest). Zhaan serves as the spiritual center of the triptych, the wise woman, who has had several cycles during which to accumulate knowledge and cultural capital.[6] Aeryn is, in many ways, Zhaan's disciple, learning patience, compassion, and tolerance from her, even as she in turn instructs Zhaan in the necessities of power, control, and hegemony—a term which I'll complicate later in this discussion. Chiana, the most immature, is also the most sexually expressive of the three. She teaches Zhaan and Aeryn (and Crichton) how to inhabit their own bodies comfortably, how to trust their deepest and (often) most frightening intuitions, even as they both teach her how to focus her own selfishness and aimless pursuit of pleasure into a powerful sense of loyalty, ambition, and emotional strength.

But none of these women are what they seem at first. Chiana is young, but also wise; inexperienced, but also intuitive. Zhaan is learned, but afraid; battle-scarred and tested, but also uncertain about her own ethical commitments. And Aeryn, despite her rigorous training, her near-perfect control over her body and its desires, is the least sure of anyone about where she belongs, what she's doing on Moya, or what the purpose of her life might be. 'I am a Peacekeeper soldier' begins to ring false, or at least incomplete, just as John's various cultural affiliations—astronaut, American, scientist, male—begin to fall apart beneath the weight of the Uncharted Territories and the unconscious Other that they represent.

With the revelation that Aeryn is pregnant, which comes at the end of Season 3, her role in the series changes markedly—just as Moya's role changes once she gives birth to her offspring, Talyn. Aeryn's body, always under scrutiny by the men in her life, becomes an artifact, an essence to be fought over, the field upon which human, Scarran, and Sebacean interstellar and ideological warfare is able to take place. Who does the baby belong to? Who will claim it, control it, name and rightfully own it? If the baby is indeed John's, will it genetically contain his coveted wormhole knowledge? This is what the Scarrans are hoping for, and it is probably the only reason why Scorpius aids John in rescuing Aeryn from the Scarran base where she has been taken prisoner. He doesn't want the Scarran imperium to control John's knowledge, and by extension, John himself. This is a Gramscian war of position, and Scorpius was here first. He has ownership of John's mind, his essence, and he isn't about to let the Scarrans decode this hidden knowledge before he does.

When Aeryn is taken prisoner, she is replaced with—of course, since this is *Farscape*—a copy: a 'bioloid,' which is like an enfleshed simulation of the real Aeryn, a bio-mechanoid copy of her, perfect down to every pore, every eyelash, every intonation of speech and gesture. Almost perfect. The bioloid fails to convince John, and not through a failure of body language or sensitivity, as we might expect, but through a crucial failure of *language*. When Crichton asks 'what about the baby?', bioloid-Aeryn seems confused. She has been programmed with extensive knowledge gained from Aeryn's military profile and personality data, information known about Crichton, Moya, and the rest of the crew. The Scarrans think that they know everything about Aeryn, but they are unable to perforate the deepest levels of her biology, the subcutaneous corridors where,

10. The bioloid Aeryn

slowly, patiently, a seed is growing, a tiny cell is dividing, and div-
ing again, and again. They don't know about the baby, and so
bioloid-Aeryn doesn't know about the baby ('Bringing Home the
Beacon,' 4.16).

When John realizes this, he switches tactics immediately—his
conversation becomes an interrogation, which will perversely
mimic the interrogation that the real Aeryn is being subjected to,
back on the Scarran military base. Crichton doesn't have to use
physical intimidation, though—in fact, bioloid or not, he must know
that Aeryn is still technically stronger than him, still more logical
and focused, still his 'species-superior' in almost every visible way.
Therefore, he tests her not through reason, but through absurdity.
Not through recollection and philosophy, but through desire, possession, and the impossible gap between them that language is
always trying to bridge—the aporia in signification that Lacan identified when he said that all speaking is desiring, and that all
communication is cathected around a singular lack, an absence. We
are always talking because we can never quite say what we need to,
and so we keep talking, and the desire just gets further and further
away. Communication is an endless chain of desires, which Lacan
describes as an interlocking series of metal rings, each ring leading
to another, ad infinitum, like 'the rings of a necklace, that is, the ring
in another necklace made of rings' (2002: 66). It is also like the liquid
heart of a capricious wormhole, where space and time merge into
something unknowable.

Crichton's interrogation revolves around two words, 'beacon'
and 'baby.' Bioloid-Aeryn understands 'beacon,' since this is a bit of
technical jargon, but she doesn't understand 'baby.' Or rather, she
doesn't understand the significance of the word. The translator
microbes in her brain decode the English word, but the translation
crucially fails because it can't denature the feeling, it can't separate
the emotion that infuses 'baby' into its proper components. Bioloid-
Aeryn knows what a baby is, but she doesn't know why it should
matter—and, most specifically, why it should matter to Crichton. So
she is confused. Crichton seizes on this, and begins to describe a
slow circle around her, playing a torture game of language and rid-
dles: 'Where's the beacon, Aeryn? Where's the baby? Where's the
baby? Where's the beacon? Beacon, baby, beacon, baby . . . who's the
beacon? Who's the baby? Say "baby," Aeryn. Aeryn, say "baby."
Say "baby." Spell it' ('Bringing Home the Beacon, 4.16). Of course,

bioloid-Aeryn can't spell 'baby,' because—unlike the real Aeryn—she has never learned English. She tries, though. 'Bb . . .' she says. 'Bb . . . .'

Crichton shoots her.

This is a profoundly violent moment in the show. No, Crichton does not shoot Aeryn. Yes, Crichton does shoot Aeryn. Who's Aeryn, and who's the bioloid? Who's the copy? Aeryn, bioloid, bioloid, Aeryn. Say bioloid. Say Aeryn. Who's Aeryn, and who's Aeryn? Can we spell her? Can we define her? Does her name, rank, and regiment somehow mark her, somehow make her coherent and legible to us, to Crichton, to herself?

When Crichton is cloned in the episode 'Eat Me' (3.06), this at first seems to instantiate a tried-and-true stereotype of the SF genre—the clone narrative. A central character gets cloned, and everyone is forced to ask themselves crucial ontological questions. Who's the clone, and who's the original? How do we tell them apart? What makes him 'him,' and what makes the clone a clone? This crisis of origins lasts for about twenty minutes or so, until the crisis management (what Roger Ebert also calls the 'Law of Economy of Characters') kicks in, reminding us that unanswered philosophical questions are hazardous to the coherence of action narratives. The clone disappears—he returns to whatever strange ether he emerged from—and everyone is left scratching their heads in wonder.

Farscape takes this myth a step further. When Crichton is cloned by a mad scientist, the clone doesn't disappear. He remains, like a strange cipher, a shadow of the original Crichton who looks exactly like him, who shares all of his personality traits, and who proves entirely unable to beat him at paper-stone-scissors because they both think alike. This anxiety around origins and authenticity doesn't disperse, but instead concatenates, thickens, until the audience actually becomes uncomfortable with the developing storyline. Who is the real Crichton? Who are we supposed to care about, and who should we disengage from? Which one is going to die, and when it happens—as it inevitably must—will it be the 'right' one? Will we be left siding with the uncorrupted original, or will we, like Moya's crew, be duped into loving the imperfect copy? The show raises all of these questions without attempting to answer them, and this clone ploy actually becomes a pivot of narrative significance, leading us to this very moment between the 'real' Crichton and the 'fake' Aeryn. Or is it the other way around?

Remember that John has already killed Aeryn once. While being controlled by Scorpius' neural chip, he attacks Aeryn, forcing her to eject from her Prowler—she then plunges into an icy river, and drowns ('Die Me, Dichotomy,' 2.22). Now he has killed her for the second time, and this murder is no less significant than the first, because he is no longer certain that he has done the right thing. 'You know,' D'Argo tells him, 'it wasn't Aeryn.' John replies firmly that 'it was never Aeryn,' but he isn't so sure. Looking at the bioloid, watching the strange fluids and unknown chemicals leaking out of its head, seeing its 'brain' pulsing in a feeble simulation of automatic life, John feels the terrible gravity of what he has done. Perhaps he has only slain Aeryn's copy, but he has still, in effect, destroyed a shadow of her—a part of her. When he killed her for the first time, he was completely under the control of Scorpius. This time, he is under no one's control—he is 'his own man.' This is what makes the act so terrifying. John understands now, feels intimately, that he is capable of doing it. He is able to kill the one that he loves.

The next five episodes become a tight story arc that revolves around Aeryn's rescue. Not since Season 1 has she been a victim-subject like this, an object of lack, a person who needs to be saved. Aeryn is usually the one who does the saving, the Peacekeeper soldier who marches into any situation with her pulse rifle drawn, ready to meet the enemy. Now, held captive by the Scarrans, her body subjected to horrific torture, she becomes reduced to a reproductive surface—a baby vessel—upon which the Scarrans and the Sebaceans can wage their ideological warfare. Held on a secure military installation called Katratzi, she is subjected to probes, needles, drugs, psychological torture, and extreme isolation, all designed to determine how her unborn child might be of use to the Scarran imperium. At this point, Aeryn is no longer a Peacekeeper soldier. She is a mother under duress. And, as she admits in the episode 'Prayer' (4.18), she will do anything to protect her baby.[7]

I have already talked in detail about reproductive technologies and the image of the mother in SF narratives in Chapter 2, but this discussion focused primarily on Moya rather than Aeryn. Now I want to talk about how Aeryn herself, as a Sebacean and 'near-human,' becomes uniquely figured in a reproductive struggle, and how this repositioning as 'problematic mother' also serves to align her with the female subaltern. Aeryn's body must be conquered by the Scarrans, her offspring must be extracted, just as surely as she/it must be rescued by Crichton and Moya's crew. Who, precisely, is John trying to save here? Aeryn? His baby? The easy answer is both, but on *Farscape*, there are no easy answers. Aeryn has been divested of her personhood, rendered into the signifier of 'alien mother,' and she must watch helplessly as the Scarrans probe and penetrate her body in search of their precious technological secrets. For the first time, she is praying for rescue. She is praying, in effect, to Crichton himself. He becomes a godlike figure, the only one capable of saving her. In *A Critique of Postcolonial Reason*, Spivak sketches out the role of the native informant—a historically crucial position that is also impossible, since s/he can only *tell* but never *be*, only *relay* but never *exist* as such (1999: 49). The native informant, constructed by the west in order to understand everything 'not the west,' is like empty language, a vessel waiting to bear the imprint of colonial classification and taxonomy. S/he exists in a mimetic (defiance through simulation, revolution through 'miming') relationship to the west, but never as a subject. Third world mothers, Spivak goes on to argue, bear the heaviest weight of this absent subject. 'The blame for the exhaustion of the world's resources is placed on Southern population explosion. And hence, upon the poorest women of the south' (1999: 385).

Making women 'an issue' justifies western aid, and hence distracts us from western consumption and the fetishizing of useless commodities (which are constructed in the third world.) These women in particular have come to bear the burden of globalization, being blamed for 'overpopulation' even as they are credit-baited, coerced into exploitative labor, and held up as an example of a 'disappearing culture' by western postcolonial scholars and 'well-meaning' political experts.

This brings us back to Aeryn, because she has now become the curious representative of such a subaltern class, a 'problem mother' whose disrespect of the miscegenation barrier, as well as her defiance of Scarran protocols, has made her a dangerous psychotic. But she is also, covertly, being blamed by Crichton and the rest of Moya's crew. This is Aeryn's 'problem,' because it is Aeryn's body, Aeryn's child. How could she allow herself to be captured by the Scarrans? How could she put Crichton's child in jeopardy like that? If she had just told him about the pregnancy from the very beginning—if she had just been more careful—if she had just let Crichton handle it all, handle everything, control every aspect of the gestation and birth—if she had just consented to give up her body and her reproductive rights, then none of this would be happening, and no one would be in danger. So it is Aeryn's fault, whether Crichton says it or not, and now it is Aeryn who must be swiftly rescued.

'Unorganized landless female labor is one of the targets of super-exploitation,' Spivak says, 'where local, national, and international capital intersect . . . by that route of super-exploitation these women are brought into capital logic' (1999: 242). Obviously, as a member of the Sebacean military overclass, Aeryn is not equivalent to 'landless female labor.' But her divestiture of power, her stripping away of self and surety as she is reduced merely to the vessel for the baby that Scarrans find genetically interesting, is an act of physical and emotional deconstruction that transforms her into a subaltern woman. She has no rights and no voice, no juridical structure to appeal to, no military vanguard to protect her, and—quite possibly—no hope of being rescued. She is chained, drugged, and dehumanized by endless Scarran interrogation and torture. Her life is threatened daily, and at one point she even considers suicide.[8]

Like third world women, Aeryn needs to be 'brought into capital logic,' to be interpolated in a way that the Scarrans can understand and control. She is nothing to them but a troublesome chest containing genetic secrets, and they are perfectly willing to destroy her body in order to wrest the offspring from her. The Scarran interrogator constantly asks her who the father is, who the baby 'belongs' to, invading her mind and combing through her memories in order to locate the truth. None of Aeryn's answers suffice, even when she, herself, seems genuinely to believe them.[9] The Scarrans don't trust anything about her—not even what seem to be licit feelings. Through their powerful colonial focus, they are able to penetrate to the deepest core of her, the 'hidden memory' that Stark prizes so greatly in the episode of the same name (1.20), until they are able to conquer her. They will stop at nothing less than metastatic domination of her entire body, every cell, every atom, every tiny piece of her, every memory. In the true western imperialist fashion, which Edward Said describes as '[the] act of geographical violence through which virtually every space in the world is explored, charted and finally brought under control' (1993: 271), the Scarrans must own every inch of her biological and genetic territory.

Spivak writes that 'the UN must first "rationalize" woman before they can develop her . . . but the ground-level value-codings that write these women's lives elude us. We pay the price . . . when we explain them as general exemplars of anthropological descriptions' (1999: 245). It's easy for the western 'world,' then, to justify saving third world women, since through this act of salvation they are also giving these women a particular identity, transforming them into objects in need of saving. Thus, they too become native informants, capable of 'telling' about their culture, but no longer subjects as such. As Baudrillard suggests, 'in order for ethnology to survive, its object must die' (1994: 7). In order for the native informant and the 'third world woman' to exist for the west, the subaltern must die, because the west cannot process this idea of the subaltern—which Spivak defines in part as 'men and women among the illiterate peasantry, Aboriginals, and the lowest strata of the urban subproletariat' (1999: 269). Everyone has a voice in the west; we can't have people without a voice (the subaltern). Hence, we're *giving* you a voice, our voice, so that you can tell us what we want to hear. This undoing of the subaltern silence is what creates the native informant, and what allows the marginalized classes to be re-admitted 'properly' into the logic of global capitalism.

This political struggle relates to Aeryn, as well as to Chiana and Zhaan, because she has (allegedly) always had a voice up until this point. As a member of the Sebacean military, as a skilled Prowler pilot, and as—more recently—Crichton's friend and lover, she has wielded immense cultural and martial power. She has flown Talyn, and experienced what it feels like to join, bodily and psychically, with an alien being so powerful and immense. She has inverted the Peacekeeper imperialist ethos (just as Marx claimed to turn Hegel's 'upside down' dialect 'onto its feet' by making it economical rather than abstract), abandoning their history of intolerance and informing Crais, in no uncertain terms, that 'you will never order me again' ('The Hidden Memory,' 1.20). But now she has been stripped of power and speech, reduced to her reproductive capacity, and punished for her defiance of Scarran dictates by repeated acts of physical and psychological torture. John can no longer get to her. There may be no 'her' left to get to. He cannot get close to any Aeryn.

I am invoking the subaltern here—as a people, not a concept—not because it is theoretically attractive or current, but because I believe that *Farscape* itself is a kind of subaltern narrative. It is a story about escaped prisoners living aboard a slave-vessel, Moya, constantly trying to elude their former captors. All of these characters begin as prisoners of a sort, their cultural values shackled, their political commitments uncertain, but all of them evolve as the show progresses into living subjects. From the moment that Moya first removes her 'control collar' and starbursts away from the Peacekeepers, she interrupts the cycle of violence and incarceration, blasting her own history of servitude and rewriting her position as a sentient being. In the Hegelian sense of the master/slave dialectic, she is the one with the consciousness, while the Peacekeepers require her productive labours in order to feed their empire.[10] She feels, whereas they do not.

But now we see Aeryn, a former Peacekeeper (isn't she *still* a Peacekeeper?), stripped of all her powers, all of her various cultural agencies and ethical certainties, lying in a prison cell. We see the moment of fracture wherein she invokes the Sebacean god, only to reject her outright. But in order to reject her, Aeryn must first create her, just as the 'third world woman' is invoked by western ethnography as a copy without an original, an idea to be transcribed so that it can summarily be lost, misplaced, gotten rid of, set adrift in the dark. Aeryn speaks to herself:

> There was one . . . guard. I don't . . . remember her face. She never told me her name. She told me a legend about how Sebaceans once had a god called . . . Djancaz-bru. Six worlds prayed to her. They . . . built her temples, conquered planets, and yet, one day, she still rose up and destroyed all six worlds. And when the last warrior was dying, he . . . he said, 'we gave you everything, why did you destroy us?' And she looked down upon him, and she whispered . . . 'Because I can.' ('Prayer,' 4.18)

Aeryn admits that she has never believed in this god, but invokes her now for reasons that she isn't entirely certain of. But Djancaz-bru ultimately disappoints her. Like Crichton, she is incapable of reaching Aeryn, of saving her, before she experiences the worst breadth of the Scarran torture. I have excerpted Aeryn's entire speech to Djancaz-bru because I find it linguistically telling, as well as spiritually haunting. Her many pauses are testament not only to the drugged stupor that she must be in, but to the ambivalence of the 'prayer' itself. It is in these hesitations, these ellipses, these dark corridors of grammar, that the god Djancaz-bru actually lives, breathing, watching her as dispassionately as any Scarran interrogator. Aeryn wants to believe, even as she knows that she cannot. The 'guard' whose face she can't remember is also Djancaz-bru, the prayer is her, the story is her. It is the nameless and primordial god-principle that Aeryn is appealing to here, the spectral female savior in whom she has never believed, and who must then be real precisely *because* Aeryn has never believed in her. At this moment, Aeryn feels herself as absence, nothing. Everything that she has ever felt, loved, or believed in has been taken from her. Everything that she has trusted is wrong, and whatever she claims to know about herself is also wrong. The Scarrans now control her 'self.' They control every aspect of her discourse. Thus, if she is wrong, if she no longer exists, if she is nothing, then these are all the reversals necessary for the existence of Djancaz-bru. If she is wrong, then god is right. It's the only thing that makes sense to her in this moment, when everything else has fled from her, when she is completely alone with her fear and her doubt.

Nietzsche says in *Thus Spake Zarathustra* that 'when gods die, they always die many kinds of deaths' (1962: 273). His aphorism that 'God is dead' has always been a riddle as such, the notion not merely that God has ceased to exist, but that God was always contingent and mortal, and hence God's believers are the ones who killed him. If Christianity is based upon the eschatological mystery of Christ-as-God dying on the cross, then Christ's death also has to be God's death, and Christian piety becomes entirely funereal in character: the mourning of an original murder.[11] When Aeryn invokes Djancaz-bru, she knows that the god is already dead—just a story, which is the loneliest thing of all—but still needs to believe in her. Then, when she summarily rejects Djancaz-bru, saying that 'you haven't listened and you haven't helped,' she is not completely rejecting the god-concept, but rather filling up the space left behind with her own rage and despair. Aeryn infuses it with her own will to power, her own need to survive—the creative principle that she is both blamed and loved for by Crichton and the Scarrans.

I recognize that this discussion has been somewhat dense, and that it has mostly avoided the characters of Zhaan and Chiana—focusing instead on Aeryn's unique experiences. But the other two women have always existed in the background, informing my thoughts, and I intend to reintroduce them now. What I've been trying to say through this (sometimes unclear) synthesis of reproduction, servitude, and subaltern studies, is that female characters in epic narratives like fantasy and science fiction are often stripped of their power and voice, and reduced to their erotic and reproductive functions. Like Aeryn, they can be recoded quite unexpectedly as mothers, which inverts their position in the action drama—transforming them into objects that need to saved, vessels that need to be protected at all costs.

They become part of masculine 'aid' strategies, or the victims of patriarchal enforcement and genetic 'development,' thus standing in for the role of the third world woman who cannot actually appear within the dramatic text (because she is not of the correct culture). They are then simultaneously celebrated and blamed for their reproductive capacity, celebrated for its generative principle (which gives them a function in patriarchy) and then blamed for 'losing control' of this essential power—for not being good mothers, not protecting the fetus properly, or for not submitting to a convenient birth that fits within the capitalist timeframe. Similar to the way in which the third world mother is blamed for 'overpopulating' the world, even as the west ignores its own ravenous consumption of natural resources, alien mothers in SF dramas are caught within a complex web of miscegenation anxiety, physical permeability, and patriarchal control, being lauded for their creative potential so long as a properly westernized baby emerges from that potential. If not, then something psychotic has occurred (like Talyn), and the result must be 'fixed.'

I have thus cited Aeryn's prayer to Djancaz-bru in order to link the Nietzschean god-principle with the equally untenable position of the native informant. Both are impossible positions, absences that need to be filled rather than subjects who can actually be acknowledged within a framework of cultural understanding. The native informant tells about 'culture,' even as that culture is a *fabliau* created by the western listener; Djancaz-bru 'listens' to Aeryn's prayer, even as Aeryn is the one who gives the god flesh and form. She is not praying to Crichton, then, but praying to herself. When she rejects Djancaz-bru, she rejects all of the divine and world-destroying qualities in herself, all of the epic and frightening elements of her character, as well as her 'warrior nature.' She is nothing now. She has no rank, no regiment, no identification. She is, like the native informant, a vessel that has been emptied out by cultural theft, emptied and discarded.

This is Aeryn's first real encounter with the subaltern, unlike Zhaan and Chiana, who were both originally political prisoners. If I have focused so tightly on Aeryn within this discussion, it is because I believe that she is a kind of hybrid person, standing between the feminine poles that both Chiana and Zhaan represent. Just as their broader archetypes give Aeryn a sense of context, Aeryn's shifting and unique sense of her own femininity (and masculinity) is what gives Zhaan and Chiana the capacity to evolve and grow. This is not the usual case of a human teaching an alien how to 'evolve,' but rather a dialogic relationship in which three aliens both guide and instruct each other.

Chiana is first brought aboard Moya in chains, and it is Crichton who is an advocate for her freedom. She is classified by her Nebari captors as a 'deviant,' although she insists to Crichton that 'they won't tell you what I've done because they're embarrassed. You . . . wouldn't consider it a crime' ('Durka Returns,' 1.15). The Nebari, we learn, are a ritualistic society who punish sexual and gender ambiguity with exile, torture, and even death. Chiana does not fit within their parameters of appropriate sexual conduct, just as Hubero, an inter-sexed Nebari whom Chiana meets later in the episode 'Fractures' (3.18), does not conform to their gender-specific codes. That Chiana is drawn to Hubero is no surprise, given that they are both gender-rebels of a sort, although Hubero's lived reality as an inter-sexed Nebari exposes her to far more prejudice and physical danger than Chiana will ever experience. Hubero's death, I think, is a bit cliché—the gender-ambiguous person needs to die and be mourned (quickly) in order for gender normalcy to be restored—although several fans were quick to argue with me about this in the online fan-forum 'Frell Me Dead.' They insisted that *Farscape* treated the subject of androgyny in this episode with surprising sensitivity, making Hubero a highly sympathetic character, and presenting her death as pathological and unjust.[12]

The real risk taken in this episode, I think, is the sexualizing of Hubero, since it is implied that s/he and Chiana are physically intimate. We see them disappear, smiling and laughing, into am empty storage crate, and our imagination opens up all sorts of interesting sexual possibilities (and positions) for what might be happening within the protective darkness of that vessel. Chiana is similarly drawn to another marginal alien, the slave Talikaa, in the episode 'Twice Shy' (4.14). It is odd that this episode—which is really a light commentary on sexuality and appearances—occurs so late in Season

4, when the story arc revolving around the Peacekeepers and Scarrans is already well under way. It is one of those interesting
moments in *Farscape*, when we are reminded that funny and strange
things happen within the margins of the epic: Chiana befriends an
abused female slave, who, of course, turns out to be a homicidal
spider-alien who wants to devour everyone on the ship. Chiana has
never been lucky in love.

Chiana and Talikaa share a kiss, which seems to be a moment of
rather innocent sexual expression on Chiana's part, rather than
some calculated lesbian-ratings-grab on the part of the writers. It
isn't a heavy makeout session, but rather an exploratory gesture.
From what we can tell about Chiana and her sexual history, she
seems to identify as pansexual, which is precisely what makes her
such a threat to the conservative Nebari. She hasn't internalized the
strict sexual mores and prohibitions of her culture, and prefers to
express herself with complete erotic freedom. This makes her a
political prisoner among her own people, a sexual subaltern, whose
own theories of love and gender are silenced by her captors for fear
that they might incite some manner of gender revolt. Like Zhaan,
who is imprisoned because she remains a political threat, Chiana is
put in shackles because of her non-conformist sexual attitudes. This
type of sexual rebellion would normally emerge from the privileged
bourgeoisie class, but in Chiana's case, it is evident within a member
of the Nebari proletarian underclass. The only political subject more
disenfranchised—and hence more dangerous—than Chiana herself
is her brother Nerri, who is the leader of the underground Nebari
resistance. If Chiana is an urban subaltern, still enjoying a few cultural agencies, then the 'underground' represents the majority
subaltern class.

Although Spivak says in interview (1990) that she considers the
term 'subaltern' to have a great deal of theoretical flexibility, she
seems to give it very specific geographic and cultural characteristics.
Spivak's subaltern is the third world woman who is denied a political speaking voice. Antonio Gramsci, who originated the term, used
it to refer more loosely to a proletariat underclass—the subjects who
would exist in a hegemonic relationship with the state, and who
would eventually, he hoped, construct their own *alternative hegemony* in order to build a new democratic framework for civil society. I
am bringing Gramsci into this discussion not merely to contextualize Spivak's use of the subaltern, but to provide an even broader

political field within which to situate the women of *Farscape*. If Chiana is indeed a sexual subaltern among the Nebari, she still enjoys privileges that the landless third world woman obviously does not. Yet Chiana herself is 'landless,' given that she is an exile and has no home, save for Moya. She labors aboard the ship, yet—like the rest of the crew—she receives no compensation for her work.

What separates Chiana from Aeryn and Zhaan is that, more often than not, she falls outside the parameters of appreciation and respect. Zhaan's emotional labor as an empathic priestess is often noticed and rewarded, whereas Chiana's efforts to connect the group together, to push everyone past their physical inhibitions, to create a maximum pleasure principle aboard Moya, are rarely lauded or even observed. She accepts the label of '*tralk*,' which essentially means 'whore,' and shoulders this mantle with little anger or resentment. She has simply managed to carve out a living space within the problematic identity, and, as she firmly explains to Crichton in 'Taking the Stone' (2.03), although her label as *tralk* emerges from the Other, her *use* of that label is individual and autonomous. This is what Butler calls 'working the weakness within the norm' (1993: 237). Chiana queers the notion of *tralk*, transforming it into a positive and self-affirming role, and it is *she* who decides when to 'act like' a *tralk*, even if it is others who ascribe the label to her. She is certainly not Crichton's *tralk*. 'Only in your dreams,' she tells him.

Let's not be euphemistic here. Chiana has sex for money—shoes might cost 'three sex acts,' as she reminds Jool—but whether that makes her a *tralk*, and what precisely a *tralk* is, remains a point of contention. Sex-trade workers remain among the most disenfranchised people on the planet (as we assume they remain throughout the galaxy as well), but Chiana seems to enjoy too much privilege to make a claim to that kind of fraught existence. She has a (mobile) home, she has currency, she has friends who would be willing to go to war for her. Is she really a subaltern, a political subject without a voice? I would contend that *Farscape* is constantly trying to downplay the reality of Chiana's financial situation, attempting to re-cast it within a playful and 'sexy' register, when in actual fact it is a lot more serious. We don't know how long Chiana has dealt in the sex trade, how much money she has made, what sorts of things she has done in her short life. Judging by her awe-struck and often childlike responses to physical tenderness and love, it seems safe to assume that she hasn't experienced many positive relationships. Her eyes have a weight to them, an ancient sadness, which is made clear in 'Taking the Stone' (2.03) when she chooses to kill herself rather than live without her brother Nerri—the only person before D'Argo and Crichton to actually care about her.

In this episode, which I have previously mentioned in Chapter 1, Chiana visits a 'royal cemetery planet' in search of her brother Nerri. What she finds, oddly enough, is not Nerri, but his signifier—a small bio-disc that he had implanted in his body to act as a tracking device. Chiana assumes that the disc has been forcibly removed, which would have to mean that Nerri is dead. This is when she decides to take her own life rather than endure the pain of Nerri's absence. Chiana tells Crichton that 'it's not about you,' (2.03), and, importantly— despite his usual role as a nurturing force on the show—John is remarkably powerless here. Aeryn says that 'if you force her to return to the ship, she will stay just to spite you.' And when Crichton attempts to drag Chiana bodily back to Moya (and Chiana's body rarely does what she doesn't want it to do), Aeryn reminds him that the choice belongs to Chiana. For all of his empathic abilities, Crichton can't peer into Chiana's complex emotional life. He can't see what it's like to lose a sibling, and he can't live her life for her. Just as it must be Aeryn's choice to return to Moya after Crichton dies, it must also be Chiana's choice to go on living.

That choice brings her to the edge of a deep chasm, at whose bottom lies the 'stone' of the episode's title—a unique rock formation which is supposed to manipulate sound waves, forming a 'sonic net' that breaks the jumper's fall. Like any good empiricist, Crichton doesn't believe in the net. He confronts Chiana once again, but she is firm in her choice:

Chiana: I never had any courage. As a kid, Nerri gave me everything.
Crichton: You've shown me courage plenty of times.
Chiana: I've gotta see if I can do this, Crichton. ('Taking the Stone,' 2.03)

Chiana begins to hum a note—a high, resonant, beautiful note. When that note reaches its perfect pitch, so powerful and so lovely that we cannot endure it any longer, she jumps. The stone responds. It matches her note, and a field of invisible energy surrounds Chiana, allowing her to float weightlessly in the air. This is a miracle, both of physics and of metaphysics. By embracing her death-drive,

Chiana leaps straight out of the Symbolic and into an uncertain darkness, a terrifying, haunting realm that is pure, voiceless sound, energy incarnate. In this moment of perfect death-consciousness, Chiana is linked to Spivak's inaugural subaltern, the Indian *suttee,* who both chooses—and is culturally pressured—to immolate herself. The choice emerges from the absence of power, but it is also a cryptic power in itself, the agency of dying, which only the bride who chooses it understands. What Chiana encounters in the magical air, near the destructive heart of that chasm that has claimed so many lives before hers, is the Real—or something like it. The history of loss, but also the miraculated possibilities of an unfolding hope, a joyous presence, She is alive, which is the most unexpected thing of all, and that is why she laughs.

Given all of these variables, Chiana's imprecise situation seems to open up a new category of subaltern, a shaky mixture between Spivak's disenfranchised woman and Gramsci's limited political subject who exists on the margins of a social-state hegemonic relationship. Gramsci says that 'every [political] party is only the nomenclature for a class,' and that '[only] the party which proposes to put an end to class divisions will . . . achieve complete self-fulfillment' (1995: 152). Thus, his conception of the ideal hegemonic state is a classless civic society, where the hegemonic relationship is used *ethically* in order to promote maximum cooperation and political education among everyone. He sees political education as the most crucial principle of social life and responsible government, and insists that 'every relationship of hegemony is necessarily an "educational" relationship . . . [this] should not be restricted to the field of the entire "scholastic" relationships, by means of which the new generation comes into contact with the old and absorbs its experiences' (1995: 354). In this sense, Gramsci envisioned a global school, a constant process of political education which would allow the process of hegemony to play out in the most ethical and egalitarian manner possible.

Within this theoretical context, I see Chiana as both a student and an educator. She lacks a developed political awareness, but she is also over-politicized due to her sexual freedom and gender play. She is subject to the political power of the Nebari and the Peacekeepers, but she has also managed to create a living space for herself, and even attempts to educate the crew of Moya—along with everyone else she happens to meet—through a syllabus of bodily erotics, sexual expression, and epicurean enjoyment of life's pleasures (not decadence, but simply acknowledgment of the sensuous, the sublime). Chiana is a subaltern, but she is also empowered, which makes her a unique political actor. Like Aeryn, she shoulders the blame for feminine reproduction, being called a *tralk* because she embraces an ethic of pleasure, while simultaneously being solicited (by men and women) for her sexual prowess and promiscuity.[13] The more 'enlightened' aliens of the Uncharted Territories see her as childish or deviant, but have no trouble accepting her sexual advances.

In this sense, Chiana becomes the ideal participant within Gramsci's field of hegemony. She understands precisely the push and pull of domination and submission, the fragile relations between the owner and the landless, and the powerful economy of sexual performance. She actually stands between two worlds, one in which she is a sexual object, the other in which she is a sexual entrepreneur, and somehow manages to combine these disparate spheres into a liveable surface. She consents to specific types of domination and subjectification (as in the 'pull' of state hegemony), but also reacts against the forces that might directly threaten her life and her livelihood (the 'push back' of the proletarian underclass). This makes her peculiarly indefinable as an alien woman, and also fittingly archetypal as a sexual entrepreneur and gender educator. She is well versed in the political education of what it means to be this kind of woman, and, rather than flinching from words like '*tralk*' or 'whore,' she meets them defiantly, queering them to her own satisfaction and denaturing the baleful and violent energy behind them. Only in our dreams is she without agency, but it would also be a mistake to say uncritically that her sexuality gives her power, since it is also what routinely places her in danger.

If Chiana emerges from the Nebari proletariat, then Zhaan makes the opposite journey, falling from the Delvian first estate—the priesthood. After becoming a ninth-level Pa'u, she murders her lover in order to prevent a political coup, and her punishment is imprisonment aboard Moya. 'On my planet,' she tells D'Argo, 'I was the leading anarchist' ('Premiere,' 1.01). Zhaan first assumes the role of a mystical mother-figure to Moya's crew, acting as their spiritual confessor (a position which she passes on to Stark), and, eventually, as Moya's sworn protector. This altruistic persona, however, is soon perforated as we see that Zhaan is actually a woman who harbors profound anxiety and spiritual doubt. She admits that, by taking a life, 'I sacrificed my right to exist' ('Family Ties,' 1.22).

But Zhaan is forced to take more lives as she fights alongside Moya's crew, and although she never adjusts to the process, she does prove to be physically adept and martially skilled. In the episode 'Throne for a Loss' (1.04), Zhaan becomes the caretaker of a troubled young alien named Zyr, a highly aggressive warrior who is in the throes of chemical withdrawal. After calling her 'soft and weak,' Zyr attacks her—and is astonished when she throws him to the ground. 'Soft? Yes,' she says calmly. 'Weak? No.' Later, still trying to goad her, Zyr asks if she's 'ever seen a man before,' then drops his robes, forcing her to look at him. Zhaan simply smiles, and asks gently: 'Is nudity a taboo in your culture? Are you ashamed of your bodies?' She then unfastens her own cloak, and the audience is allowed to see a great deal of Virginia Hey—the actress who plays Zhaan—covered in blue body paint. In this sense, Zhaan shares Chiana's sense of sexual freedom, but, as I mentioned in Chapter 1, she expresses herself sensually rather than through explicit sexual contact. Zhaan prefers to couch her gender insubordination in pedagogical terms, opting to 'teach' Zyr about the permissibility and beauty of naked bodies rather than sexually propositioning him (as Chiana no doubt would have).

This doesn't mean that Zhaan is somehow more ethical than Chiana, but simply that she utilizes a different feminine model. Given that she is capable of having 'multiple photo-gasms' as a result of exposure to direct sunlight (Delvians are plantlife, after all), we can assume that Zhaan has had an active and fulfilling sex-life for the past 200 cycles or so, and sees no need actively to pursue erotic pleasure to the extent that Chiana does. Importantly, this type of flexible celibacy (she can have sex when she chooses) emerges not from ascetic priestly training, but from already-present sexual satisfaction. Zhaan simply chooses not to be as sexually active as Chiana, although potentially she could sleep with as many people as she liked.[14] This is a fairly radical position for a priest to be in, but, as *Farscape* continually tells us, alien mores and ethics are as complex as human ones, and they often don't look anything like ours. Being a Pa'u isn't the same thing as being a priest, nor should it be.

Zhaan is the first alien on board Moya to truly accept Crichton, and is giving him philosophical advice as early as the second episode of Season 1. We learn, over time, that Zhaan's tolerance and compassion is the inverse of her own deep sense of inadequacy and spiritual failure, a response to the perceived ethical gaps that she sees in her own behaviour, and a penance for her past mistakes. Unlike Stark, who bears a kind of mystical burden to ease the passing of souls across the great divide, each day Zhaan chooses to be a Pa'u. She also chooses to sacrifice her life in order to resurrect Aeryn—not because the situation necessarily demands it, but because she loves Crichton and Aeryn, and wants them to be happy. When Aeryn's spirit asks Zhaan why she is doing this, she replies: 'because I love you. More importantly, Crichton loves you. You must take this gift, not for my sake, but for his' ('Season of Death,' 3.01). We are never quite certain why Zhaan must die so that Aeryn can live, but it seems to be a sort of cosmic balancing—the cost of one life for another. Once again, *Farscape* presents us with a mystical problem that has no solution, and a loss that we can never fully grieve because we can't even understand it.

As I have already mentioned in Chapter 1, Zhaan's death is the ultimate rending of the *Farscape* family, but it also brings them closer together. It is a moment of profound fracture, and the only other character who chooses to die under similar conditions is Crichton himself. Crichton, however, is brought back, whereas Zhaan is lost forever. In that sense, as she disperses into spirit, she becomes the primary Christ-figure within the show. It is not Crichton, but Zhaan, who makes the ultimate eschatological gesture, giving up her own life in order to atone fully for her past sins, as well as for the sins of her loved ones. Her speech to Moya's crew before she dies is remarkably sublime, and totally shattering. When Aeryn protests that they cannot lose her, Zhaan simply raises her hand—and with that gesture, Aeryn's expression falls, for she sees what has been put into motion. Zhaan's emotional sacrifice, her logic born of affection and love, is ineluctable. There is no escaping from this act. It simply must be. Zhaan knows it, and Aeryn knows it. And that is why she chooses the words that she does:

> No more. If I am *so* needed, and *so* valued, and *so* wise . . . then you will honor my wishes. You will obey me. For the longest time I feared physical demise, because my spiritual essence was suspect, but now

I know I'm worthy. Now I know the transgressions have melted from my soul. ('Wait For The Wheel,' 3.04)

If I return to this moment again, it is because I think it represents an event of both spiritual and *political* significance, for Zhaan is not simply giving her friends spiritual guidance, but urging them to become more active political beings—to realize the full potential of their own wills, their own desires. Just as D'Argo's death sunders the masculine trinity within the show, Zhaan's death is also a death of the feminine, the destruction of a particular feminine principle— the wise woman—who is able to transcend because she is no longer needed. Like the perfect Gramscian political class that works towards its own dissolution, envisioning a state where the whole notion of 'class' is no longer an issue, Zhaan plants a particular wis- dom within her friends which will one day effectively replace her. She loves them so fiercely, so deeply, that she produces her own obsolescence—but what a glorious end it is. For Zhaan knows that, although she is leaving the physical realm, a specular presence will remain. Like the god-shaped hole where a deity once lived, an aura will be left behind, a luminescence that resembles both everything Zhaan was and everything she might become. This is what she means when she says 'a family was born,' and what D'Argo means when he replies, 'you birthed it.' Zhaan says: 'Always together. Joined as one. Peace of mind, peace of spirit, peace of soul. Goodbye, my love.'

Here, we can read Zhaan's last words as ambiguous—they seem addressed to Stark, but also to the entirety of Moya's crew. 'Peace' can also mean 'piece,' and indeed, in several different versions of the 'Wait for the Wheel' shooting script, it is spelled either 'peace' *or* 'piece' depending upon the whim of the typist. Thus Zhaan leaves them *in peace*, but also *with a piece*, a piece of mind, spirit, and soul. They are both her 'children' and her 'teachers,' and so, by re-naming them—sensitive (D'Argo), exuberant (Chiana), wise (Rygel), selfless (Aeryn), innocent (Crichton)—she also gives them new political identities, new ways of relating to the world beyond Moya, guided by the 'piece' of desire that she has infused each of them with. It is Zhaan's final act of love that allows Chiana to respond so honestly to Jool when she calls her a 'young whore.' None of Jool's epithets can erase the power of Zhaan's original naming, and no amount of provincial intolerance can pave over the compassion through which Zhaan figured and understood all of them.

This is why I claim that she has given them new political identities. If, as Gramsci suggests, politics and education are deeply intermeshed, and political education is the only force that allows us to resist oppression, then Zhaan has gifted her friends with the most formidable and enduring tool imaginable—self-knowledge, and self-love. Zhaan dissolves her own class, her own existence, so that the others can forge a stronger relationship within a galactic hegemony that, as she sees it, always possesses the capacity to become truly ethical. The Uncharted Territories are not a negative or terrifying place—just ill-mapped. They need to be mapped not in the imperial cartographic sense, but through social responsibility and emotional risk, political bravery and physical vulnerability. Zhaan dies because she understands that she can do infinitely more good as a *signified* rather than a *signifier*, as an idea of holism and beauty rather than a whole and beautiful body. She surrenders herself to the symbolic order, slipping through it, and becoming what we see in her last moments—a tongue of flame, a shimmer of golden energy, an exquisite mark upon the astonished surface of the universe.

5 'Point it Like a Gun and Shoot'
Bodies and Biological Narratives

there are no bodies
there are no bodies
I don't know you
all I know is
how to give you pleasure

—Kathleen Mary Fallon (1989: 88)

Tommy: Wh . . . what is that?
Hedwig: It's what I have to work with.

—*Hedwig and the Angry Inch* (Mitchell, 2001)

Hnnn . . . Normally you have to rub my eyebrows to make me feel like this!
—John Crichton (to D'Argo) ('Out of their Minds,' 2.09)

This chapter is about pleasure, food, and alien bodies. It is about migrating clams, crispy grolack, Hyneirian stew, erotogenic eyebrows, tentacles, mystical unity, *tralks*, and sexuality among the Uncharted Territories. Alien surfaces meeting, leather, pain, submission, control collars, body-switching, tripping the light fantastic with Noranti's elixir, Delvian schizoanalysts,[1] a three-foot slug in bondage gear, and Sebacean geometric pregnancies. Oral sex and zero gravity. Oh, and farting helium.

I should say at the outset that this discussion is really about the characters on *Farscape*, and not about 'theories of the body' as they currently exist within academic writing. These theories, which began as feminist and Marxist interventions into traditional psychoanalytic formulations of the sexed/gendered body, have now become a dense and powerful tradition within the humanities and social sciences—pulling in writers all across the board, from Freud and Marx to Hegel and Heidegger. Although I am firmly invested in these many creative and productive analyses of the body, I also think that we need to keep such analyses grounded in *live human bodies*, in lived realities and living traditions, rather than exotic signifiers.[2]

We need to avoid the exclusionary impulse by which 'transgressive' bodies—women, Aboriginal peoples, poor communities, and transgendered people—are often left out of the very academic conversations meant to discuss their 'identities' as transgressive within books, conferences, and classroom pedagogy.

That said, although I will be citing the work of important gender theorists such as Judith Butler, Elizabeth Grosz, and Elspeth Probyn, I will make no attempt to summarize the impact that theories of the body have had within academic discourse. By the same token, I will not attempt to trace the diverse ways in which the psychoanalytic ideas of Freud and Lacan have historically formulated 'the body' as we now analyze it within academic settings. I am interested in the fantastic bodies and bodily encounters that exist on *Farscape*, and if I pull a wide range of authors and critics into this discussion, it is to frame their work via *Farscape*, and not the other way around.

I feel that, with this book, I am often walking a fine line between talking about the show and talking about gender theories. Ultimately, I am trying to do both, but my task must remain focused on the characters rather than on elucidating the various tangles and snarls of critical theory, fascinating as they might be. Perhaps this is just an excuse to apologize for not knowing enough about Freud and Lacan. If so, I hope that you'll forgive me, since Moya hasn't heard of them either.

The quotes that I begin this chapter with are diverse and unmappable, like the body itself. Kathleen Fallon's *Running Hot*, a hypererotic novella about a lesbian narrator named Toto. *Hedwig and the Angry Inch*, a film/musical/playtext about a transgendered singer named Hedwig and his/her inconstant lover, Tommy Gnosis. And the *Farscape* episode 'Out of their Minds' (2.09), when all of the characters aboard Moya switch bodies (twice). The amazing and terrifying thing about bodies, these texts show us, is both their mutability and their impossible metaphysical foundation. Are we made to switch, or are we made to inhabit one body, one skin, only? Are we ever alone with our bodies, or do we always live multiply, geometrically, with constantly shifting skins and eternally performative genders? Luckily, I don't have to answer any of these questions definitively, or I'd be out of a job.

Farscape presents us with a constant datastream of moving bodies, a slideshow of alien body parts, bodily functions, and bodily contradictions. A three-foot tall slug, with three stomachs, who floats around on an anti-grav throne. A blue-skinned (slightly exhibitionist) priestess who can achieve multiple orgasms when in contact with particularly strong sunlight. A Luxan warrior with a prehensile tongue, erogenous tentacles, and military tattoos (which we later learn are deceptive) inscribed into his flesh—along with the chains that made him a Peacekeeper prisoner, their remnants still festering in his skin as corrosive metal rings, subcutaneous, keeping their discourse continuous and below the skin. Moya herself seems impossible. A vast, living 'biomechanoid' ship, sentient in mysterious and unpredictable ways, 'controlled' by a Pilot who exists in trans-species symbiosis with her, embodying the realization of Haraway's 'companion species' ethic, which we discussed in Chapter 2.

In the episode 'Premiere' (1.01), we learn that the Peacekeepers are unduly concerned with bodily and racial contamination. Aeryn is deemed 'irreversibly contaminated' by Crais for having come into contact with John, whose exact species remains unclassified (hence he is a possible contaminant to Sebacean genetic purity). In Crais' framework, simple physical contact with a non-Sebacean (who has not been enslaved and subjected to behavior modification) is enough to transform Aeryn herself into an exile, an unwanted hybrid. She later throws this back in his face when, standing before him while he sits in the infamous Aurora Chair, not even deigning to touch him, she asks: 'Does this contaminate *you*, Crais?'

Moya would thus be Peacekeeper High Command's personal nightmare, since she is filled with organic chambers and orifices, doors that swing open like hinges, mysterious chambers and *chora* where the Leviathan's very biological essence—blood, lymph, amnexis fluid, nutrients—are on display, gummy and wet, slimy and tactile, Crais' own haptic hell. In the *Timaeus*, Plato describes the *chora* as a space that is 'eternal and indestructible . . . [providing] a position for everything that comes to be, and which is apprehended without the senses' (1999, 1205). Elizabeth Grosz clarifies this mystical, pre-material space as 'a mythological bridge between the intelligible and sensible, mind and body' (1994: 112). Moya is the *chora* in a sense, since she represents the decidedly feminine space upon which the characters of *Farscape* inscribe their social and physiological relations.

And this is to say nothing of the flexibility, permeability, and physiological 'openness' of Moya's crew, which remains the object of my discussion here (and, really, the object of this entire volume). Moya is a 'desiring machine,' to Deleuze and Guattari's term, where energetic, organic, and machinic webs all converge, like gossamer traceries, neural clusters, fibroid bulbs of cyber-flesh and *aphrodisia*, linking human with alien, bioloid with biologic, neuronal (Freud's word) with the language-Unconscious (Lacan's innovation) of connected human and alien selves. Signifiers slide all over the place in a neverending chain of slippery, *frelled*-up surfaces, partial objects, *objet-a*, fantastically unmoored cultural synapses.[3]

Blood mingles with amnexis,[4] life mixes with death, all of the valves, hinges, and atria fluttering open like astonished neural blooms, awash in cultural and verbal synesthesia. Is anyone having trouble deciphering this? If not, I'd be worried. Language is our precondition for subjectivity, but it also swirls like a perpetually draining sink around a lack, a black hole, a negative wormhole. Our bodies are said, spoken, processed through Lacan's imaginary anatomies, but despite all of that 'saying' we can never really come round to speaking them properly, to describing them fully. We always end up whispering ourselves, saying/not saying what it feels like to inhabit a particular body, to be 'us.' We cannot get close to any you/me/Moya, nor to the souls that inhabit her.

Not all bodies are pornographic—some are fortunate enough to fall within the ethical parameters of the right or the left—but most bodies, especially those with nonconformist shapes or sexual practices, tend to be 'pornographized' (Linda Williams' brilliant term) within both visual and verbal representation. Don't look at them, and don't talk about them. I thought I saw a real live anus over there, but it was probably just one of those giant mushrooms from the Smurf village. Shows like *Farscape* challenge this pornographizing of the body by providing a constant parade of fascinating and remarkable alien forms. In doing so, the pornographic signifier also gets exploded, and 'pornography' is rewritten as a valuable literature that applies to all genders, all sexualities, rather than an illicit backroom pleasure that only 'those' people (read: working class) talk about or enjoy.

Linda Williams describes this as the shift from *obscene* to *on/scene*, which 'marks both the controversy and scandal of the increasingly public representations of diverse forms of sexuality *and* the fact that they have become increasingly available to the public at large' (2004: 3). We aren't supposed to see graphic bodily representations, but how can we not look? And how can we keep from noticing that *our* bodies are just as graphic, that our bodies can do all of the same things, that we're all just potential porn stars in the making? In trying to construct an expressive pedagogy around the history of porn, as well as the historical and political issues that porn embodies, Williams describes a fundamental disconnect between the moving image and the spectatorial response. The problem, in the classroom at any rate, lies not in creating a feminist valuation of porn—since her students seem to have no problem doing this, once they get over their initial squeamishness—but in allowing the spectator to honestly voice what she desires about the porn on-screen, how it affects her, how it repulses her, and how all three of these modalities can occur simultaneously (2004). When we see naked bodies on-screen engaged in sex acts, can we even articulate how this makes us feel? Is it safe to articulate this? Can we separate our prejudices around queerness (or heterosexuality) from our complicated physiological reactions?

Farscape's parade of the alien body is an intervention into dialogues on obscenity, a valorization of the *on/scene* ethic of graphic representation, of bodies stripped to the flesh. We get to see both aliens and humans in all of their corporeal beauty, kissing, fondling, squeezing, loving, striking, and pushing toward/pulling away from each other in a continual dance of physical interaction. Even when Crichton and Aeryn don space-suits, they just end up tearing them off again to have sex with each other. Rather than making us wonder what sex between two Hyneirians might look like, *Farscape* actually shows us.

The three episodes that I will focus on primarily in this discussion—'Out of their Minds' (2.09), 'The Choice' (3.17), and 'Lava's a Many Splendored Thing' (4.04)—all display amazing, gratuitous, and sometimes abject bodily expressions and bodily relations. We will talk a bit about explosive diarrhea, about sensuality between a humanoid and a pulsing fetal brain, and about some heavy petting between a Luxan and a Human (or is it a Nebari and a Hyneirian?). Along the way, we will hear from bodily authorities such as the

Marquis de Sade, Kathy Acker, Kathleen Fallon, and John Cameron Mitchell. We will ask what it means to see a vulnerable alien body, to witness an alien sex scene, and to (illicitly) enjoy inter-species eroticism.

When I originally set out to write this chapter, I was worried about my ability to represent theories of the body in all their complexity accurately. I was also unsure of which episodes to select, since almost every episode of *Farscape* features body politics and bodily relations of some sort. In fact, I worried about it so much that I had a nightmare specifically involving bodies on the show. This proves Deleuze and Guattari's notion (1983) that the unconscious is more like a factory than a theater, a site for *production* rather than a holding tank for mythological and primordial imagery.[5] My fevered brain was trying to work out academic arguments, as well as personal beliefs and insecurities, long after I had turned off the computer and gone to bed.

In my dream, the crew of Moya is attacked by an deranged Scarran, a military commander who is obsessed with racial purity (a bit of a mixture, I think, between Crais and Durka, with his predilection for torture). While Crichton is away, the rest of his companions are all hunted down and killed by the Scarran. Aeryn is the last to die. The Scarran corners her in the maintenance bay, attacking her with some kind of large knife, almost the length of a short sword. Aeryn resists, but the Scarran is naturally stronger than her. The odd thing is, they fight silently. There are no sarcastic quips, as would occur on the show. There are no pulse-rifle blasts, or *deus ex machina* interruptions to save them at the last moment. This fight is clearly to the death, and it unfolds in a visceral, almost animal register, fist to fist, blade to skin.

The Scarran finally stabs Aeryn in the shoulder, and this seems like the end—but it is only the beginning. He keeps cutting, through her shoulder, her breast, her abdomen, literally vivisecting her, reflecting the organs that lie beneath. Aeryn screams. I have never heard her scream so loudly on the show before, so I have no idea where this sound is actually coming from. Not from memory. Is it my own scream? Is it a bizarre instance of heteroglossia, an amalgam of every scream that I've ever heard, the very cosmos screaming? Like the *ecthroi* in Madeline L'Engle's *A Wind in the Door* (1973)—the sound of the universe X'ing itself. Aeryn's cry is terrible and full of anguish; it seems to explode from every atom in her body.

My position as spectator keeps changing. One moment I am on the ship, watching all of this transpire, the next moment I seem to be viewing it on television—as if this is just another episode. The violence is occurring in three different media—in 'real' time (the 'Real' of the dream), on the specular television set, and in the unreality of the dream world itself.

Finally, I begin to notice that, although Aeryn is continually screaming, no blood is flowing from her mortally wounded body. Instead, a strange clear fluid seeps from her mouth and eyes. The Scarran notices this at the same time as I do, and we both make a similar connection. This is not Aeryn. It is, instead, the bioloid Aeryn—the same bioloid who originally fooled Crichton in the episode 'Bringing Home the Beacon' (4.16). But she seems so real. It seems like the real Aeryn is being tortured, that we have watched the real Aeryn die before us. And haven't we? This seems to be the point. The body is false, but the pain is real. The Scarran has only tortured a simulacrum, a collection of wires, fluids, and microchips, yet her realness was undeniable, tormenting in its convincibility.

The dream, like the bioloid Aeryn, is both insubstantial and material, ephemeral and haunting. I can't get back to sleep afterward—I keep turning it over and over in my mind, knowing that I have to integrate it into this volume somehow. What are these bodies that we dream about? How do they matter, in what ways are they 'real,' and how can we escape from them?

In Sade's writing, sex and violence are always linked—in fact, they are the same thing. Sade insisted that nature itself was violent, murderous, and criminal, so it only made sense that violence, sex, and criminality should emerge from the same *chora*, the same primordial and pre-Oedipal drives.[6] Deepak Sawhney says that we are 'simultaneously attracted to and repulsed by Sade, who asks that we, as readers, actively participate in the cold calculus of rape, sodomy, and murder, while philosophizing on the uses and abuses of Christian theology' (1999: 25). Sade created lurid and fantastic worlds, arenas of sexual perversion and violence where orgasm and evisceration were combined—women being chased by phalluses (*phalli*?) like battering rams with an 'eight inch circumference,' chains of nuns joined by dildos, and libertines joining together to feast on excrement in a 'Circle of Shit' in *120 Days of Sodom* (1966). In *Juliette*, the Pontiff observes sagely that: 'There is nothing then wrong or bad in restoring to the elements the means to recompose a thousand insects at the expense of a few ounces of blood diverted out of its usual canals, in a somewhat larger species of animal conventionally known as man' (1968: 777).

In *120 Days of Sodom*, the sex-act becomes fatal—people die in the midst of frantic copulation, having their organs perforated and torn out by alien objects, being strangled, crushed, garroted, disarticulated, until sex and murder recombine to form a single deadly strand of annihilative DNA. Sodomy becomes the sign of this chaos, both because it is non-procreative and because, in the words of Alphonso Lingis, it is 'coprophilic.' The Sadean libertine chooses sodomy because it generates nothing, because it flouts biological conventions. I find it more than a little aggravating that, in his essay on Sade called 'Deadly Pleasures,' Lingis describes sodomy as 'a black hole' and links it inseparably to coprophilia (love of shit) and destruction (1999: 41). Although I recognize that he is framing sodomy as it occurs nihilistically within Sade's work, it seems irresponsible that he cannot at least provide positive examples of anal eroticism, such as same-sex desire, or even consensual straight sex. How do we in fact know that, for Sade, sodomy is always a nihilistic act, always purely transgressive? Couldn't it also be just another erotic site on a broad spectrum of perverse pleasure, proscribed desire? I think that if we always read Sade through the lens of political transgression, we risk essentializing his work, and we miss out on the unique and compelling ways in which he mobilizes non-normative pleasures.[7]

I mention Sade because, although *Farscape* is miles away from his literary or cultural project, its displays of sexuality and violence share much in common with some of the less 'upsetting' ideals of Sade's libertinage. Characters on *Farscape* are just as often assaulted, beaten up, bloodied, seriously wounded—even killed—as they are stroked, caressed, fondled, or kissed. Often, these activities occur simultaneously. Think of the episodes 'Sacrifice' (4.02) and 'Resurrection' (4.03), when John is essentially raped by Grayza. I say 'essentially' because this violation, although painful and humiliating, lacks the violence of forced penetration. John's life never seems to be in any danger, and, as far as we know, he suffers no physical injury from Grayza's sexual attentions. However, although she claims that 'my interrogation methods are far more pleasant than Scorpius',' what she does to Crichton is still a form of rape. Grayza uses a chemical stimulant that she extracts from an artificial 'gland' (in her cleavage, no less), which arouses and intoxicates Crichton even as it neutralizes him, rendering him physically defenseless and completely vulnerable. We witness him tied up, shirtless (we don't get to see him from the waist down, but let's assume that he's naked), exhausted and demoralized by Grayza's enforced 'recreation.'

This is an unconventional place for any male on television to be, and doubly so for Crichton, who is the alleged 'action-hero' of this SF narrative. His ironic refrain of 'humans are superior' can often be more specifically translated as 'males are superior,' and to see a male character in a position of such extreme physical vulnerability is definitely unusual. In 'Sacrifice' (4.02), as Grayza cups his head in both of her hands, John tells her that 'you can have anything . . . anything you want.' His mouth forms the words, but his eyes stare straight ahead, flickering and haunted. Although, as he admits, Grayza's methods are indeed 'better than what Scorpius used to do,' they are still a violation of Crichton's body. Much is made of how, later in the show, the Scarrans use 'mind-raping' techniques—specifically on Aeryn—for the purposes of interrogation, but Crichton talks very little about his carnal experience with Grayza. Like D'Argo's imprisonment, or Rygel's own experiences of torture at the hands of Durka, it becomes a dark episode that he is too ashamed to speak of.

In 'Out of their Minds' (2.09), John and company are attacked by an alien vessel whose 'energy weapon' interacts in a bizarre way with their 'defense screen,' unhinging their individual psyches and replacing them in different bodies. The body-switch is another staple of SF genres (exploited by *Star Trek*, who even have a race of body-switching symbiotic aliens called the Trill), but in this case, the results are a bit different. This is *Farscape*, after all, and whereas the characters on *Star Trek* would deal with such a situation in a regimented, military fashion, Moya's crew reacts as they always do to new and dangerous phenomena—they break down and panic. The body-switches are doubly ironic, since the characters with opposing physiologies and worldviews are, of course, the ones who exchange psyches. D'Argo's mind inhabits Pilot's body, and his natural frustration and impatience make him, at first, incapable of running the ship. Then Chiana switches with D'Argo, and we get to hear Anthony Simcoe (who plays the Luxan) using his most convincingly girlish voice to portray the female Nebari (wouldn't he simply retain his usual speaking voice?).

Rygel inhabits Crichton's body, but he encounters a bit of a problem while trying to use his . . . equipment. He has to pee, but doesn't actually know how. In the same way that D'Argo's original 'I have to pee' comment becomes the laughable core around which the 'serious' episode 'Family Ties' (1.22) revolves, the characters' own bodily quirks and functions become the heart of this later episode—above and beyond the hackneyed 'aliens are attacking us again' narrative. When Rygel-in-John asks John-in-Aeryn 'how do you work this thing?', John's 'psyche' is exasperated—he's never actually had to give instructions before. So he tries his best:

> John-in-Aeryn: Oh my God. Unzip.
> Rygel-in-John: Um . . . Right.
> John-in-Aeryn (rolls her eyes): Pull it out. Point it like a gun and shoot.
> Rygel-in-John: Is it aimed the right way?
> John-in-Aeryn: Yes, that's fine. ('Out of Their Minds,' 2.09)

Later, when one of the potentially hostile aliens vomits all over the floor, Rygel-in-John says: 'Don't worry. We do that sort of thing all the time here on Moya. I just peed in the maintenance bay!' Rygel's statement is more precise than even he realizes. That 'sort of thing,' meaning bodily evacuation, bodily function, sexuality, and biological boundary-crossing, does indeed happen all of the time on Moya. This is what makes her so very different from the USS Enterprise, and what makes Farscape a radically different show—its willingness to cross bodily boundaries.

John experiences the ultimate straight (and gay) male fantasy—he gets to inhabit Aeryn's body. While he is supposed to be fixing some problems with Moya's defense screen, he takes a brief moment to further explore Aeryn's body. This is no deep, spiritual connection, however. John is content to simply wiggle his breasts from side to side, completely entranced with the way that they bounce. When he spots Aeryn-in-Rygel, he defends his behavior by saying: 'Oh, come on, man! They're here! They're right here! They've been here for a couple of arns, and I just had to—'[8] I understand completely. It reminds of when Steve Martin said in interview once that, if he were a woman, 'I'd never leave the house. I'd just stay at home and play with my breasts all day.' Crichton's fixation is so typically sophomoric that he can't even say the *word*—he simply says 'they' instead of 'breasts.'

The scene that I excerpted for one of the chapter's opening quotes occurs later, in private, between Rygel (in John's body) and Chiana (in D'Argo's body). Of course, this is the type of exchange that can only occur when Chiana is around, since she is so often a locus for free sexuality and libidinal expression. Ever the pragmatist, Chiana tries to convince Rygel-in-John to run away from her. Rygel resists because he wants his real body back, but Chiana is very persuasive:

D'Argo:	Now why would you want to do that? This body's much better.
John:	You think?
D'Argo:	I know [. . .]
John:	But this body is so *white*. . .and it only lasts for another forty pathetic cycles. *My* body will last for—
	(*D'Argo puts his hand on John's groin*)
John:	What are you doing?
D'Argo:	I want someone to go with me. It gets lonely out there.
John (startled):	Hnnn . . . Normally you have to rub my eyebrows to make me feel like this! ('Out of Their Minds,' 2.09)

I have excerpted this dialogue using the simpler 'John' and 'D'Argo,' rather than the more precise 'Rygel-in-John' and 'Chiana-in-D'Argo,' to show what a remarkable difference a hyphen or so makes. This scene is nowhere near as threatening if we convince ourselves that D'Argo isn't 'really' D'Argo, that he's actually Chiana, and that Rygel is 'really' John. In that case, we have an erotic scene between a male and a female—admittedly, a male three-foot tall slug and a female Nebari—but, for *Farscape*, this is actually pretty normal. However, when we consider that D'Argo's body is, in some sense, 'doing this' to John's body, that their bodies are engaged in a queer encounter—even if their minds are protected from it—the scene is a lot more interesting. To me, this is Rockne O'Bannon's and David Kemper's answer to the slash fanfiction revolving around Crichton and D'Argo, as well as the winsome fan knowledge that these two characters are 'more than just friends.' Here, Crichton and D'Argo finally get to make out, even if it's by proxy, and even if we don't get to see all of the action. The real sexuality is all in the dialogue, as well as the actors' facial expressions. Have we forgotten that John is wearing leather pants, and that D'Argo has a tongue that would rival Gene Simmons'?

Much of the Crichton/D'Argo slash on the net is, interestingly, concerned with a kind of erotic pedagogy—D'Argo is often the 'teacher,' and Crichton the pleased and bewildered pupil, exploring D'Argo's alien body with an almost childlike delight. There is also a collection of Crichton/Stark slash, mostly concerned with Stark's possessive love for John. In a Crichton/D'Argo fiction entitled 'Happy and Gay' by the author pleasureandpain (an apt username), Crichton and D'Argo explore their sexual attraction to each other while trapped in a locked cargo bay, and then later, in Crichton's quarters. D'Argo patiently explains to Crichton that Luxans have no social prejudices around homosexuality, and then gives John the opportunity to explore his own uncharted territories:

> D'Argo's skin almost glowed, a few shades darker than the slick gold sheets they lay on, and John noticed for the first time that he had unbraided his mustaches, leaving them to flow in a rippling tide over the tattoos that lined the side of his chest from throat to belly. He glanced back up at D'Argo's face, and D'Argo nodded, as if he understood that John just needed to look, to examine him. Reassured, he continued looking, noting the fine dusting of light red hair, the same color as the long hair that hung down D'Argo's back, over his chest and stomach. The pattern of the hair narrowed to a point above a set of five ridges across D'Argo's lower belly, stopping there completely. Curious, he reached out and brushed a finger along the topmost ridge, jumping a little when D'Argo gave a gasping sigh under the touch. (pleasureandpain 2005)

In this scene, power seems to be a floating signifier—both men are exploring each other's bodies—while, in the previously cited scene from 'Out of their Minds' (2.09), the sexual encounter is more calculated. Chiana wants to get off the ship, and is willing to manipulate Rygel erotically in order to do it. But who really has the 'power' here? Is it D'Argo? Chiana? It can't be John, since he's on the receiving end of this particular sexual advance. But John/Rygel also directs the flow of the scene, inviting Chiana's physical attention, then shutting it down when he decides that she can't help him reclaim his body. The phallus is a hot potato, getting passed from person to person (who's got it, who wants it, does anybody have it, does nobody have it?). The concept has never been sufficiently clarified. Beacon, phallus, beacon, phallus, who's got the beacon, who's got the phallus? 'The question, of course,' says Judith Butler in *Bodies that Matter*, 'is why it is assumed that the Phallus requires that particular body part to symbolize, and why it could not operate through symbolizing other body parts' (1993: 84). Why can't the phallus be an elbow, or a tongue, or a toe, or all five fingers?

Why can't our whole body be the phallus? This would be quite a lot like one of the ancient Greek conceptions of orgasm, which was thought by Hippocrates to begin in the blood (roiling and boiling like a sexy milkshake) or the bone marrow, and to emanate from the entire body (Foucault 1983). He also thought that conception involved irritating the womb (a historically fragile organ), and that '[when] the womb is disturbed, an irritation is set up in the womb which produces pleasure and heat in the rest of the body' (Hippocrates, quoted in Foucault 1983: 323). The womb always seems to be frigid, on fire, distended, disturbed, or wandering about in ancient medicine.

We're never going to be sure who has the phallus, then, but we can tentatively conclude that the dialogue itself is phallic—that language has the phallus (because it is the phallus). In *Farscape*, sex and language are often conflated, and the real erotic encounters occur through dialogue rather than through direct physical contact. Note the erotic tension between Scorpius and Braca, despite the fact that they barely touch each other, or the sexual unity between Zhaan and Aeryn that is made safe by its enshrinement as a 'mystical' act. John describes it much better as being 'a lot like an acid trip.' When Scorpius appears before John in 'Sacrifice,' (4.02) tied up and on all fours, slobbering like a dog, we are given the ultimate S/M reversal of their relationship.[9] Normally, John is on the receiving end of Scorpius and his 'interrogation' methods. Scorpius takes the active and penetrative role.

Now, in the sexual reversal that every fan has been hoping for, Scorpius is finally the submissive one. Grayza even clarifies this by inviting John to 'do anything to him . . . anything at all.' But John doesn't have to do anything (and, indeed, he can't really think of anything to do, although we know that's probably not entirely true), because the power-switch has already occurred. The erotic transgression of this scene emerges not from any physical contact between the two men, but from the positions that they actually inhabit. Isn't watching Scorpius, on his knees, lapping up water from a bowl and licking Grayza's boot, far more titillating then some hot, swarthy kiss between the two men? Personally, I find the episode that I mentioned in the last chapter—when Scorpius sucks on Crichton's finger in a gesture that makes every Lacanian lean

11. *Zhaan and Chiana in S/M gear*

12. *'All of you bitches out now! Crichton is mine!'*

forward with bated breath—far more transgressive than full-on sex between the characters. We don't *really* want to see what Scorpius looks like under that body suit, but the curiosity itself is erotic.

Sex and language don't just occur within the same frame—they are the frame; they exist in total contiguity with each other. All that we know about sex is the language that we use to describe it, just as Toto, in Kathleen Fallon's *Running Hot*, says that 'there are no bodies . . . I don't know you / all I know is / how to give you pleasure' (1989: 88). Our bodily knowledge is only expressible through language, just as 50% of our language (or maybe even 100%) is carried purely through our bodies, through gestural communication, through positioning and physical syntax. Lacan clarifies this when he observes that, if bodies and words are the same thing, if our unconscious is a language and our language is a living organism, then it stands to reason that speaking and sex are also the same: 'In other words—for the moment, I am not fucking, I am talking to you. Well! I can have exactly the same satisfaction as if I were fucking. That's what [sublimation] means. Indeed, it raises the question of whether in fact I am not fucking at this moment' (1977: 165). Even if you detest Lacan's theories, you have to love his critical sauciness. *How do you know that I am not fucking at this moment?* An important question—especially if the neighbors are watching, or if we don't know each other that well, or if, on the contrary, we're related, brother and sister, mother and son. Talking, fucking, and psychoanalysis brings us to *Hedwig and the Angry Inch*; however, the quote that I proved at the beginning of this chapter will seem cryptic to those who have never seen the movie (or the play). Hedwig, who begins his/her life as Hansel, describes him/herself as 'a slip of a girlyboy from Communist East Berlin.' In order to escape from East Germany, s/he undergoes a sex-change operation. However, the operation gets botched, and Hansel (now Hedwig) is left with 'an angry inch.' The real moment of erotic fracture occurs when Tommy Gnosis, who has become Hedwig's muse, finally reaches down his/her pants for the first time—encountering 'the inch':

Tommy:	Wh . . . what is that?
Hedwig:	It's what I have to work with.
Tommy (hesitating):	My mom is probably wondering where I—
Hedwig:	Sissy. Nancy, girly, lispyboy. What are you afraid of?

Tommy:	I love you.
Hedwig:	Then love the front of me. (Mitchell 2001).

Tommy can't handle (literally, as well as symbolically) what Hedwig 'has to work with,' the angry inch, which Hedwig his/herself describes as 'a one-inch mound of flesh / where my penis used to be / where my vagina never was.' Hedwig's use of hate speech—sissy, nancy, girly—is important here, since s/he is reconfiguring the parameters of the homophobic epithet, throwing Tommy's own homo- and trans-phobia back at him using the terms of his own disgust. It is no longer enough for Tommy to love the uncomplicated parts of Hedwig, the parts that are sexually familiar, or the parts that fall under a clearly defined gender. He must love 'the front' as well, and the front embodies all of Hedwig's gender dysphoria, all of his/her multiple sexes and subjects.

I invoke *Hedwig* not simply because I love the text, but because I think that *Farscape* shares many of its commitments to gender inclusivity and sexual openness (not 'tolerance,' the great crutch of western liberalism, but *openness*, dialogic space, crucial attention and respect). The aliens (and human) aboard Moya all have unconventional bodies in our eyes, and those bodies form the matter of what they 'have to work with,' the psychic and physical surfaces along which they produce their own relations of desire and dialogue, inclusion and acceptance. What Rygel 'has to work with' (an imperial inch) is very different from what D'Argo or John has, but he uses it just as effectively.

Although Mitchell makes a lot of mistakes (as does *Farscape*) within his film and playtext, his ultimate endorsement of biological and psychic wholeness—outside of and beyond gender prescription—endures as *Hedwig's* evocative political message. It is what makes the film so infinitely viewable, and what makes me, as a queer spectator, return to it again and again. *Hedwig* haunts me and moves me—not because I believe in a dream of mythic gender holism, or because I need to empathize with Hedwig and all that s/he might represent, but because, like Mitchell, I am convinced that it is possible to feel beautiful and powerful within your own skin. Beautiful and powerful because of your scars, because of your body's complex, fragile, and amazing surfaces. To be fearfully and beautifully made, and *re-made*, in whatever direction your own living biological narrative takes you, and in the end, in the final cut, to know that you fit somewhere.

The 'point' of *Farscape*, if it has one, is that nobody—human or alien—fits anywhere except with each other. We have to lovingly create the spaces in which we fit, we have to create spaces in which others can fit, and to allow others into our own private spaces rather than shutting them out with psychological boundaries. We can't expect these spaces to emerge *ex nihilo*, to precede us, as realms that we can easily access without any emotional labor. Everyone aboard Moya has to build a family with each other, and even within the tender margins of this family, they still experience moments of profound physical fracture, irreconcilable psychic loss. Such a moment occurs for Aeryn when one of the Crichtons (we can never know which one) dies, and she must find a way to process this death, even as she knows (however impossibly) that *another* Crichton, a perfect copy of her lover, is waiting for her back on Moya. Accompanied, albeit reluctantly, by Crais and Stark, she flees to the planet of Valdon—a site of magic and criminality, sex and death, betrayal and confusion, where Sade would feel right at home. Aeryn goes there to forget Crichton (and herself) and to remember him (and herself). The result is mixed.[10]

While on Valdon, she encounters a horribly disfigured man (he has actually been genetically 'modified' in order to escape Peacekeeper attention) who claims to be her dead father, Talyn ('The Choice,' 3.17). This turns out to be an elaborate ruse, constructed by her mother, Xalex, in order to trap her. Aeryn's 'father,' who is actually an alien in Xalex's employ named Lyczak, tells Aeryn that he might be able to contact John's departed spirit. Aeryn never really believes this to be possible, but she allows him to try anyway. Between the margins of impossibility, however hard they are, she finds a tiny space that could admit miracles, an inch or two in which to dwell, hoping. As she waits for Lyczak to return with 'the Seer,' Aeryn sees John several times—his ghost. He lies down with her, holding her, silent. She asks him: 'Was it easy to be the hero? Leave me behind?' ('The Choice,' 3.17). His answer doesn't satisfy her.

When Lyczak returns, he brings with him an alien called Cresus—a writhing, fetal-like brain, with four eyes and a tiny, shriveled body, tucked like some kind of closeted monster into an electronic capsule. Cresus invites Aeryn to touch him, promising that 'I won't bite . . . much.' He utters a weird, high-pitched giggle, like a small child playing with a toy (and Aeryn is the toy). She reaches out to touch him, but Cresus flinches. 'Huh! Soft. Touch me . . . soft.' Aeryn makes her touch gentler, and Cresus closes his eyes in a kind of ecstasy, almost purring. Then, in halting words, she begins to tell him about Crichton:

Aeryn:	He—uh—
Cresus:	Did he . . . love you?
	(Aeryn looks away. She swallows.)
Cresus:	Hold you? Touch you . . . soft?
Aeryn:	Yes. He loved me. He was very—he made me better. ('The Choice,' 3.17)

There are only two erotic moments in this episode. The first occurs psychically, spiritually, when Aeryn lies down with her image of Crichton. She is embracing mist and shadows. The memory of hair, lips, smell, taste, skin. How the warmth of his body felt against her back. How he folded into her like a paper crane, one leg dangling over the bed, one arm tucked beneath her, his breath in her hair as they both slept. How his tears tasted when he cried for everyone, and everything, in the Uncharted Territories—for the fact of death, and the crucial unfairness of it.

There is nothing holding her, but also, everything. John's body is insubstantial, but his memory is phallic. It is his language that sees her, cradles her, serving as lone witness to her unendurable sadness (even as it recognizes her astonishing strength). We are transported back to the moments before Crichton dies, when Aeryn, her face contorted into a sob that never quite escapes, declares that 'I'm very *angry*' ('Icarus Abides,' 3.15). The statement seems incongruous, but it also makes perfect sense, because John has done something completely stupid and reckless. He has gotten himself killed to save millions of lives, a whole planet, in fact, but most especially Aeryn herself. 'Me too,' John says. Aeryn's reply, 'we had good times,' is strange and funny, filled with an inarticulate despair.[11] It's as if they're having a simple conversation between friends, just two people relaxing after a long day at work, trading memories. Only, this is the last time that they'll ever speak, the last time that they'll ever know each other. The goodbye is anecdotal and heartbreaking, with all of the love, regret, and rage gathering in the margins, between the words, in the same space where Aeryn now waits. Hopes.

The second moment of intimacy that I mentioned occurs in the exchange between Aeryn and Cresus, where she modulates her touch, going from 'hard' to 'soft.' She strokes his face gently, and he acts as a speculum for her memories, taking in everything that she knows about Crichton even though she barely says a thing. It's all in that first word—'He—'—the sentence that Aeryn can never finish, because she's been living within it up until this very moment, harboring within John's language, waiting and searching. Like Gatsby, staring, always staring, at the green light across the harbor (could it be—no—it's not), Aeryn waits within his language. Cresus shares this moment with her, this longing. 'Did he hold you?' he asks tentatively. 'Touch you . . . soft?' Yes, he held me. Yes, he touched me soft, touched me fine. Even as Aeryn rejects both Crais and Stark in this episode, spurning their advances, she has these two significantly erotic moments, occuring light years away from both 'real' men—between her and a ghost; between her and an abject creature, a djinn trapped in a bottle, the chimera named Cresus. She touches him soft, even though she doesn't have to. She shares her language, and with it, her desire.

This brings us to the final episode that I want to look at—'Lava's a Many Splendored Thing' (4.04). This episode does have a 'plot,' but it isn't important, nor does it really make sense. What makes the narrative, instead, so fascinating is that it precisely mirrors an alimentary model—the process of digestion. The story begins with hunger, then ingestion, then purgation—through vomiting—and, finally, concludes with an extended diuretic episode, Rygel's 'schlock.' So, we start with eating, move into puking, and end with a coprophilic finale. The digestive process in miniature. Where else on television can we find this kind of grotesque mimesis?

Noranti, ever the old trickster, gives John and company an herbal concoction which she calls a 'restorative.' Unfortunately, it turns out to be a purgative—a very strong one. This is where *Farscape* deviates from the average SF program. Where most shows would merely gesture towards the fact that their characters were ill, the crew of Moya actually change their flightpath in order to make a 'pit stop' on a barren world. An intergalactic bathroom break. Imagine that you're driving, and you suddenly have to 'go.' (*go where*? I've always wondered about the syntax). Could you make it all the way home, or would you be forced to stop at a gas station? The lava world here becomes the gas station of the Uncharted Territories, a place for the crew to empty their stomachs (and bowels) in a violent *danse macabre* of reverse peristalsis. That the show organizes an entire episode around this fact is quite remarkable.

D'Argo:	Where's Rygel?
Chiana:	Down that hole. Taking a giant *shlock*.

('Lava's a Many Splendored Thing,' 4.04)

However, Rygel never gets the chance to take his giant *schlock*.[12] He springs a booby trap left by alien scavengers, and finds himself encased in amber. Not a tenable position for someone whose bowels are full to bursting, especially a three-foot-tall Hyneirian with three stomachs. By this time, Rygel is definitely wishing that he hadn't eaten three portions of the herb (rather than the one portion allotted to everyone else) which makes this episode as much about gluttony as it is about bodily revolution and colonic revolt. Sikozu even observes how ridiculously inefficient their bodies are for having to eat every three arns or so, when her own body can go without food for several weeks (although she has to binge first, an amazing sight which we witness in 'Coup By Clam,' 4.10). It isn't until the end of the episode, after he has been freed, that Rygel is finally, mercifully able to relieve himself. 'I'll never eat again,' he groans, but we know that this isn't true. He'll be eating again in a few arns. That's just Rygel.

13. Rygel is always happiest while eating

Before this resolution, however, the crew hits a snag. Chiana and Sikozu need to operate D'Argo's ship (in his absence), but in order to do that, they also need his DNA. The ship is biologically keyed to his body (a peculiar kind of bodily ownership.) Chiana's solution is elegantly simple—she reaches into D'Argo's (impressively large) mountain of vomit, scooping out a great handful, and then slathers it all over the interior of the ship. Biological waste matter meets advanced electronics, and miraculously, the two connect. The ship works. Sikozu is less than impressed by the method, but she has to admire its ingenuity. The solution is in the puke.

As the camera pans across the piles of vomit, we see that D'Argo's 'pile' is more like a towering mass—at least twice as large as the others, even Crichton's. The puke is also the phallus. Waste matter gets conflated with sexuality here, just as food is always being conflated with desire. Consuming hunger and violent release are experiences that can apply to both eating and sex. Elspeth Probyn, in her book *Carnal Appetites*, explains that 'as individuals, we eat into culture . . . rather than simply confirming who we are, eating conjoins us in a network of the edible and inedible, human and non-human, the animate and the inanimate' (2000: 17). We eat our way through life, through culture, but it also eats its way through us. 'As alimentary assemblages, eating recalls with force the elemental nature of class, gender, sexuality, and nation' (Probyn 2000).[13] Food can also be rape, as Rygel discovers in 'Crackers Don't Matter' (2.04) when D'Argo violently shoves crackers down his throat in order to punish his gluttony.

Eating a peach is never just eating a peach, as anyone who has ever eaten one can tell you. Everything, even and especially food, occurs within an ideological matrix, as well as a nostalgic register. To this day, I can't eat salmon and cream cheese without remembering the time that I ate it with my very first boyfriend, when I was barely nineteen, amazed at how wonderful it tasted and how lovely he was. Curiously, while reading Probyn's book, I also found myself watching a culinary program—*The Naked Chef*, starring the adorable Jamie Oliver. Watching him grin implacably while he cooks voluptuous food is one of the sexiest things imaginable. I perfectly understand the link between food and sex. It's on the Canadian Food Channel, between 8:00 and 9:00 p.m.

An interesting reversal of Rygel's usual gluttony occurs in the episode 'Family Ties' (1.22), when Chiana unexpectedly prepares everyone's favorite dishes for what might very well be their last meal. She says: 'So I, uh, I wanted to let you all know how much I appreciate everything you've done for me. For each of you . . . your favorite dishes. Krawdlar, smoked prongo sinew, hepatian minced stew, and of course, crispy grolack.'

It would have been peculiar enough for Chiana to prepare a single meal (since we've never witnessed her in any kind of domestic activity before, least of all cooking), but for her to prepare *individual* meals, tailored to everyone's specific tastes and cravings, is an act of surprising tenderness. Crispy grolack is, of course, the most important, because it is Rygel's favorite—for once, Rygel's obsession with food becomes a pleasure to be indulged rather than a vice to be critiqued. Just as food is linked to sexuality and class, it can also be linked to warmth, conviviality, family, and belonging. That the characters are eating *together* is what's important here, since eating is so often a solitary activity, something done behind closed doors. And even when we eat in the presence of others, we're still alone, since we experience the food, the taste, the whole alimentary experience in an entirely individual way. Perhaps we love eating, perhaps we hate it, perhaps we can't wait for the meal to be over— but we rarely voice these feelings. In this episode, for just a moment, everyone is enjoying food and company at the exact same time. Impending death pales in comparison to crispy grolack.

As I have tried to show in this chapter, bodies always exist relationally to political, ethical, and sexual mores—indeed, bodies themselves are completely relational, nothing but context, extensions of the ego that are nonetheless fabulous to hold (and behold). The alien bodies on *Farscape* are constantly rebelling against the constraints set upon them by the network, by cable television, by a staff of white male writers, and by the expectations of various fan communities. They exist within a complex *bricolage* of social forces, and are shaped by the politics of television even as they attempt to force a rupture within those politics. This is what Kathy Acker means when she says, in *Blood and Guts in High School,* that 'having any sex in the world is having to have sex with capitalism' (1978: 135). Her narrator in that book, Janey, moves from one unfulfilling sexual experience to the next, never quite able to wrap her mind (or body) around what it means to be 'sexed' in a world where sexuality is necessarily organized along a continuum of capitalist expansion and Marx's notion of 'labor time.' All time is work, all work is production, and so sex is also production, gender is also work, a labor.

Acker, who died of breast cancer in 1997, was a revolutionary force, always polemical in her writing against sexual essentialism and capitalist exploitation. She was most intrigued by the work of the Marquis de Sade and William S. Burroughs, whom she saw as being emblematic of a revolutionary deconstruction, rather than the *laissez-faire* deconstructive efforts of some members of the French and Frankfurt schools that merely substituted an open power for a secret one, an obvious oppression for the exclusion of a cryptography. True agency, for Acker, resided in piracy. She wanted to be a pirate, but knew '[even] as a child that the separation between me and piracy had something to do with being a girl. With gender. With being in a dead world. So gender had something to do with death' (Acker 1997: 160). But if gender has something to do with death, it also acts as a ground for experiencing life—as a sort of *chora*, both natural and constructed, that relays us 'in' the world even as it limits our perception of its wonders. Gender can always be used as a tool of oppression, but it can also always be used as a flexible weapon of resistance: 'The trading arena, the market, is my blood. My body is open to all people. This is democratic capitalism. Today pleasure lies in the flow of blood . . . language isn't just translation. The word is blood' (Acker 1988: 55).

Everything is blood. Capitalism regulates blood, birth, flow, energy, holding, breathing, and dying, but it also occurs within a wash of blood, within an ocean of bodily fluids and permeable membranes opening up to spill out their steaming contents. Everything is blood. Everything is killing, loving, kissing, shitting, puking, all stretching across the surface of bodies that are both limited and have no limits. The aliens of *Farscape* are constantly slipping and sliding through this matrix, rebounding off each other, striking and stroking each other, holding and pushing away, all regulated by the advanced economic forces that shape them even as their creative genesis goes beyond those forces, as 'the sword, the will turns on, interiorizes or eats itself so that pure power turns into play. This play is the ground for art' (Acker 1997: 90). Play turning into power, and power into play—this generative labor is at the very heart of *Farscape* as a television show that pushes against so many social boundaries.

When all is said and done, we may have no control over our bodies. They may simply speak us, even as we attempt to speak *them* into being. In *Running Hot*, Toto explains this aporia, this paradox of the body—always submissive and always in control—to her lover, even as she remembers the previous night's sexual encounter:

> I was only a force last night you know I lost my body my sex my humanness the heart knew nothing of the onslaught—just a force—

gravity momentum whatnot I was malevolent ecstactic I went into you over you between you the heart knew nothing of the onslaught I made you sing out my name . . . I have too many tongues too many sweet tongues. (Fallon 1989: 84)

Multiple bodies and multiple tongues, multiple surfaces for desire to lodge, for exploration without colonization to occur. This is the bodily utopia, but it is also a wrenching and violent moment, a moment where psychic acumen disappears completely, where the body takes over. 'I was only a force,' a force with too many tongues. Like the cherubim Progonoskes in *A Wind in the Door* (L'Engle 1973), nothing but blinking eyes, wings, and tongues of flame, a cloud of burning and amused desire.

Having a body in *Farscape*, whether it''s alien or human, is being part of an interface, a biomechanoid union, and a becoming (enflaming). Piece of spirit, piece of mind, piece of soul. Living on Moya is living on a pile of dren, living within a writhing mass of fleshy bodies, living in a pool of blood, saliva, and tears. Labor is joy and joy is labor. The body is always being pushed to the point of failure, as any bodybuilder can attest—shearing muscle, bruised flesh, myelin and acton heads pounding together like pistons, lactic acid burning—evolution occurs within the spaces of failure, within the gaps and fissures where change is possible. Rygel is always going to fill all three of his stomachs, but he has learned to share—somewhat. For a Hyneirian, that's not just progress. That's a bloody miracle.

'I thought that, one day, maybe, there'd be a human society in a world which is beautiful, a society which wasn't just disgust' (Acker 1988: 32). The narrator of Acker's *Empire of the Senseless*, Thivai, makes this observation while he is being psychoanalyzed—by Dr. Schreber, no less. This isn't simply a disavowal of the world as disgusting, a rejection of liberty (which Thivai calls 'shit . . . a nail in my head'). Liberty is shit. The world *is* disgust, *is* disgusting. There is no world other than the world of disgust, because bodies are disgusting, bodies are unpredictable, bodies make life 'disgusting.' Heraclitus observed that 'asses prefer garbage to gold' in the fifth century BC, and that was a precapitalist rupture. Everything is disgusting. We live in the heart of disgust, in Mallarmé's overflowing reservoir of 'mud, filth, and ruby' collecting in the sepulcher of Baudelaire. Every human interaction occurs within the register of the obscene. Desire is *on/scene*, love is *ob/scene*. We can't help that.

We can only attempt to construct an egalitarian world that respects this disgust, that limns the beauty around it with a passionate light.

This isn't just an overwhelming effort—it's an extraterrestrial task.

6 *Frell* Me Dead, You're Totally *Fahrbot*
Language-Power and Language-Play in *Farscape*

> There is neither a first word nor a last word. The contexts of dialogue are without limit. They extend into the deepest past and the most distant future . . . at any present moment of the dialogue there are great masses of forgotten meanings, but these will be recalled again . . . for nothing is absolutely dead: every meaning will someday have its homecoming.
> —Mikhail Bakhtin (1986: 373)

> Time wounds all heals.
> —John Crichton ('Unrealized Reality,' 4.11)

This chapter will focus on language and speech practices within *Farscape*—how the show's characters gain subjectivity through (but are also subjected *to*) various languages, and how their individual and communal speech-acts tend to be structured in opposition to conventional expository and exemplary dialogue within SF genres. By expository I mean the recurring 'this is how the warp drive works' speech,[1] and by exemplary I mean the tradition of moral example that proliferates within SF, and which achieves ethnographic perfection in the moment when a human patiently separates 'right' from 'wrong' for an alien. Contrary to the notion that dialogue operates wholly in the service of situating technology within SF (Jones 1999), I would contend that the characters on *Farscape* are, if anything, over-invested in—and over-determined by—their dialogic relations with each other. And by 'dialogic,' I am referring chiefly to Mikhail Bakhtin's work on intertextuality and heteroglossia, which I will discuss in more detail later. For now, let us simplify *dialogism* as the idea that 'existence, like language, is a shared event' (Holquist 2002: 28). Bakhtin's reading of *carnivale* as the 'cosmic terror' (1984: 335) of mingling bodies, along with the pleasure of collapsed categories and topsy-turvy social roles, also applies to

Farscape, which appears at times as a kind of intergalactic *Feast of Fools* wherein no social convention is safe from the forces of parody.

The characters on *Farscape* speak themselves into being, rearticulate their own identities through speech, and become linked to each other through chains of recursive dialogue; that is, through speech-practices that, according to Luce Irigaray, work to ensure that 'linear reading is no longer possible . . . the retroactive impact of the end of each word, utterance, or sentence upon its beginning must be taken into consideration in order to undo the power of its teleological effect' (1985: 80). Everything that they say *matters*, and it matters because it is fluid and interconnected—all of their dialogue has a continuity, in that a past speech-act (for example, something that Chiana said in Season 1[2]) can return as a narrative rupture, a determining echo, yet that 'continuity' is not rigid because language remains an adaptive tool within the show: it allows these characters to escape from life-threatening situations, just as it catapults them *into* those situations. Whereas most serial narratives have 'story arcs'—episodes linked by a common narrative thread, often occurring near the end of a season—*Farscape* encodes language as a kind of always-present and living story arc, a *language arc* with which spectators need to interact in order to understand the complex motivations of the show's characters.

I am going to attempt, with this chapter, to situate *Farscape*'s various languages, speech-practices, namings, and other addresses/interpellations within both current and traditional discussions of semiotics and linguistics. I say 'attempt' because this is a near-impossible task, especially given these fields' resolute indeterminacy. Even isolating something like 'speech-act theory,' inaugurated more or less by J.L. Austin in *How To Do Things With Words* (1980), sends one careening into (surprisingly vitriolic) debates around Saussurian vs. post-Saussurian linguistics, the relationship between sign, signifier, and signified, between *langue, langage,* and *parole*,[3] between concept and referent, between performative and constative utterances, and—that maddening question—whether language speaks us or we speak language. That is, whether we can impose contextual limits upon our own speech, or whether speech always exceeds, through its essential iterability, the individual contexts and safeguards that we attempt to place on it.

This is no easy terrain to traverse, and, given the rich and extensive mines of dialogue within *Farscape*, any substantial discussion would have to be a book in itself. For the sake of brevity, then, I will offer only a surface reading of semiotic and linguistic traditions as they apply to the show, using them as general frameworks through which to discuss the flexibility and ingenuity of the show's many bizarre, offensive, and wonderful speech-acts. Working chronologically would be more or less useless, but, if you need a temporal benchmark, the earliest semiotician (in terms of when the bulk of his work was published) will be Ferdinand Saussure (the creator of semiology), and the most recent will be Judith Butler—specifically her work in *Excitable Speech* (1997). Along the way, we will cover, in brief: J.L. Austin, Mikhail Bakhtin, Louis Althusser, Jacques Derrida, Julia Kristeva, Luce Irigaray, and Helene Cixous. Since much of linguistics and semiotics criticism remains masculinist in its interests—shooting for the 'big' language issues while ignoring the 'small' ones, like gender, sexuality, and race—I intend to position the work of Butler, Irigaray, Cixous, and Kristeva as a kind of humane antidote to the more epistemological concerns of traditional male writers.

My goal here is not, as I have stated in earlier discussions, to create a convenient envelope of theoretical validity into which we can 'stuff' the show, thereby justifying its status as an object of scholarly debate (i.e. Derrida's work applies here, which means that the show must be worth watching). And this is no mere lip service or self-conscious gesture on my part, meant to peek my head out of an ivory tower window for a moment in order to wink and say *I get what's going on here, I'm not fooled by the academic machine.* I can't pretend to be writing from outside this machine, and I constantly live this tension (what Spivak might call 'riding the hyphen'), the tension of being an outsider/insider, of being rewarded for biological things that I can't control (being male, being white) and feeling exiled for other things that I can't control (being queer, hence, politically over-determined), or that I choose not to control (being *openly* queer, being a writer). Working with academic theory is supposed to produce these tensions—as well as the most obvious tension between conceptualizing and 'doing'—and if that tension lets up for even a second, then, as Stuart Hall describes it, 'theory has let you off the hook' (Morley 1996: 272).

Thus, when I say that I am not 'merely' situating *Farscape* within semiotics and linguistics criticism in order to ensure its scholarly legitimacy, what I mean is that I am trying to maintain two discussions simultaneously: one thread is text based, treating the show 'in itself' (though as an intertextual subject, obviously), and honoring what it does on its own, without any academic intervention; the second thread is more like a series of frames, of potential readings.[4] These scholarly 'frames' (deconstruction, semiotics, queer theory, etc.) inform each other, as they inform the show, and as the show informs them. This is not just a happy rhizome—Gilles Deleuze's (1983) organism with a network of infinite points, all connected— but a way of reading that honors the text while acknowledging its contributions to scholarly analysis, and honors the interrogatory and transgressive potential of these academic 'frames' while acknowledging that they do not make a text 'real,' that shows like *Farscape* were disruptive and wonderful long before academia found them, and that they continue to exceed the classificatory and organizational readings that we (Cultural Studies academics) offer.

Many shows, of course, depend upon innovative dialogue. In terms of fantasy/SF television, *Buffy the Vampire Slayer* became such a critical success primarily due to its quick and brilliant dialogue, along with its capacity to address its own status as a television show ironically (through various episodes that drew attention to the show's means of production). *Farscape* is not, therefore, alone in its dialogic character relationships. However, unlike *Buffy*, which both entices and alienates through its adaptation of extant North American 'English'—employing such neologisms as *wiggins, insane-o, nouned,* and *slut-bomb*—*Farscape* actually incorporates alien languages into its characters' dialogue, effectively re-rendering English as extraterrestrial speech.

It is John's extensive pop-culture knowledge that remains a foreign language to his friends on board Moya, bizarre and impenetrable, while John himself begins to pick up words like *arn, metra,* and *microt,* adapting his own speech to admit a common language (what is probably a 'pidgin'[5] language within the Uncharted Territories). When D'Argo or Aeryn try to speak Crichton's 'language'—that is, the language of popular culture—they inevitably produce comic results, whereas Crichton has little trouble building up his own alien lexicon.

Whether this is a comment on the adaptability of the human subject, or the *indecipherability* of North American English, is a point to be debated. What remains more interesting is that, aside from Aeryn—who begins casually to study English near the end of the third season[6]—nobody seems particularly interested in learning Crichton's language; Crichton, on the other hand, *must* understand the meaning of crucial alien words and concepts if he is to survive. Standing on Moya's bridge-area in the 'Premiere' episode, freshly transplanted into this alien environment and without the aid of translator microbes (they haven't been injected yet), Crichton cannot understand Zhaan or D'Argo—he hears nothing but disconnected sounds. In that moment, the spectator understands that language will be a very important part of this show, and that Crichton's ability to negotiate this alien universe will be intimately connected with his ability to master particular forms of linguistic interaction.

But 'speech-acts' don't occur within some hermetically sealed language realm—the speaker's body communicates, through a gestural language of its own, as much as her words do; in fact, it often transmits a context entirely separate from her words. Bakhtin calls this context *extraverbal*. It is the messy component of human linguistic interaction that so annoyed J.L. Austin, who was looking for 'felicitous' speech-acts to occur in the right place and time, under the right circumstances (1980: 22).[7] In order for a 'performative'—that is, a speech-act that 'does' something rather than merely describing something—to be felicitous for Austin, the speaker needed to mean what she was saying, to *know* what she meant, and to speak within the right context. But what happens when we say one thing, and our bodies say another?

Gestural language remains a crucial component of the signification process, and the characters on *Farscape* communicate as much through their bodies as they do through strict phonation (that is, speech). A character like Chiana often says more through body language, gesture, *kinesics*—which is the study of gestural codes—than she ever does by speaking out loud. D'Argo's tongue is a weapon, and a sign of physical superiority, as well as a speech organ. And Rygel speaks, perhaps, *too* often with his body.

In order to understand these characters' dialogic relations, we need also to incorporate gestural communication, as well as bodily configuration—how their bodies are deployed in relation to their speech-acts, what spaces (of vulnerability or superiority) they occupy, and how they relate to one another spatially. *Space*, both within Moya and beyond her—the breathable kind and the fatal kind—remains a crucial determinant and 'third witness'[8] within *Farscape*, as it does within all SF narratives. Chapter 5, on bodily functions and bodily permeability, discussed the space/body relationship in greater detail; this present chapter will instead focus on the body's role in language-making, on a show that is, arguably, all about language and all about bodies.

The two most oft-used alien words on the show are curse-words: *frell* and *dren*. *Frell* translates 'literally' as 'fuck,' although, like fuck, it has a delightfully broad spectrum of connotative meanings.[9] *Dren* translates as 'shit,' and, like its English counterpart, can be used either as a noun (look at that pile of *dren*) or as an expletive (*dren!*). Because the characters on *Farscape*, including Crichton, swear in a language other than English, they are able to get away with a great deal of luridly inventive phrasing that would never normally get past a network censor. This strategy is similar to the one used in Joss Whedon's *Firefly*, wherein characters swear exclusively in Mandarin and Cantonese (which I've been told is somewhat 'creatively' translated). The difference with *Farscape* is that the English-speaking spectator knows precisely what is being said, but the alien word, *frell* or *dren*, creates a rupture in the normal chain of signification, a bit of Derrida's *différance*[10] within the utterance, making it mean 'what it means,' but also mean something else simultaneously—that is, making it different, alien, to itself.

One of many examples occurs in the episode 'Suns and Lovers' (3.02), when Aeryn, upon finding a group of lost children in a derelict space station, looks up in surprise and says '*frell* me dead!'[11] The utterance is made more complicated, though, by her intonation: she says '*frell* me dead' in a light, somewhat curious register, as one might say 'well *I'll* be!' upon witnessing something surprising. Austin would see this statement as infelicitous, because Aeryn is obviously being sarcastic, rather than literally inviting someone to '*frell* me dead.' In this sense, she is 'abusing' the *locutionary* or descriptive power of the act, as well as its *perlocutionary* or agential power, its power to affect a change (1980: 13, 99). It neither describes a reality nor produces a consequence—and a perlocution is really just a consequence of an illocutionary speech-act—but rather separates itself off from the physical universe, being neither true not false, neither *constative* (a statement that produces no *direct* consequence, but which can produce indirect ones) nor *performative* (a statement that is also an action, thus, also a consequence).

The fact(s) that Aeryn is being sarcastic, that she is carrying a pulse rifle, and, of course, that she is a character within a fantasy program, all act as vitiating forces to the constative 'truth' of her utterance — what Austin calls 'etiolations,' (1980: 22) which are, quite literally, 'withering' forces that blast away the value of the speech-act because they represent a disruptive and fallacious context. These forces include most of literature (so we're *frelled* there), poetry especially (double-*frelled*, since much of *Farscape*'s dialogue exhibits the same linguistic patterns as poetry), and any lack of honest intent on the part of the speaker (Aeryn's sarcasm, then, makes this a triple-*frell*-threat, in terms of etiolating forces).[12] Three strikes, and we're out — which is another Austinian example of the performative at work: that is, the umpire's call that makes 'out!' a physical reality.

But why stop there? We can also use *frell* to 'clarify' Saussure's thorny notion of the *sign*, which is the double-sided psychological/ physiological event that produces signification among humans. A sign is the combination of a sound, which Saussure calls an 'acoustic image,' with a concept, in order to produce a 'complex physiologi-cal-psychological unit' (1983: 8). Kristeva clarifies this by explaining that 'the sign is a psychological reality with two sides, the concept and the sound image . . . which Saussure describes as two sides of the same piece of paper' (1989: 14). These two 'sides' form the *signi-fier* and the *signified*, which Saussure originally posed (in his *Course in General Linguistics*) as 'acoustic image/concept,' but which were changed by his editors into the much catchier 'signifier/signified' (Holdcroft 1991: 50).

In order to understand *frell*, then, as a sign (and what a flexible sign it is), we need to divide it into its psychological and physiolog-ical components, which will combine within the act of phonation to produce a linguistic reality. The word itself, 'frell,' is a combination of *phonemes*, or units of sound, which here combine to produce a *morpheme*, or unit of meaning. *Fe-rell* becomes *Frell*, which actually means something, as opposed to just the fricative '*f*' or the liquid '*r*', which don't mean anything on their own. That sound-unit, the actual word that can either be spoken phonically or written graphi-cally, is the *signifier*, the psycho-linguistic 'envelope' for the word's concept. And that concept, the image of what *frell* is, of what it might mean to *frell* or be *frelled*, is the *signified*, the concept that the word references.

All signs represent something *in absentia*, in its absence, which means that language itself is built around absence rather than pres-ence, like something swirling around the event horizon of a black hole, always about to fall in. Derrida is thus referring to this absence when he describe the 'iterability' of the sign or 'mark' (1988: 48), its potential to outlive the addresser and addressee, and hence to exist, in a way, outside of time (like something within a singularity, wherein the laws of physics break down, and time/space becomes infinite), never subject to an origin, always 'marked, from the beginning or even before the beginning, by iterability, that is, by impurity' (1988: 80).

This sense of linguistic impurity, of a word or speech-act never quite doing what we want or need or expect it to do—because no originary template for it exists beyond its own already-ruptured state of flux—suggests a compelling parallel with the doctrines of genetic purity that the Peacekeepers adopt on *Farscape*. When Aeryn first comes into contact with Crichton and the others, her (then) commanding officer, Captain Bialar Crais, tells her that she has been 'irreversibly contaminated' ('Premiere,' 1.01).[13] This is an inversion of *Star Trek*'s 'prime directive'—rather than the threat of an advanced civilization interfering with a pre-spacefaring one, the Peacekeepers are more concerned with the threat of a 'primitive' civilization (that is, anyone who isn't Sebacean) contaminating their own genetic purity. Given that, in Crais' view, Aeryn is contaminated simply by being *near* Crichton and the others, we have to assume that this dictate of purity is violated by any kind of contact, social, proximal, spatial, and—most importantly—psychological. Any form of contact with an outsider carries with it the threat of irreversible contamination, but the most insidious kind of contact, for Crais, seems to be any form of emotional sympathy.

The feeling of being contaminated by another subject—specifically of being contaminated through psychic or emotional affinity—echoes Judith Butler's ideas on hate speech and its effects on the subject in her work *Excitable Speech*. 'To be injured by speech,' she says, 'is to suffer a loss of context, that is, not to know where you are' (Butler 1997: 4). This is a kind of anti-interpellation, a 'shattering' that exposes 'the volubility of one's 'place' within the community of speakers; one can be 'put in one's place' by such speech, but such a place may be no place' (Butler 1997: 4). The Peacekeepers have arranged many of their cultural practices in general to avoid this moment of potential shattering, to avoid the contamination by external ideas, by other subjects, for fear that *their own* subjectivity as a dominant cultural force in the Uncharted Territories will be somehow unmoored by this contact. The contamination that they fear is not, although it seems outwardly so, a genetic one, but is rather a psychic contamination, a sense of iterability, of emotional and ethical flexibility, that will expose their own speech-practices and cultural mores as being ambivalent, marked, impure.

The Peacekeepers want their language, their context, their speech-patterns, to be the only ones accessible within the galaxy, thereby creating a speech machine that does nothing but approve and validate its own unique ethical (and unethical) contexts, re-rendering them as universal. At the heart of this effort, which is, after all, the effort of the western epistemological tradition in general, is the fear that their own efficacy as cultural subjects will be contaminated—not by the alien others that the Peacekeepers try so hard to quarantine, but by the ineluctable impurity that has always lain at the bottom of their language and cultural practices, like silt and detritus at the bottom of the ocean.

Aeryn tells Crichton in 'The Way We Weren't' (2.05) that 'most Peacekeepers are bred, and reared, for one purpose: military service. Procreation is . . . assigned.' Peacekeeper High Command monitors the interpersonal (and physical) relations of its soldiers through a powerful surveillance system—the same system that catches Aeryn on camera, years before she boarded Moya as a prisoner, when she was still a soldier. There is a discussion of this event in Chapter 4; but, for the purposes of this chapter, Aeryn's own speech-practices in that episode are of interest. She never questions what cargo she has been assigned to carry (the cargo is Pilot, she discovers later), and, when the officer Velorek[14] questions her about this, she replies simply that 'I do what I'm ordered to do, but it doesn't mean I have to be interested.' Peacekeeper Command controls its soldiers, like any military apparatus, by limiting both their knowledge and the parameters of their speech. Aeryn knows only what she needs to know, and asks only what she needs to ask. Her speech-practices are thus, in an Austinian sense, *felicitous*, because she only ever says what she means, and only ever knows the 'right' thing in the 'right' context.

Pilot, on the other hand, employs a language that operates on precisely the opposite principles. In fact, he employs two languages—his own native speech, which is untranslatable, and the 'common' speech that the translator microbes pick up on, which is severely limiting for him. When Pilot is distressed, he reverts to this original language, which nobody else can understand. 'One sentence,' Velorek says, 'can carry over a hundred different facts . . . concepts, emotions—far too complex for our translator microbes' ('The Way We Weren't,' 2.05). Pilot's language is a mass of colliding contexts, an Austinian nightmare, wherein one word can mean a hundred different things, and a few simple morphemes might convey a whole book's worth of information.

In this sense, Pilot's language is a material representation of the fundamental iterability that Derrida finds within all speech-acts. That is, the original 'contamination,' the impurity, the lack of originary meaning, which 'leaves us no choice but to mean (to say) something that is (already, always, also) other than what we mean (to say), to say something other than what we say *and* would have wanted to say, to understand something other' (Derrida 1988: 62). Pilot, because his language is constructed around iterability (rather than in illusory opposition to it), actually *means* to mean something different with every utterance, to say 'what he says' but also something always beyond that. Whereas Aeryn's language is a closed context that, nevertheless, remains contaminated by such iterations as her memories, her own gestural communication, her relationships, and countless other things, Pilot's language is an exercise in iterability from the start, and thus completely indecipherable to the Peacekeepers.

We now have two 'official' models for linguistic communication within *Farscape*. There is Aeryn's model: say only what you mean, know only what you're meant to know, and suppress any extraverbal context so that your utterance remains felicitous. Then there is Pilot's model: communicate in two languages at once, one of which is context-controlled and limited, the other *over-invested* with context, beyond framing, impure in every mark, and nearly infinite in its possibilities for simultaneous signification. Let us add to this two more competing models, as demonstrated by the characters Chiana and Stark, who rarely say what they mean, but often mean something above and beyond what they say; that meaning lingers, ghost-like, visible through sometimes-hysterical gestures and psychologically fractured histories, along with the ideological codes—'crazy' and 'woman'—that inhere within them.

In summary, both these characters operate much closer to Pilot's model, always communicating an overabundance of information whenever they speak.[15] But Chiana's extraverbal context is gestural, communicated through her body—and through her subjectivity as a sexualized female character—whereas Stark's is phonetic, communicated through excessive language that often seems to lose all meaning and become virtually aphasic: a 'word salad.' But Stark always means *something* through his excessive speech, and that liminal meaning tends to be more crucial than the literal one that conceals it. In the same way, Chiana always communicates something vital through her gestural representation, although that information often gets read simply as erotics, rather than as a unique fusion of body language and phonation.

When Chiana first appears on board Moya, as a prisoner of the Nebari, she begs Crichton for 'amnesty.' Her captor, Sallis, then activates a sort of mental-torture device that subdues Chiana, sending her into convulsions and effectively cutting off her speech. When Crichton protests that 'she was *just talking* to me,' Sallis asks him coldly: 'are you now the arbiter of our justice system as well?' ('Durka Returns,' 1.15). Clearly, Chiana is not 'just talking' in Sallis' view, because her speech patterns, her propensity for saying what she likes, are the reason why she has been imprisoned in the first place. There can be no 'just talking' for Chiana, just as women's speech has historically been a threat to various patriarchal ideologies, which has necessitated its strict surveillance and containment—often through instruments similar to the Nebari torture device, such as the gags and other silencing devices common in the Victorian era. Chiana expresses, through speech, not only her dissatisfaction with Nebari political policies, but her own desires as a physical being, which are actually a great deal more threatening to the physically repressed Nebari.

More than any other character, Chiana comes to be signified by what other people call her, by the hate speech that defines and limits her own sexuality: *tralk*. Even Aeryn, who is normally nonjudgmental of sexual practices (it's the emotional practices that scare her), calls Chiana a *tralk* when she is angry with her. In this sense, *tralk* becomes a double-voiced instance of hate speech. It comes to represent not merely 'slut,' but also 'idiot,' 'child,' and other addresses that are most common to Chiana. The linkage here of feminine sexuality with imbecility and childishness remains a severely problematic factor within the show, although I do think that *Farscape* works to 'un-address' its own epithets by eventually rendering Chiana as one of its most mature and perceptive characters—a character who risks frequent bodily harm, as well as permanent blindness,[16] on multiple occasions in order to save her friends.

Although Chiana always says what she *wants* to, this is not the same as always meaning what she says, or, for that matter, saying what she means. Like Rygel, she is at first relegated to a selfish outsider position, a childish margin, only to be given a great deal more character development as the show progresses (and perhaps it is fitting, then that Chiana, like all Nebari, is *gray* in color). In the episode 'Nerve' (1.19), for instance, Chiana proposes to Crichton that they both infiltrate a Peacekeeper command carrier together, in order to find a 'tissue graft' that will help save Aeryn's life. Everything that Chiana says in this scene is mediated, and extended, by a wealth of extraverbal context, including her gestural communication, her spatial relations to Crichton, and the curious outfit that she is wearing. She enters Moya's maintenance bay in a flowing gray coat and shawl,[17] very Hepburn, and, upon seeing Crichton, says 'gotta love a man in uniform.' Crichton's reply, 'gotta love a girl in gray,' is fitting—for Chiana *is* a 'girl in gray,' in that her femininity is constantly a background force, constantly influencing all of her speech, and yet it becomes so visible to the other characters that it is eventually rendered *invisible*, peripheral, gray.

Chiana speaks in a light, airy register, and seems to dance as she moves, passing between Crichton and his ship in a manner that is, while playful, also disruptive. Crichton sees her, here, as a child in his way; but Chiana's aim is anything but childish. She is absolutely intent on following Crichton to the command carrier, although her breeziness might suggest the opposite. The casual pleasure with which she says 'gotta love a man in uniform' suggests that she enjoys how Crichton looks in his Peacekeeper outfit, but has absolutely no sense of reverence or trepidation about what that uniform is supposed to signify. Just as Crichton pays no heed to her traveling outfit—nor to her grayness—Chiana is not concerned by the authority that his uniform represents. Both appear, in this instance, to be ignoring what is most visually obvious about each other. The difference between them is that Crichton really *doesn't* care what Chiana is saying, really isn't paying her any attention at all, whereas Chiana—as she always does—is carefully cataloging his every movement and gesture, his every word. She has him fixed in her gaze, and he doesn't even know it.

When Crichton asks her if she is 'volunteering,' Chiana makes no verbal reply, but merely stares at him. Although it may seem here as if *Farscape* is about to commit a traditional SF misogynistic gesture—that is, setting up a female character to appear sexually powerful and flirtatious, only to have her be physically overpowered by a male character in the next instant—we should pay close attention to Chiana's gaze. She raises her eyebrows, and just barely smiles; Crichton, who is significantly taller than her, rises to his feet, but her head mimics his motion, following him exactly. 'What's the angle?' he asks, leaning in closer.

Chiana executes a kind of paradoxical movement here. She leans away slightly, but doesn't *retreat*—instead, she angles her face upward, so that there is a small but intimate distance between her and Crichton. He replicates her movement, and then she his, until they appear to be sliding against an invisible field, their faces drifting as if through some frictionless environment. Who is in control here? Every time Crichton attempts to make a physically overpowering gesture, Chiana not only matches it, but *re-translates* it into a subtle erotic movement—and physical eroticism remains her sphere, not Crichton's. She is fluent in intimate body language, whereas Crichton tends more often to be on the receiving end of sexual contact, clumsy and generally unprepared. Just as Crichton, by leaning in, attempts to subsume Chiana's sexual agency with an overpowering physical one, so does Chiana reverse that maneuver, continually reinscribing power as erotics, erotics as power, until the two blur and become unrecognizable from each other.

When she offers him a 'Peacekeeper ident-chip, maximum security clearance,' her smile is not ironic, but visibly and obviously pleased. As Chiana dangles the chip in front of him, she is also saying *I got this for you; I did something that you couldn't*. The authoritative power of the chip—the power that Crichton needs in order to get past the Peacekeepers' security checkpoint—is conflated now with Chiana's femininity, her resourcefulness, her perceptiveness and willingness to act. Thus, the technological sign here, which is almost always a masculine sign within SF, mingles and becomes inseparable from a sexualized female body.

Crichton takes the chip, but appears troubled. Not only has he lost some of his (illusory) power—although nobody else is around to see it—he also appears to have misjudged Chiana. In an effort to reassert some sense of 'normalcy,' Crichton grabs Chiana, although not in an overtly threatening way,[18] and says 'then help ... if you're gonna help.' His implication is as strong as Chiana's was a moment ago: *are you coming to help, or coming to play?* But Chiana just looks at him, and, ultimately, he is the one forced to break eye contact. Her look—not angry, not petulant, but more *irritated*, as if to say *can we just get past this prejudice of yours, since there are more important things to do?*—is enough to convince John of her intentions.

In 'Bad Timing' (4.22), when Crichton has 'writer's block' and can't figure out a particularly thorny wormhole equation, Chiana suggests, simply: 'sex'. 'That works for *you*,' D'Argo clarifies; but her rebuttal—'it works for *everyone*'—is a pretty compelling one. Most of the time, Chiana can't fathom why everyone around her isn't having sex all of the time, since this would be the scenario that generated a maximum pleasure principle. When she first says 'sex,' and Crichton playfully asks 'with you, or with him?' (meaning D'Argo), Chiana merely shrugs: 'either.' Bisexuality holds no quandary for her, nor does the thought of Crichton having sex with D'Argo, whom she happens to be in love with. In this sense, she is a lot like Aeryn, who is willing to 'recreate' with Crichton, but doesn't want to establish an emotional relationship with him. Unlike Aeryn, however, she is capable of expressing both sexual desire and physical intimacy, without trying to control or narrowly contextualize either. She talks about sex in the same way that Aeryn talks about pulse rifles, or John talks about human pop-culture: not because she is obsessed with sex, but because it seems eminently normal and rational to her, which is precisely the ideology that made her a threat to the Nebari in the first place.

Chiana's speech-acts often appear as ruptures, but only because their content—infused with her own hyper-feminine presence—is generally at odds with the transparent ideological codes that govern speech within a patriarchal register. When Chiana talks about sex, it 'sounds' odd, because women are not supposed to talk about sex in general. When she is physically intimate or sexually playful, it translates as being 'forceful,' because women are not supposed to exhibit control of their own biological desires. It is a lot easier, then, to call Chiana a *tralk*[19] than to admit that she is actually a powerfully disruptive force to the masculine constraints that make narrative possible, that make *discourse* possible.

In this sense, she aids what Irigaray calls the 'sexualization of discourse' (Irigaray: 1985: 73); that is, she shifts the material of discourse from 'neuter'—the masculine disguising itself as the norm—to 'feminine.' In so doing, she is able to communicate in Irigaray's notion of the 'feminine syntax,' which involves 'nearness, proximity, but in such an extreme form that it would preclude any distinction of identities, any establishment of ownership' (1985: 134). In fact, Irigaray states that feminine syntax, although understandably difficult to pin down through masculine language, 'could best be deciphered . . . in the gestural codes of women's bodies' (1985: 134). It remains Irigaray's project to create a rupture within masculine discourse rather than establishing a place for women's speech *inside* of it—to '[jam] the theoretical machinery itself' (1985: 78). The strategy for this is primarily self-conscious mimicry, which re-emphasizes the feminine by articulating it through women's speech, on women's terms. Not to be subjected *to* a version of femininity by masculine discourse, but 'to assume the feminine role deliberately' (Irigaray 1985: 76).

Helene Cixous also supports the agency of feminine gestural communication, insisting that, when a woman (and she is self-conscious about collapsing 'woman' into an intelligible term, whereas Irigaray seems less so) speaks, 'it's with her body that she vitally supports the 'logic' of her speech . . . she signifies it with her body' (Cixous 1997: 1457–8). This is not to suggest that men communicate through some laser of intellection, whereas women must communicate materially, through their bodies, through Kristeva's 'primordial act of signification' (1989: 304). Cixous is instead suggesting that women's speech is a powerful unity of phonetic and gestural context, whereas men's speech denies this physical interdependence because it needs to shore up the individualizing power of masculine linear communication. This emphasis on linearity, on the necessity of one concept to follow the other—without being unduly contaminated by extraverbal context—remains a criticism of Saussure's work. It is in direct opposition to Bakhtin's notion of heteroglossia, which 'insists on difference and simultaneity, rather than symmetry' (Holquist 2002: 47).

Cixous calls women's speech, and women's writing, the 'anti-logos weapon' (1997: 1457). Like Irigaray, she sees a feminine rebellion against masculine linguistic constraint—against masculine 'normative' discourse—as arising from radical disruptions of that discourse rather than accommodations to it. She urges women, with every speech-act, to 'blow up the Law,' and to affect this explosion 'right now, in language' (Cixous 1997: 1461). Chiana seems to represent the most explosive potential within the show, although her linguistic 'detonations' can sometimes be reinscribed as patriarchal, reconfigured through various filmic techniques and representational codes—specifically her identity as *tralk* and her physical inferiority to D'Argo, Aeryn, and Crichton. But the same holds true for these acts of physical superiority, which, by virtue of Chiana's transgressive potential, can be seen self-critically as the attempts of a masculine discourse to reassert itself, rather than as simply the norm.

If I seem to be talking a lot about Chiana, it is because I see her as an often-misrecognized character, a subject reduced to certain codes—like *tralk*—that the show is actually employing self-critically, not transparently. I have talked more specifically about her sexuality in Chapter 4. For now, let us turn to Stark, who is in some ways her opposite. In Chiana's case, much of what she says makes perfect 'sense,' but nobody is willing to listen. In Stark's case, very little of what he says is intelligible at all, yet the crew is generally *forced* to listen—since they can't get away from him. Stark also, I think, has a unique relationship with Crichton; discussion of that is included in Chapter 3, which focuses on Crichton's masculinity.

Stark is a Banik, a 'slave race' ('The Nerve,' 1.19) who are utilized in an unknown capacity by the Peacekeepers, probably for labor. That the Banik resemble the Sebaceans, just as humans do, is a point of curiosity never actually taken up by the show (one could wonder why Crais, upon first meeting Crichton, doesn't simply mistake him for a Banik with his mask off). The Banik must all wear masks (very Andrew Lloyd Webber) in order to signify their servitude, but some of them, like Stark, also have unique psycho-mystical powers. These few are called the Stykera, and they are able to guide dying souls beyond the physical realm.

When Stark first removes his mask in 'The Hidden Memory' (1.20), he reveals a mass of energy where the other half of his face should be. Later, in 'The Ugly Truth' (2.17), Stark admits that 'my physical form is only part of my reality.' It's difficult to tell whether *all* Baniks can manipulate energy and exceed their own corporeality this way, or if only Stykera can do this. I get the impression that Stark's mystical powers began more as an interesting narrative trope than as a serious piece of character development, and that the show avoided over-explaining them for fear of wandering into some

14, 15. Crichton as *wounded Christ, comforted by Stark*

strange paradoxes. Still, this gesture towards the spiritual is one of the things that separates *Farscape* from most SF narratives. Its characters, like Zhaan and Stark, have ties to the mystical realm, and their powers are never sufficiently explained within an analytical or technological framework. Everyone simply accepts that they can accomplish feats beyond the power of technology.

Stark appears, at first, to be crazy (hence his name). When Crichton is forced to share a prison cell with him on Scorpius' Gammak base, Stark begins yelling at him immediately: 'My side, your side! My side, your side! You were just in my chair, too, weren't you?' ('The Nerve,' 1.19). Crichton assumes that the Aurora Chair—a physiological torture device, designed by Scorpius, which reads people's minds by brutally extracting their memories—has driven Stark mad, but Stark is, in fact, perfectly sane. Well . . . not perfectly. Stark is always a little bit insane, which is one of the things that makes his character so interesting. He exhibits the general sense of insanity, of disjuncture, that everyone on board Moya should be feeling all of the time—Stark is simply the only one who expresses it openly. His initial obsession with 'my side' and 'your side' is also a coded gesture towards the violability of his own body—which is partly made of energy—as well as Crichton's (always vulnerable) body, which will very soon be penetrated by Scorpius' Aurora Chair.

'The Ugly Truth' (2.17) is probably the last episode in which Stark is still able to communicate more or less lucidly and analytically. Told from multiple points of view, it represents an interesting cinematic intervention, an attempt to narrativize the properties of a dialogic 'event' as it is perceived by a number of speaking witnesses. What results is 'false testimony,' a web of differing stories and oppositional perceptions, as well as a series of multiple and overlapping realities. This seems to anticipate the multiple realities that John will encounter in Season 4, when he journeys through a wormhole and experiences a number of 'unrealized realities.' But for now, these realities occur within dialogue, spreading outward and threatening to warp space/time as they each try to assert themselves as the truth. The effect is one that can only be told through multiple camera angles, speech-acts, stories, and realities—that is, a manifestation of Bakhtin's heteroglossia.

Like wormholes, heteroglossia is a bit difficult to pin down theoretically, let alone to express in the kind of linear communication that actually militates against its existence. Bakhtin defines it as not necessarily a state or experience, but more like a 'situation'—that is, 'the situation of a subject surrounded by the myriad responses he or she might make at any particular point, but any one of which must be framed in a specific discourse selected from the teeming thousands available' (1983: 69). To live within heteroglossic tension is to live within a constantly relational context, or a relation of infinite contexts, a state of flux. Unitary language (Saussure's linearity) is 'opposed to the realities of heteroglossia' (Bakhtin 1981: 270), but those *realities* (unrealized?) remain. Between every word and its object, every sign and its referent, 'there exists an elastic environment of other, alien words about the same object' (Bakhtin 1981: 276).

Alien words. I am, of course, appropriating this, since Bakhtin surely wasn't referring to extraterrestrial languages. But the comparison is a provocative one. Behind every 'normative' word, every context that we attempt to control, there is another word, an *alien* word, with just as much meaning; a word that deserves to exist just as much, that *does* exist, not in spite of our imposed context but within it, alongside of it, in simultaneity. Behind all of Crichton's 'English' (North American) words, there are alien words waiting to be said, words that mean something similar but different, words that he must accept if he is to communicate at all. These alien words seem, at first, to be a threat to his human subjectivity, but they are merely traces of the heteroglossic nature of his own language, emanations of his own unrealized realities, his own suppressed contexts and restrained identities. Speaking them ruptures the linear chain of signification (which Bakhtin tells us never existed to begin with), and allows Crichton, like Pilot, to inhabit multiple linguistic streams, to understand that 'no living word relates to an object in a singular way' (Bakhtin 1981: 276), that, as the quote beginning this chapter suggests, every lost or unrealized context has its own 'homecoming,' just as 'time heals all wounds'/'time wounds all heals.'

As the multiple narrative threads of 'The Ugly Truth' unfold, spectators are able to view a single dialogic reality, a reality made possible by multiple speech-acts, proceeding *as it always does*, over different tracts of space/time, over different visual and auditory terrains, seen and heard differently by each speaking-viewer. The first perspective is an outside one—Chiana and Rygel watch, from onboard Moya, as Talyn appears to destroy another vessel, a Ploka-vian ship. They have the least amount of information about what has happened, since they were entirely removed from the event. Throughout the remainder of the episode, the Plokavians interro-gate the crew (using an elevated chair-device that suspiciously resembles a gynecological exam chair, and which places the male characters in a rather interesting position of physical vulnerability).

Everyone's version of the story is told characteristically, infused by the traits that make each speaker legible to the others. Aeryn's version is highly logical; Zhaan's is inflected with compassionate moments that nobody else seems to have remembered; Stark's is dis-jointed and patchy; D'Argo's is aggressive, with everyone seeming to miraculously agree with his judgment; and Crichton's, suppos-edly the 'objective' testimony, is the least illuminating at all—though it is funny when, within his own retelling, all of the charac-ters duplicate Crichton's own mistakes, calling the aliens 'Plokavites' instead of Plokavians. Crichton even calls them 'Plokavites' to their faces, which suggests that he has unswerving confidence in his own perception of the events, even going so far as to edit out what he sees as incorrect pronunciation. We do, after all, most often reconstruct ourselves positively within stories, especially if we're the ones doing the telling.

At the end of this episode, Stark is accused of destroying the Plokavian vessel himself, and must suffer molecular 'dispersal' as (remarkably non-fatal) punishment. He does, eventually, return (by reassembling his body), but his behavior grows increasingly erratic throughout the end of the second season, and the beginning of the third. It seems as though, in being physically dispersed, Stark was psychologically dispersed at well. He can re-corporealize his body, but he can't just as easily mend his fractured psyche, which was always a bit fragile to begin with. His straddling of sanity/madness degrades completely when Zhaan dies, and he is left with all of her responsibilities—safeguarding Moya, tending to the medical and emotional needs of the crew, and offering spiritual guidance. While Zhaan had a gentle touch in most of these regards, Stark is erratic and unstable, getting the crew into danger more often than he saves them from it.

His frequent descents into linguistic 'nonsense'—mumblings like 'decompression, decompression!' ('Wait for the Wheel,' 3.04), or 'no hands, no hands!' ('Plan B,' 2.21)—do have their own 'sense,' their own rhythm, which is almost prelinguistic. They are similar to the ruptures of poetic language, whose use of rhythms and tones is, for Kristeva, an irruption of the 'semiotic' into the 'symbolic.' Kristeva describes poetic language as that which 'compels language to come nearest to the human enigma' (1980: 206). It carries with it the force of unconscious drives, of what Kristeva calls the 'semiotic chora'— that is, the relation of bodily drives that makes signification possible in the first place, but which is 'anarchic' because it represents the infant's presymbolic, *in utero* connection with the mother. I am not going to attempt a psychoanalytical reading of Stark here (with Zhaan as his potential mother), but I do think that his disruptive and disjointed language often mirrors these same drives, the unspoken desires of the other crew members, as well as the double-voiced quality of every speech-act within the show.

In *The Peacekeeper Wars*, when Stark is called upon to marry Aeryn and Crichton—this being their third attempt at marriage so far—he responds quickly, but is totally ineffectual. Standing in a pool of water with Crichton and a very-pregnant Aeryn, he begins to incant: '*Ra'tuga La'kuga La'keena—*' when D'Argo interrupts him, insisting 'that's a Sheyang prayer for the dead!' (*PKW*, Pt. 2). Aeryn then punches him, although the gesture seems less angry, more exasperated. She is, after all, under a lot of pressure. Now a bit baffled, Stark begins again with '*Sin'klilo Rashnishi Kashninah,*' but this isn't right, either. 'That's a Delvian puberty rite!' Chiana yells. And, once again, Aeryn hits him. This time she appears a bit more on the angry side. The implications of this scene—'improper' language acts being punished by physical violence, as well as a marriage ceremony that keeps failing until the context is perfectly right (or perfectly wrong, given that there's a war going on in the background)—are numerous, and probably deserve a lot more attention, but I just want to focus on Stark for the moment. He seems to be nothing *but* competing contexts now, entirely unmoored, all vying for linguistic control. He can speak, but that speech is now beyond his control, sliding off into different historic and cultural realms, pulling with it fragments of knowledge that probably even Stark doesn't know he possesses.

It seems possible that Stark's misfiring language, as well as his psychological violability, could stem from his very positioning as a Banik slave.[20] He has not simply experienced a few years of personal incarceration at the hands of Scorpius—he also experiences *daily* the reality of his ideological imprisonment, his subjection to the terms that the Peacekeepers have given him, the terms of being a Banik slave. Peacekeeper command, here, is Althusser's 'ideological state apparatus,' which manipulates Stark's own personhood, his sense of who he is and what he might become, in order to render him as a concrete laboring subject. And all of this is in order to '[reproduce] the relations of production . . . [the] capitalist relations of exploitation' (Althusser 1971: 146). Stark's servitude thus becomes what Althusser calls an 'obviousness,' similar to that which 'make[s] a word 'name a thing' or 'have meaning'. . .the 'obviousness' that you and I are subjects—and that that does not cause any problems—is an ideological effect' (1971: 161). The Peacekeepers' certainty that words must do as they ask them to, must signify contingently, is identical to their certainty that Stark—along with the other races they've subjugated—will remain indentured and beneath their control.

But if ideology constructs Stark as a subject, above-and-beyond his 'prior' self-construction, then Stark is in so many ways being spoken and narrated by the Peacekeepers, having, to paraphrase Trinh T. Minh-ha, 'the blanks filled in for him on his behalf,' being *said* (1989: 80). His growing insanity only exacerbates this situation, transforming him into a character that needs to be translated, spoken for, because he allegedly cannot speak for himself. 'Who can I become,' asks Butler, 'in such a world where the meanings and limits of the subject are set out in advance for me? By what norms am I constrained as I begin to ask what I may become?' (Butler 2001: 621). But Stark proves, strangely enough, in support of Austin's work, that he can speak for himself—when the context is right; when he is in control, and most importantly, when he *wants* to speak. At the end of *The Peacekeeper Wars*, when Crichton is still in a comatose state, Stark does speak to him.

'Whenever we cross paths,' he says, 'I leave the encounter transformed . . . thanks to you, I have found my own internal peace' (*PKW*, Pt. 2). Stark then removes his mask, to reveal, not the familiar mass of energy, but flesh: a mass of scar tissue, sutured by some unknown force, and not cleanly—since this is *Farscape*—but violently, painfully, bearing witness to the force of its own inscription. Stark is, indeed, transformed. Unlike Zhaan, who becomes pure energy when she dies, Stark is rendered *more* material, more flesh. Crichton has left his imprint on Stark's body, an imprint of kindness and love, just as Stark once cradled John in his lap, telling him to rest, to sleep. Now, as Stark gently places his mask—which he no longer needs—beneath John's hand, we understand that he has gotten loose from ideology, from interpellation; he has unmoored himself, un-fixed the epithet of 'slave' and renamed himself. Althusser, of course, suggests that we can never get outside of ideology, that we can never outrun it, because it runs with us, speaks through us (and speaks *us*). But this is, after all, the Uncharted Territories. Anything seems possible.

There are many other examples of language-power and language-play within *Farscape*, too numerous to mention.[21] This chapter has treated only a few of them, and I have attempted to discuss many others, peripherally, throughout the rest of the book. Stark, Chiana, Aeryn, and Pilot, for me, remain the characters who are most keenly subjected to language, and who in turn reconfigure language most inventively, most surprisingly. Crichton also has many crucial dealings with language, and is both controlled and liberated by it, but those dealings have uniquely 'human' complications that are addressed in the earlier chapters. Ending this discussion with Stark's transformation (which is both linguistic and physical), let us now turn once again to Moya, 'this living ship,' and her complex relationship to the living nation.

7 One Nation Under Moya
Alienation and Imperialism in *Farscape*

> The globe is on our computers. No one lives there; and we think that we can aim to control globality. The planet is in the species of alterity, belonging to another system; and yet we inhabit it, on loan . . . we must think of our individual home as written on the planet *as planet*, what we learn in school, astronomy.
>
> —Gayatri Spivak (2000: 14; 18)

> The only thing worth globalizing is dissent.
>
> —Arundhati Roy (2001: 33)

> I don't care about the things that you care about. Peacekeepers rule the Scarrans. Scarrans rule the Peacekeepers. Both of them can put your ass in a cage.
>
> —John Crichton ('Prayer,' 4.18)

Farscape begins with the phrase: 'My name is John Crichton . . . an astronaut.' As Ben Browder narrates, we see an image of his space module with 'IASA' emblazoned on the wing, and the words 'United States of America' flash across the screen. Thus, from the first moment of the show, John is given a very specific position as an American astronaut; not just an intrepid explorer lost in space, but a lost American in the Uncharted Territories, searching for the nearest border crossing (which happens to be a wormhole). John's repertoire of pop-culture imagery is well-stocked with traditional Americana—Ford pickup trucks, Good Humor bars, the WWF, *'Lil Rascals*, *Abbott and Costello*, Jimmy Stewart, and a pulse rifle named Winona. He is never unmoored from the ideological frameworks that compose the United States, no matter how far he penetrates into Scarran territory or Tormented Space. He even describes his rear end as 'Grade-A Prime American beef' ('Crichton Kicks,' 4.01).

However, we can't be certain what it means to be an American in the Uncharted Territories, thousands of light years away from Earth. Can the American sign endure over such a vast distance? Does John's nationality come apart as he steps onto Moya's bridge for the first time, or does it hover around him like some kind of aura, naturally inflecting all of his interactions with different aliens across the galaxy? This chapter will focus on national ideology and imperialism as it exists within *Farscape*, and I will be trying to determine whether Hyneirians, Luxans, and Nebari have a 'nationality'—or if Crichton remains the sole representative of the nation-sign among them. Does Chiana belong to a nation? Do the Sebaceans have national histories, national cultures, or do they simply embody imperialism as it is written across the surface of the cosmos? How do John's political ideologies help him in his transition to the Uncharted Territories, and how do they prevent him from necessary transformation?

SF programs often pirate existing cultures in order to recode them through benevolent or hostile aliens. The dispassionate and coldly logical Romulans first became a threat in the original *Star Trek* at the height of the Cold War. Both the evil Empire of *Star Wars* and the Peacekeeper military machine of *Farscape* bear more than a passing resemblance to German Nazism. In the characters of Grayza and Scorpius we have what first appear to be a mad scientist and a megalomaniacal dictator, both bent on enslaving the intrepid American (Crichton) and extracting the wormhole knowledge from his mind. But as the show progresses, both Grayza and Scorpius grow more layered in their personal ambitions, more complex in their passions and hostilities.[1] In the end, neither become reducible to the political tropes which they seemed to embody, and both of them appear to violate their own 'rules' on more than one occasion.

The ultimate imperial force in *Farscape* seems to be the Scarrans— they even call themselves the 'Scarran Imperium,' and exhibit a colonial intensity that drives them to conquer and enslave races across the galaxy. But a strange reversal occurs near the end of Season 4, when we discover that the Scarran economy—indeed, their very evolution—depends upon something incredibly fragile. A flower. We learn from Scorpius that the Scarrans were 'brutish creatures' who evolved mental cognizance as a result of ingesting a particular flower. Without it, their evolution would reverse itself (why, I'm not quite sure), and they would devolve back into lizards walking on all fours. Thus the Scarran imperial drive has, at its very core, a powerful sense of insecurity and doubt, a hidden frailty.

Is alien imperialism the same as human imperialism? What happens when we rewrite human imperialism within an alien register? If the Peacekeepers are supposed to be Nazis—with their regimented culture, police state, and obsessions with racial purity—then what does that make the rest of the Sebaceans? And what would the point be in re-invoking this historical specter of Nazism within a contemporary SF program? The easy answer is that, by replaying the histories of warfare and dictatorship over and over again within popular media, America is able to continually restage its wartime victories, to repeat its military successes again and again, thereby strengthening the public valuation of whichever government happens to be in power. By summoning up epic narratives, we recast the current era *within* the epic, empowering the current administration as if they were the reincarnation of Achilles, Alexander the Great, General Patton, or even 'Stormin' Norman Schwarzkopf. In the same way that capitalism exploits the laborer, popular media exploit cultural histories in order to squeeze extra value from them—value that will, it is to be hoped, reinforce the political crises of the moment.

This is the easy answer, but not the only answer. Politics are an integral part of all popular media, but they infuse SF even more so, because SF remains a genre that is closely concerned with ethics and cultural development. Moya is always marked by a web of competing ideologies, above and beyond the 'unique' alien cultures that her crew invoke an reproduce in their daily interactions with each other. As Althusser insists, we can't get away from ideology, because there is no 'away.' The exit sign is ideological, the rear entrance is ideological—even the getaway car is tainted. 'The author and the reader of these lines both live "spontaneously" or "naturally" in ideology in the sense in which I have said that "man is an ideological animal by nature"' (Althusser 1971: 160). It's like wandering through a massive Wal-Mart superstore, and every time you think you're about to find an exit, you only end up in a new section. Leisure. Housewares. Entertainment. Everything is a happy euphemism for credit-baiting and capitalist exchange. You aren't spending money—you're 'purchasing entertainment.' You're purchasing leisure, a lifestyle, a life, whose limits are the force field of ideology.

Since Crichton is desperately trying to return home (at least for the first half of the show's duration), the audience expects that at least a few episodes will refer to Earth, or even take place on Earth. *Farscape* delivers this, but not in a predictable way. The episodes that deal closely with aliens and their effect on earth—'A Human Reaction' (1.16), 'Kansas' (4.12), 'Terra Firma' (4.13), and 'A Constellation of Doubt' (4.17)—are all unique and peculiar in their treatment of human culture and American national ideology (with 'American' often a metonym for 'human'). This is even further complicated by the fact that *Farscape*, although created by two American writers (Rockne O'Bannon and David Kemper) and a very well-known American producer (Brian Henson), is filmed in Australia. The majority of the actors (and all of the extras) on the show are Australian or British, with conspicuous accents which interestingly become 'alien.' John Crichton may be American, but the aliens of the Uncharted Territories are definitely Australian.

In 'A Human Reaction' (1.16), Moya and her crew 'accidentally' fly through a wormhole and end up orbiting a very unexpected planet—Earth. We discover later that this was all planned by a spacefaring race known as the Ancients, and that 'Earth' is merely a simulation designed to test Crichton's reactions. 'We needed a human reaction,' the Ancient tells John.[2] But what could this mean? What happens to John and company when they return to this imaginary Earth, and why does Crichton's behavior in these events so assuredly fall within the parameters of 'human?' In fact, since the Ancients are ostensibly seeing humans for the first time here, how can they be sure that any of Crichton's reactions are human at all? By some fluke of cultural agency, John becomes the representative of his entire species. But it isn't really a fluke, since John has been representing his species since the first episode, and the various privileges that he inhabits as a hetero white male allow him to be the ideal representative for Earth.

When Rygel, Chiana, and D'Argo first see Earth, they have a reaction of their own. Perhaps we must classify this as an 'alien reaction,' which the show in some way 'needs,' just as the Ancients need a human one. Are we inside ideology, or outside of it? Is there an outside? If not, then we should buckle up.

This alien reaction is not one of awe, or even one of interest. Only John is impressed by Earth. Rygel and Chiana could care less:

John:	Oh my God.
Rygel:	What? It's just a tiny blue planet. What are you getting so worked up about? It's got no particle rings, no red moons—
Chiana:	Totally unimpressive.
John:	That's Earth . . . that's my home.

('A Human Reaction,' 1.16)

Rygel is correct in his assessment—Earth lacks a lot of crucially interesting features, such as particle rings, red moons, a retrograde orbit, methane storms, a space armada protecting it, or the ability to cloak itself. As planets go, it's kind of like the Citroën of uncolonized worlds. Later, in 'A Constellation of Doubt' (4.17), Aeryn points out that Earth isn't on anyone's radar. It lacks the military scope to be considered a threat, and isn't even technologically advanced enough to rate as an ally. This isn't the same as *Star Trek: The Voyage Home*, when Kirk and company travel back in time to visit late twentieth-century Earth. In that film, America is humbled by the Federation's technological might, and realizes that 'we aren't as powerful as we thought.' However, given that they're being visited by a future reflection of *themselves*, the suggestion is that we simply aren't there *yet*. Eventually, we'll grow into this new technology. *Farscape* turns this cultural collision upside down, suggesting that, not only does Earth lack anything close to intimidating technology, but that it might *never* be as advanced as either the Peacekeepers or the Scarrans. This is quite the ego-wound.

The word 'alien' always has multiple contexts within science fiction, although they are rarely explored as being specifically *political* within SF criticism. Usually, alien cultures are explained away as purely ethnographic, allowing 'us' to see how 'our' culture really behaves, like a mirror image. Aliens are supposed to be an anthropological function, a museumification of 'Earth' culture that presents unique slices of political and ethical behavior, as if the world has one culture—the west. Or, aliens are useful representations of human xenophobia, teaching the world that 'we shouldn't be afraid of difference.' But *xenophobia* has experienced a grammatical narrowing in contemporary usage, coming to signify almost exclusively a fear or hatred of 'alien' as foreigners or 'extraterrestrials,' when in the original Greek it meant something closer to a fear of 'strangers.' In fact, *xenia* was often the Greek word used by Plato and Aristotle to refer to hospitality. *Xenia* was a complex process of entrances, niceties, invitations, and deferrals, the very same codes of hospitality and entertainment that would later be put under intense scrutiny in the case of Sodom within the Old Testament.

Intergalactic aliens and illegal aliens share a symbolic resonance with each other, and extraterrestrials are always emblematic, or at least suggestive, of *terrestrial* ideals of immigration, border-crossing, and state control. Just as aliens are always threatening to invade Earth, policymakers insist that disparate cultures are always threatening to invade the United States—the USA/Mexico border is a space station. You can't step out of ideology—it only gets recoded within media genres, becoming fantastic but still recognizable. Galactic xenophobia has to emerge from a human social equivalent, and so, when *Farscape* deals with borders and invasions, it is always necessarily staging a repeat and recapitulation of imperial scripts around invasion and colonization.

Perhaps it is most surprising that, of all the aliens aboard Moya, it is Rygel who first has an emotional response to human interrogation—and Rygel who becomes the primary sacrifice around whom the episode revolves. Scared, confused, in pain and feeling ill, Rygel demands to know what their human interlocutors want. But the question that he asks Crichton is very un-Rygel-like. In fact, it sounds more like something that Chiana would ask:

Rygel:	Why are they treating me like this?
John:	They're freaking out. You're an alien and . . . they're freaking out.
D'Argo:	I vowed I would never be taken prisoner again.

While John originally sees the human/alien encounter as a primarily ethical one, an opportunity for exchange and growth, Rygel sees it as a physical assault, and D'Argo conceptualizes it as a form of imprisonment (they are in a holding cell, after all). Rygel's question is strangely innocent, almost childlike—*why are they treating me like this?* It is a question that anyone who's ever experienced an unpleasant interrogation while crossing a border might also ask. *Why am I being treated like a criminal?*[3]

John's response—'you're an alien, and they're freaking out'—is almost aphoristic in its density. Who are 'they?' The United States. Who are you? An 'alien.' What does this mean? *Alien* means not human, but it also, and just as importantly, means not American. They're 'freaking out' because you're not human, because you don't look human, and because you're not American, because you don't look American. I am not being deliberately anti-American here, nor am I sheltering in some conveniently Canadian neutrality that allows me to feel politically and ethically superior to 'The South' as a mobile complex of imperialism. Canada has its own colonial histories, its own acute racisms and military interventions—the head tax on Chinese immigrants at the turn of the century, the Japanese internment, the *Komagata Maru* incident, the rejection of Jewish refugees during the Second World War, and the widespread land-theft from, and marginalization of, First Nations and Inuit peoples. We are no less a part of the global imperial project than the United States, and to assert that our political quietude as a nation makes us somehow ethically superior is frankly senseless and hypocritical. Discourses around alien invasion necessarily recode and reflect discourses around immigration policy and border security. Saskia Sassen, in *Globalization and its Discontents*, sums up the public political response as a mixture of cynicism and outrage, aimed at the immigration 'waves' that are always threatening to overwhelm vulnerable American and European borders:

> First, the sovereignty of the state and border control, whether land borders, airports or consulates in sending countries, lie at the heart of this regulatory effort. Second, immigration policy is shaped by an understanding of immigration as the consequence of the individual actions of emigrants; the receiving country is taken as a passive agent. (Sassen 1999a: 7).

The receiving country is always on the defensive, always shoring up its borders against the immigration threat, which is characterized as a literal ocean of illegal aliens who are poised to overwhelm, a deluge of foreign culture that will subsume the target nation's 'authentic' culture (a culture that is actually composed of diffracted foreign, hybrid, and *patois* cultures, both within the border and beyond it). As Sassen explains in *Guests and Aliens*, these waves of immigration are actually cyclical in nature, occurring in quite predictable iterations throughout European history. 'The most important migration impact for Central Europe,' she says, 'resulting from the political changes and economic restructuring in the former Soviet Union, has been the development of circular migration streams, including commuting' (Sassen 1999b: 114). These circular migration streams have followed noticeable patterns, mirroring the course of seasonal labor as it oscillated throughout Europe from the beginning of the seventeenth century. This is why western Europe has an allegedly 'foreign' population of well over fifteen million, 'mostly from other European countries' (Sassen 1999b: 113). 'Foreign' becomes a flexible sign that can apply to anyone, on either side of the border—it can even emerge from 'nativeness'—although it is most often mobilized to segregate people of color.[4]

In 'A Human Reaction' (1.16), the aliens become this overwhelming force, this deluge of foreignness and unknown cultural representation, threatening an invasion that is more psychological than physical. The American army is able to apprehend John and company quite easily, showing that these 'invaders' actually pose no significant military threat—they are promptly thrown into a holding cell and subjected to scientific experimentation. It is during the course of these experiments that Rygel becomes the sacrifice necessary to galvanize John's own suspicion of American values. John is ushered into an examination room, where he discovers an object of singular horror: Rygel has been killed and dissected, and his disarticulated body is lying on a stainless steel exam table.

The sterility of western medicine here is revealed to be in sharp contrast with Moya's biomechanoid architecture, the gentle curves and soft surfaces of her medical chamber, the tender ministrations of Zhaan or Jool—visualized as 'real' healers, as opposed to the simulacrum of the western doctor—who genuinely care about their patients and would never harm anyone as obviously defenseless as Rygel. The Hyneirian dies precisely because he is no threat, because he is small, vulnerable, and has no practical means of defending himself, but also because he is the most vocal opponent of IASA's experiments. He doesn't trust the humans from the start. Aeryn's death would be shattering to John; D'Argo's death would strike him to the core, especially since D'Argo's warrior persona dictates that such a death would be entirely dishonorable. But Rygel's death here becomes the most unforgivable, because he has been reconfigured as a child, a defenseless organism:

D'Argo:	You know that those animals killed him!
Aeryn:	And then they cut him open.
John:	They said they were just trying to restart his heart.
D'Argo:	They were studying him like an animal, like an alien.
Aeryn:	You know, Crichton, Peacekeepers wouldn't even kill their prisoners to study them. ('A Human Reaction,' 1.16)

This is the ideal of the native informant taken to its ultimately destructive conclusion. Spivak describes the position of the native informant as 'impossible' because s/he is 'a figure who, in ethnography, can only provide data, to be interpreted by the knowing subject for reading' (1999: 49). Rygel has been interpreted here, vivisected by an intense anthropological scrutiny. Like the native informant, he has been forced to narrate, to speak, to tell everything about his culture—only this time he has narrated with his body, 'told everything' with his blood, lymph, spinal fluid, viscera. His culture, his story, has been ripped out of him, and so the very act of storytelling is revealed here to be intrinsically violent, displacing, traumatic. A story always kills as it creates, and when storytelling is removed from the hands of the living subject and placed within the apparatus of western ethnography, it becomes a fatal narration, mutilating and destroying the body of the native (just as the machine mutilates the body of the laborer, rendering her as merely an appendage).[5]

As opposed to John's 'human reaction,' which the Ancients seem so intent on extracting from him, we are given the alien reactions of D'Argo and Aeryn. Remember that this is still the first season of *Farscape*, and D'Argo and Aeryn still have a largely adversarial relationship—given that Aeryn is a Peacekeeper, and the Peacekeepers enslaved D'Argo and imprisoned him, robbing him of his family. But they unite in this moment, and are able to share a common anxiety about John's own cultural values, his own notions of what it means to be human. Thus the title of the episode is grammatically rich, because it encodes several different reactions at once. We have John's reaction as a 'human,' but we also have the 'alien' reactions of D'Argo and Aeryn, which leads us to question just what a *human reaction* really might look like. How do we know that Aeryn's reaction, or D'Argo's, is not in fact more human than John's? Are we, the audience, human enough to understand any of these reactions? And how would our own reactions take shape if we were in John's place?

D'Argo's wording is crucial here. 'They were studying him like an animal, like an alien.' Animal and alien become interchangeable terms, just as he earlier called humans 'animals,' making their dissection of Rygel an act so heinous that it goes beyond the ethical parameters of any civilization—a brutality that could only go unpunished within the amoral animal kingdom. Humans become animals, animals become aliens, aliens become humans. This is metonymy in action Lacan-style, the unconscious linking of part-

and-parcel concepts that take on a psychic proximity to each other, the same proximity that metonymic words take on within a grammar. Rather than a distal relationship, which would be symbolized by metaphor—alien is nothing like human, but we are condensing the two into a single image—these terms have a more threatening metonymic relationship, a proximal intimacy, with 'alien' and 'human' becoming parts of the same whole, words that interchangeably represent the same concept.

So what is D'Argo really saying? They were studying Rygel like an animal, like an alien. 'They' [the humans/animals] were studying him like an animal [human], like an alien [animal]. They [the aliens] were studying him like a human [alien], like an animal [human.] Everyone takes on a sliding scale of identities here, because animal, alien, and human are no longer discrete signifiers, but rather intermingling surfaces that can't be logically separated from each other. 'The body,' says Katherine Hayles, 'is the original prosthesis that we all learn to manipulate' (1999: 3). If humanity itself is prosthetic, flexible, then the decomposition of the human sign into animal/alien creates a world where 'signifiers collapse like stellar bodies into an explosive materiality that approaches the critical point of nova' (Hayle 1999: 45). What if we're all just animals? What if we're all just aliens? How do we sort out a human reaction when we might, after all, not even *be* human, since humanity—like nativeness—emerges from the impossible position of the native informant, the human informant? We have produced our humanity like a machine, an appendage, and relegated it to a machinic consciousness that we can oil, lubricate, and maintain, but never significantly change. Our product is out of our hands.

'Animals continue to haunt man's imagination, to compel him to seek out their habits, preferences, and cycles, and provide models and formulae by which he comes to represent his own desires, needs, and excitements' (Grosz 1994: 278). As Elizabeth Grosz suggests here, our infatuation with the animal kingdom arises from an (often uncomfortably) shared proximity—we are animals ourselves, with animal desires and animal habits. Marx said that humankind was the most peculiar member of the animal kingdom, able to live an existence of almost complete deprivation and lack, reduced to the meanest implements of survival and pleasure. 'No other animal can repress his needs in as extraordinary a way, and limit his conditions of life to such a minimum' (Marx 1995: 397). This is perhaps ironically echoed by Crichton in the episode 'A Constellation of Doubt' (4.17), when, upon being asked what the worst thing about being in space was, he replies: 'an utter lack of toilet paper.'[16] In 'A Human Reaction' (1.16), after witnessing Rygel's mutilated and disarticulated body, John is no longer able to ride the hyphen between human and animal—the distinction has vanished. The culture whose collective dreams and memories have kept him going up until this point, confined to a realm of perfect nostalgia, has now betrayed him. Or he has betrayed himself. Aeryn says that 'not even Peacekeepers' would so such a thing. The Peacekeepers, the very epitome of German Nazism at the height of its genetic paranoia, are suddenly 'too moral' for this. More human than human.[7]

Near the end of the episode, John and Aeryn escape, taking refuge in an old beach house (the Crichtons' summer home). While pausing a moment to stare out the window, to absorb the scenery, Aeryn says: 'You know, you were right . . . it's actually very beautiful.' She sounds neither sad nor hopeful, but rather slightly surprised, as if she doesn't quite know how to deal with or live through this contradiction, this planet. Crichton was right about it being beautiful, but what has this earned him? What price is now attached to this beauty? As Aeryn gazes at the mountains and skyline, she seems to be looking at something lovely and terrible at the same time—a wormhole, a dragon just barely asleep on its golden hoard, a cut slowly forming in the flesh of the world whose blood wells up but doesn't quite fall, a miracle of physics, pooling into a perfect vermillion line that is beautiful even as it horrifies her.

It reminds me of a scene from Steven Spielberg's film *Jurassic Park* (1993), when Laura Dern, playing the brave and plucky scientist, takes a break from chasing dinosaurs (and alternately running away from them) in order to catch her breath and formulate a plan of escape. Lacking anything else to do, she finds herself absently eating some of the ice-cream that was left out for the theme park's grand opening. 'You know, it's good,' she says, in a kind of sad disbelief, 'it's really very good.' These strange moments of desire and wonder often occur within the margins of the terrifying, acting as hinges that link one experience of pain with another, the traumatic ontology of being human (or alien). The Earth is really very good, really very beautiful, despite the fact that it has murdered one of her friends, that its organisms are even now hunting her down. From the outside, as a hovering globe, the Earth seems beautiful and harmless—

neither an ally nor a threat. From the inside, it is a lot more complicated: 'Planet earth is simultaneously a kind of fetus floating in the amniotic cosmos and a mother to all its own inhabitants, germ of the future . . . [this] particular image of the earth, of Nature, could only exist if a camera on a satellite had taken the picture' (Haraway 1999: 343).

Here, Donna Haraway is talking about the iconic representation of Earth, the photograph taken from space—our shimmering, vulnerable planet—which is a position as impossible as the native informant. The globe is on our computers, and the earth is in space, perceptible as a whole only by the miracle of satellite photography. We are seeing the Earth here as if through some Lacanian mirror-stage, where its apparent mythical wholeness belies what is, on the surface, a complete lack of articulation. From space, we see the planet as unified and adult; from the ground, it is actually childlike and clumsy, lacking motor control, still taking its first uncertain step and trying to hold its head up without the help of some specular and invisible parent. Like an astronaut seeing the Earth from space, the child sees her own reflection. She turns around to look at the Other (the parent), and then looks back at the reflection, 'understanding' for the first time that she and the Other are somehow separate, and that the *imago* in the mirror—like the image of the planet Earth—is somehow also her, a *whole* version of her. By means of this oscillating gaze, the child 'fashions the series of fantasies that runs from an image of a *fragmented body* to what we may call the *orthopedic vision of its totality*—and to the armor, donned at last, of an alienating identity, whose rigid structure will shape all the subject's future mental development' (Lacan 2002: 4).

The Earth seems whole, 'orthopedic,' armored, from space, just as the human subject seems whole and fully articulated from within the subject-relation itself. But when Crichton is alienated from his own notion of humanness, when he is given the chance to see the Earth through alien eyes, his armored subjectivity begins to oxidize rapidly and crumble. Although it is, in Aeryn's words, 'actually very beautiful' to be human is also a violent, traumatic, and negative process whose cultural movements produce exclusion, bigotry, hatred, and murder. Just as Rygel is reduced to a childlike subjectivity when he asks Crichton 'why are they doing this to me?' so is John reduced to a state of childlike confusion and dread as he faces the mirror-image of his species, his culture, which has proved to be rad-ically unstable.

In the end, John learns that it was all a dream — the Ancients engi-neered this 'false Earth' purely in order to gauge his reaction, the coveted 'human reaction' that will allow them to ascertain how Earth might deal with true interstellar contact (not well, obviously). John is well on his way to discovering this quite early, however, when he begins to notice that the people around him are 'repeating.' Everyone seems to be either someone he knows, or someone he met in the past, which leads him to suspect that this version of America is actually an imperfect copy extracted from his mind. But if the Ancients are able to construct such a detailed, accurate, and highly plausible copy, then how do we know that America itself isn't the real copy, the bioloid, the clone?

This is what Baudrillard means when he states that 'Disneyland exists in order to hide that it is the "real" country, all of "real" Amer-ica that *is* Disneyland' (1994: 12). America, Disneyland, the Uncharted Territories, Tormented Space, are all the same simulacra, copies that have no original, 'middles' without beginning or end. To feel that your nation has legible values, that you understand and produce those values, that you are 'valued' by a country, is a posi-tion as impossible as that of the satellite photographer, the ancient ethnographer, the native informant. It presumes a violation of the mirror-stage, a misrecognition of the fragmentary for the whole, a perspective that no single human being could possess unless s/he were as wide and far-reaching as outer space itself.

We don't return to Earth until much later in the run of the series, when it is predictably recast as an object under threat — the victim of Peacekeeper and Scarran imperialism. John returns to his home planet to ensure that it hasn't been altered in any way (as a result of his creative time-hopping), but also in order to make certain that isn't being threatened by alien attack. In the end, he is forced to admit that the planet is indeed too vulnerable, and as a consequence, he must collapse the wormhole that links Earth with the Uncharted Territories — thereby destroying any reasonable chance that he has of ever returning 'home' again. If he even knows where home is any more.

In 'Kansas' (4.12), John returns to his hometown to discover that things have changed for the worse. Through his mutilation of the timeline, he has inadvertently changed crucial events within the history of his own family—his father is now slated to pilot the doomed Challenger space mission. Both this episode and the next one, 'Terra Firma' (4.13), ostensibly deal with John's attempts to clean up this massive temporal mistake, but they are actually more concerned with human/alien relations. As Aeryn, D'Argo, Chiana, Noranti, and Rygel attempt to 'blend in' with humans, we see the impossibility of cultural fusion, as well as the multiple ways in which well-meaning social interaction and anthropological contact can produce disastrous results.

The aliens are able to move about unnoticed at first due to a fortunate coincidence—it happens to be the weekend of Halloween. Crichton doesn't bother explaining this concept, assuring them only that nobody will notice their 'costumes.' Of course, everybody does notice, which is the whole point. Even when the aliens try to dress like humans—Aeryn dons some impressive 1970s duds, left in a goodwill box, which Crichton says make her look a lot like Cher— they only end up looking more like aliens. Halloween becomes a crucial failure, because it does nothing to hide them, and similarly does nothing to include them. It has no cultural function, save for highlighting the artifice and alienation that already exists within the world that is Disneyland.

In the film *In America* (2002), which narrates the lives of an Irish immigrant family who move to Manhattan, Halloween also plays an interesting role. First, the two daughters, Ariel and Cristy, are singled out at their school Halloween party for being the only kids with homemade costumes. Then Cristy grows exasperated as she tries to explain the Americanization of Halloween to her father, who can only associate it with goodwill and social assistance:

Ariel: Everybody else goes trick-or-treating.
Johnny: What's that?
Ariel: It's what they do here for Halloween.
Johnny: What do you mean? Like, help the Halloween party?
Cristy: No. Not help the Halloween party. You don't ask for help in America. You demand it. Trick-or-treat. You threaten.

Halloween becomes an occasion for the renewal of American superiority, the laying claim to certain 'in*alienable*' rights, regardless of race or class, rather than a holiday concerned with myth and magic. Which is strange, because the nation is also concerned with myth and magic—it is arguably a product of myth and magic, smoke and mirrors, standing in for the less obvious work that is enacted through separate state legislation. States play an integral role in supporting transnational organizations, ratifying global policy, and regulating their own micro-borders. As Sheila Croucher observes, states

> join organizations ranging from the WTO [World Trade Organization] and IMF [International Monetary Fund] to the ITU [International Trade Union] and International Organization for Standardization, and states sign onto treaties, protocols, and conventions, all of which set standards and establish procedures for global trade and commerce, and technological, financial, and cultural exchange. (Croucher 2004: 33)

What, precisely, do nations do, if anything at all? This is somewhat like the question: what does Halloween do? In *Farscape*, it comes to represent the absolute failure of *mimesis* or 'passing,' the inability to blend in, because one's foreignness, one's alien qualities, will always be forcibly rooted out and subjected to cultural scrutiny. In order to save his father, John must, however impossibly, 'pass' as a complete stranger walking among them. He stages an accident that will force his father to rescue 'young Crichton,' thereby refusing to go on the Challenger mission because he is too concerned about his son's welfare. Along the way, young Crichton ends up losing his virginity to Chiana, who also passes as 'Karen Shaw.' Much earlier in the series, John declares that he remembered losing his virginity to Karen Shaw in his dad's four-wheel-drive truck. Now, Chiana whispers into the young Crichton's ear: 'Remember nothing . . . except for Karen Shaw in the four-wheel-drive.'[8]

Just before he is about to place 'himself,' his younger version, in peril—thereby necessitating that Papa Crichton will come to the rescue—John can't help staring into his own reflection. He studies this younger, sleeping version of himself (Noranti has knocked the boy unconscious) as a father might study his son. Then he bends down and kisses himself gently on the forehead, whispering: 'Don't frown so much . . . it's bad for you.' Up until this point, Crichton has had to deal with many copies of himself. In the episode 'My Three Crichtons' (2.10), his consciousness is split into two additional bodies, representing both the bottom of the evolutionary ladder (caveman Crichton) and the uppermost pinnacle (evil genius Crichton). Then he had to contend with an exact duplicate. Now, he is staring at the most confusing clone of all—this younger version of himself, who perhaps he doesn't even remember any more. Or remembers just barely.

Later, in 'Terra Firma,' the tables get turned—John's father makes a surprise visit to Moya, revealing that Earth has been in contact with the aliens for some time now, and that they are eager to exchange cultural knowledge. This, of course, does not go well, and its various pitfalls are literally documented within the 'alien documentary' that Crichton watches in 'A Constellation of Doubt' (4.17). As head of IASA (when did this happen?), Jack Crichton is torn between giving all nations (that is, all members in good standing with the UN) access to information about the aliens, or keeping that information local to the United States, who by all accounts 'discovered' the aliens. John is frustrated by his father's moral bind, since he sees the big (intergalactic) picture, and realizes that alien contact can only matter if it is shared globally:

Jack:	The best and safest thing to do is keep it to ourselves.
John:	Space travel was your dream to unite mankind. When did that change?
Jack:	September the eleventh. This isn't the same world you left four years ago son. People don't dream like they used to. It's about survival now.
John:	Whose survival?
Jack:	Olivia's survival. And Susan and Frank and Bobby's. Imagine them blown up by a suicide bomb, or coughing up blood from a poison gas attack. This country is under siege. You just don't understand the global situation.

This dialogue is remarkable for a number of reasons. First of all, it is a surprising intrusion of 'the real' into a science-fiction narrative, which, although it draws upon the real, still relies more heavily upon its own futuristic fantasies. September 11 might be mentioned in passing by an SF show, but it's unusual for it to be foregrounded with such intensity within a story that is allegedly about interstellar travel. Second, what's doubly remarkable is that this anti-terrorist mantra—America under siege—is actually being set up *for criticism* within this 'American' show, created by American writers and being beamed out of Australia. Crichton doesn't necessarily contradict Jack here, but Jack's own uninformed passion is what makes his rhetoric seem like a failure. He's telling John that 'you just don't understand the global situation,' but John has an intergalactic perspective, now far more expansive than Earth's terrestrial politics.

Understanding the 'galactic situation' somehow translates into not understanding the global situation here, with the global now becoming local (Earth) and the galactic becoming global (the Uncharted Territories).[9]

'People don't dream like they used to. It's about survival now.' Crichton's response is pointed: *'Whose* survival?' Indeed, who are these 'people' that Jack keeps referring to, these people who no longer dream? Are these Americans? Do they represent a homogeneous global culture, a collective dreaming nation whose limbs and articulations stretch magically across the globe? Jack is unwilling here to admit responsibility for the west's own poison gas attacks, their own suicide bombs, their own political and economic entanglements with the third world military regimes that they claim to disavow (while covertly profiting from). Just as the American border is constantly under threat, so the Earth now seems to face continual invasion by foreign militants, suicide bombers, poison gas attacks, all emerging from some kind of demonic vacuum—some outer-space wormhole that pukes forth all of the rapacious and devouring evils of the universe and spills them onto the shocked and paralyzed west. None of this conflict emerges from within. It is always an external threat, just as the ego cannot possibly admit that its own incoherence, above and beyond some exterior menace (other people), might be the real danger.

In *Precarious Life,* Judith Butler links the events of September 11 to a massive wound in the American national ego, a tear in the very fabric of ideology itself whose repercussions are felt above and beyond the material destruction of the twin towers falling. It is the life of America the Unconscious, as well as the lives of individual Americans, that was mutilated and struck down as a result of these events:

> An [I] narrative form emerges to compensate for the enormous narcissistic wound opened up by the public display of our physical vulnerability . . . each of us is constituted politically in part by virtue of the social vulnerability of our bodies—as a site of desire and physical vulnerability, as a site of publicity at once assertive and exposed. (Butler 2004: 7; 20)

The 'real' of the events of September 11 is unfathomable, despite the global news-machine's obsessive attempts to fathom it from every conceivable angle. What was lost cannot properly be accounted for within any framework of national or international grieving, just as what is lost every day in Iraq, Iran, Afghanistan, Algeria, Haiti, Zimbabwe, southern India, and other spaces that the west relegates to an imaginary third world—the loss of human lives, the annihilation of cultural traditions, the curtailment of religious freedoms, the murder of gays and lesbians, the credit-baiting and forced prostitution of the poorest rural women—this is a loss that cannot be taken stock of, cannot be calculated, and hence cannot be processed. All four corners of the world, north, south, east, and west, are all in some way responsible for these daily depredations against human liberty and freedom, these incalculable losses and enormous psychic and material wounds that have been torn in the fabric of the Earth itself.

Now it somehow boils down to 'us' and 'them,' the aliens and the humans, the Americans and the terrorists, and the only choice that remains legitimate within the bounds of a parliamentary democracy—embrace the government, reject the terrorist Other—is a manifestly impossible one. In *Welcome to the Desert of the Real*, his commentary on 9/11, Slavoj Žižek states that 'What is problematic in the way the ruling ideology imposes this choice on us is not "fundamentalism" but, rather, *democracy itself*: as if the only alternative to "fundamentalism" is the political system of liberal parliamentary democracy' (2002: 3).

When Jack says that 'the best and safest thing is to keep it [alien technology] to ourselves,' he is assuming a paternalistic role for the entire globe, claiming to know what's best for everyone by virtue of his faith in American democracy—the sanest alternative. But, as Žižek reminds us, 'a country can be "financially sane" even if millions in it are starving' (2002: 36). A particular model of democracy, the American model, can be seen to run just fine, even when—like the capitalist world-system upon which it is based—it appears to function entirely on contradictions, grinding and spinning forward like an unholy machine that nobody quite knows how to repair anymore, because they've lost all the blueprints.[10] The challenge is not to issue strident criticisms of American democracy and its failings from the relative anonymity of public or academic channels (that's easy, I'm doing it right now), but to formulate a sustainable leftist alternative, which would have to involve a massive amount of cultural education, language acquisition, and border-crossing if it was to be at all responsible or successful.

At first, Crichton thinks that this alternative might be possible, and that alien contact will be the propulsion behind it. But, as he watches the many hours of documentary footage in 'A Constellation of Doubt' (4.17), recording actual cultural exchanges between humans and aliens, he realizes that he was wrong. It isn't possible — at least not yet. Not while the current political atmosphere of xeno-phobia persists, and not until the United States, as a first step in healing its own psychic and material injuries suffered as a result of 9/11, acknowledges its place within a global articulation of coun-tries, rather than its inherited position as the supreme articulator of international relations.

In the same episode, while being interviewed by a reporter who seems to amalgamate every negative aspect of both the American and European press, Aeryn tries to explain what the Earth's position is, in terms of intergalactic relations. She is careful and non-critical, almost as if speaking to a small child:

Aeryn:	Well, what you have to understand is, while cultures and civilizations may vary wildly, from socially primitive to hyper-mechanized, there is still a uniformity in the way that people conduct their lives.
Monroe:	You're saying wherever you go in the Universe. . . we're all the same?
Aeryn:	Essentially, yes. In that way, Earth is no different from other planets.
Monroe:	Other species, from different worlds . . . do they have relationships, marriage, children?
Aeryn:	Most definitely. There are limits. The genetic patterns would have to support such a union.
Monroe:	And could a Sebacean, such as yourself, procreate with a human male? ('A Constellation of Doubt,' 4.17)

Aeryn is trying to give Monroe a lesson in intergalactic etiquette, but he's more interested in the same ideals of genetic purity and racial impermeability that the Peacekeepers espouse—he wants to know if humans and Sebaceans could procreate, if Aeryn's foreign DNA might somehow invade and corrupt the Earth, producing hybrid children for which the parameters of 'human' would have to be (dangerously) expanded. Aeryn is clearly taken aback by the question. Not only is it personal, but it seems like the wrong thing to be asking, given the opportunity that they currently share for cul-tural and technological exchange. This is like the public's fetish for celebrity marriages and breakups; Monroe might as well be asking whether or not the Peacekeepers have their very own Brad Pitt and Angelina Jolie. They don't care about the things that Aeryn, or John, cares about.

But the ultimate display of imperial power comes in *The Peacekeeper Wars*, when John constructs a wormhole weapon capable of destroying the Scarrans, the Peacekeepers, and potentially the rest of the galaxy as well. Given the exponential rate at which his wormhole-of-death grows, duplicating its size like a cancerous macrophage, we have to admit the possibility that it could become infinite—that it could devour the rest of the universe, even if it took forever to do it. At first, when John activates the wormhole weapon, nothing seems to happen. Scorpius asks, 'is this a joke?' and John replies, 'Cosmic. Keep watching. Blink and you'll miss it' (*PKW*, Pt. 1). The result is a massive black hole that begins literally tearing through the Scarran and Peacekeeper armada, threatening to engulf everyone and everything in its path.

John's revelation of this weapon, his unveiling of it, is an act drenched in imperial and sexual power. This is Scorpius' madness, Scorpius' wet dream, and so he addresses his old enemy first and foremost. This a moment between the two of them, an intimate dialogue, punctuated by Crichton's disgust and Scorpius' erotic pleasure—he is about to get his intergalactic money shot:

John:	The wormhole weapon. You want to see it?
Scorpius:	Yes.
John:	Beg.
Scorpius:	I beg you.
John:	That's not good enough. Say please.
Scorpius:	Please.
John:	Pretty please.
Scorpius:	Pretty please.
John:	With a cherry on top.
Scorpius:	With a cherry on top. (*PKW*, Pt. 1)

This moment of imperial aggression—the launching of the ultimate weapon, which will somehow destroy Empire itself, is both erotic and destructive. It is palpable in its phallicism, a hard, sharp, razor-edged, climactic emission of colonial power that is fueled by John's rage, Scorpius' desire, and the military greed of both Commandant Grayza and Emperor Sta'leek. John is successful in this final dramatic gesture, but it costs him his life. This is the very last time that Crichton dies for the Uncharted Territories, going out in a bang, like a shooting star, blazing a fearless trail of light against the all-consuming darkness of the ultimate wormhole. 'Wormhole weapons don't make peace,' John says, *'people* make peace.'[11] He thus becomes a part of the equation of peace, but only a part, since his friends, Scorpius, the Scarrans, and the Peacekeepers must all play their role.

We cannot escape from ideology. While writing this chapter, it seems I've done nothing else but watch endless televised and internet news clips about Hurricane Katrina and its decimation of rural black communities in Mississippi. As of today, September 9, 2005, 80% of New Orleans is still under water. Tens of thousands are feared to be dead, and the Bush administration, along with the Federal Emergency Management Agency (FEMA), is under constant attack for their slow and disorganized response and inadequate disaster relief efforts. Today, Michael Brown, the former head of FEMA, was officially fired. In interview with (who else?) Barbara Walters, Colin Powell says that 'it was not racism, but economics,' that hampered relief efforts; that it was the poverty of these rural communities, not the color of their skin, that made it more difficult for them to receive aid—as if aid was simply waiting in the wings, like a magical helicopter capable of transporting all of Mississippi out of danger, and certain citizens were simply unable to reach it. Aren't race and poverty intimately connected? Why is it that, when someone suggests this—like the rapper Kanye West, who dared to claim that 'Bush doesn't care about black people,' or the displaced people themselves, who have cited racial discrimination in numerous interviews—why is it that, when this connection is made, it always gets relegated to the function of extremism? The same area that 'Muslim extremsists' and 'fundamentalists' reside in within the western consciousness?[12]

The quote from Spivak that I opened this chapter with is particularly resonant now. In order to effect global changes, we need to see the globe as a world. In order to acknowledge and honor all of the cultural contradictions that make up the Earth as interconnected matrix of competing nations, bordered communities, we need to see education as 'astronomy,' eco-politics as planetary ecology and ecofeminism, language acquisition as star-mapping, cultural exchange as interstellar navigation. We have our own Uncharted

Territories to explore, and they exist both within our own borders, and in the fragile spaces between those borders, the delicate tendons, marrow, and psychic cordage that binds cities, nations, humans, and genders together—not in a comfortable 'multi-culti' quilt, or even in a Canadian laddered-mosaic, but in a mass of raw silk, unrefined and dangerous and lovely humanity, a flax of knowledges, touches, betrayals, and loves, all joined by permeable membranes. The Earth is Moya, fragile and enduring, impenetrable and open, unfathomably vast and entirely local, completely bizarre and wonderfully familiar. What we need is not a Pilot, but a crew.

In Tony Kushner's *Angels in America* (2003), which is also, in some ways, about being an extraterrestrial—that is, being a gay man in the Reaganite 1980s—there is a remarkable dialogue between the characters of Belize and Roy Cohn. Cohn, of course, is a real person (Joseph McCarthy's right-hand man), and Belize is merely a fictitious creation. But as Kushner's 'gay fantasia' progresses, we begin to doubt our ability to tell these two apart, to determine who is real and who is fictional. By the end of the play, Roy is dying of AIDS— a disease that he swore couldn't conquer him—and Belize is his nurse. One night, while Roy is sick with delirium and wandering around the hospital, Belize tells him a bedtime story. It is the story of the afterlife:

Belize:	It's like San Francisco.
Roy:	A city. Good. I was worried . . . it'd be a garden. I hate that shit.
Belize:	Mmmh. Big city. Overgrown with weeds . . . but flowering weeds. On every corner a wrecking crew . . . piles of trash, but lapidary, like rubies, and obsidian, and diamond colored cowspit streamers in the wind. And voting booths.
Roy:	And a dragon atop a golden hoard.
Belize:	And everyone in Balenciaga gowns with red corsages, and dance palaces, full of music and lights and racial impurity and gender confusion. And all the deities are creole, mulatto, brown as the mouths of rivers. (Kushner 2003: 76)

When Roy asks, 'what about Heaven?', Belize just takes a long, languorous drag of his cigarette, and replies: 'That was Heaven, Roy.'[13]

This is, in many ways, the blueprint for the Uncharted Territories. Dance palaces, racial impurity, gender confusion. And voting booths. Jewels among the waste, ruby among the filth, unendurable beauty within the disgusting, and grace within all of the clawed appendages, dripping bodily fluids, and cacophonous alien languages. These spaces are precious because they are uncharted, because they resist the cartographic stamp, surrendering instead to the sensual rhythms and flows of body language, the semiotic, the *in vitro*. If the Uncharted Territories represent a unified nation, then it is Marx's ur-nation, ruled by Etruscan and Babylonian godkings, the primordial sign of the nation for whose loss we are forever compensating, and whose blood gives birth to our current model of capitalist accumulation. The problem with capital is that it has no limits, save for its own internal contradictions, the limits that it constantly crashes against, in wave after wave, only to continually reabsorb them through the same crisis management that FEMA uses to deal with nature, the same model of global crisis management that results in a terrain of uneven development and differential poverty as vast and uncrossable as the Sahara itself.

In the end, Zhaan is perhaps the only one who understands this aporia, this contradiction that we must live through every day, even if she is never fully able to articulate it to her friends:

Zhaan:	There is no guilt. There is no blame . . . only what is meant to be. Grow through your mistakes.
John:	Wait for the wheel.
Zhaan:	Thank you John Crichton.
	(She kisses him.) ('Wait for the Wheel,' 3.04)

Thank you John Crichton. 'Thanks for your memories,' as Harvey would say. Thank you *Farscape*, for your memories, your many nations, genders, sexualities, and cultures, your recklessness, your bravery, your contention, and your honesty.

The transmission doesn't end here. It's just beginning.

*16. Crichton and baby D'Argo—new life emerges
from the destruction of the wormhole weapon*

Farscape Lexicon

This extensive list of slang, terminology, and alien verbiage has been taken with kind permission from The Farscape Encyclopedia website (http://www.farscape-1.com). Thanks to webmaster and author Adam Garcia, and writers Hollie Buchanan, Amanda Reynolds-Gregg, Josh Weigelt, and Midnight.

altex: noun
Hyneirian bodily organ.
— As in: 'I can prepare another slide of Rygel's blood and check his liver and altex functions again.' — Aeryn

a-lu-e-masata: greeting
Acquarian greeting meaning 'hello' or 'welcome'. Since the Acquarians are lost 'colonists' of the Ancient Hyneirian Empire, it is very possible that this phrase originates from an ancient Hyneirian saying.

ammiox: noun
Tool to alleviate Moya's amnexus problems.

amnexus: noun
Part of Moya's internal systems.

arn: noun
Measurement of time; roughly equivalent to one standard hour on Earth.

aura morph: noun
See definition for *freslin*.

barkan: noun
Hyneirian animal analogous to a bat.
— As in: 'He blasted out of there like a barkan out Hezmana!' — Rygel

bassim oil: noun
A possession of Zhaan's that Chiana snurches.

blez: verb
Meaning to relax or to 'chill out'.
—As in: 'Tell Moya she's just gonna have to blez out!'—Chiana

blotching: adv/intensifier
Extremely, very; similar to *'frelling'*; believed to be solely a Dam-Ba-Da
 term.
—As in: Aeryn: 'How long is this going to take?' Furlow: 'Twice as
 blotching long as if you weren't here.'

bonosphere: noun
Outer layer of atmosphere of Dam-Ba-Da.
—As in: 'I picked up bursts of unusual gravity waves not long ago in the
 upper bonosphere.'

borderwarks: noun
Tears, watermarks.
—As in: 'Toad, what's with the borderwarks?'—Chiana to Rygel, who
 is crying because he has a chemical imbalance after the transfer of
 Aeryn's baby out of his body, akin to post-partum depression

brandar tiles: noun
Brandar tiles are a form of currency, possibly equivalent to a *credit*.

broka seeds: noun
A medicinal seed that helps arrest infection.

cacking: verb
Dying. Slang analogous to 'croaking' or 'kicking the bucket'.
—As in: 'Crichton . . . We ah . . . we don't know what to tell him about
 the guy *cacking*.'—Chiana explaining to D'Argo about the death of
 another.

calcivore: noun
An eater of bone, such as M'Lee.

chakan oil: noun
Derived from the *tannot root*, it is used to power Peacekeeper weapons.

cherklan jerky: noun
A food which Rygel is fed on the planet of Aquara.

chelsik fire hose: noun
Presumably a hose which shoots liquid, or possibly flames, with great
   power.
—As in: 'We couldn't have got you off of each other with a chelsik fire
   hose?'—Rygel

cholian curd salad: noun
Hyneirian delicacy.

clorium: element
One of the six cargos Leviathans are forbidden from carrying, because
   it has a numbing effect on them; an atmospherically induced isotope
   of twinium.

commerce planet: noun
The term used to describe any planet on which trade or bartering
   occurs, and where supplies may be bought.

contala tea: noun
A Luxan drink.

crank: adv/intensifier
Mild Zenetan expletive.
—As in: 'They blasted the crank out of me!'

credit
The most general term for currency in the universe.

crindars
Scarran form of currency.

cronite: noun
Shavings from Moya's cargo-hold floor; highly explosive when mixed
   with *lutra oil*.

cycle: noun

Measurement of time; approx. one standard Earth year (365 days).
—As in: 'I have spent eight degrading cycles aboard this ship and now I am finally liberated.'—D'Argo to John

dag-yo: adjective

'Cool'; Nebari origin.
—As in: 'So, the baby's really dag-yo?'—Chiana

das-trak krjtor: intensifer

Scarran expletive.

delta: directional vector

The first part of a set of coordinates.
—As in: 'delta 6, premno 9, lurg 8'—Zhaan

dench: noun

Unit of measurement equivalent to an inch.
—As in: 'I want a three point grid of every square dench of this asteroid.'

dominar: noun

Title for the 'emperor-king' of the Hyneirian Empire, such as Dominar Rygel XVI. Also, presumably, Rygel's cousin would use the title Dominar Bishan.
—As in: 'You're a Dominar—it has to count for something!'—Stark

drad/dradest: adjective

Best or wildest.
—As in: 'Molnon says it's the dradest. Says it will blow my mind.'—Chiana
Also meaning cool.
—As in: 'Hey princess, the narl is in your stomach? Drad!'—Chiana

draz: expletive

Curse word; Nebari origin.
—As in: 'We can Starburst the draz out if here!'—Chiana

dranick: noun

Rough equivalent to the derogatory term 'bastard', or 'asshole.' Used to describe a person who is being arrogant, stubborn, or cruel.
—As in: 'You are such a dranick.'

drannit: adjective
Sebacean slang for a part of the anatomy, often used as an insult.

dren: noun
Equivalent to 'shit', or an unwanted substance or act.
—As in: 'You smell like dren. You look like dren.'

driblocks: noun
Derogatory term, roughly equivalent to slut.
—As in: 'Get your own fantasy, driblocks, they're having my baby.'—
  Rygel to Jool

dridgenaughts: noun
A derogatory term; possibly of Nebari origin.
—As in: 'We can take those dridgenaughts on.'—Chiana referring to the
  Scarran soldiers marching by, from whom the group is hiding

eema: noun
Backside; Luxan origin.
—As in: 'You are a real pain in the eema!'—D'Argo

fahrbot: adjective
Crazy; insane; potty; mad; nutso; demented; Hyneirian word. See also
  magra-fahrbot.
—As in: 'Stark went completely fahrbot when he heard that the Scarrans
  blew the hezmana out of the Eidilons'—Chiana to D'Argo
Also 'fahzbot', as in: 'What is it exactly about these guys that makes you
  so fahzbot?'—Chiana to Stark

fapootah (or fa-pu-tah): noun or exclamation
Bastard, or asshole. Can also mean 'Like Hell!' A distinctly unfriendly
  term; Hyneirian word.

farko: noun
Analogous to 'hogwash'.
—As in: 'Well, need I say more? If you learned about it in military
  school, it's certain to be farko.'—Jool

fek: noun
Multi-usage Nebari word, not easily translated; probably 'ass' or
  'asshole'.

fekkik: noun

Stupid waif; naive fool; dipshit; Nebari word used by Chianna when she saw Jool being 'milked' for *freslin*.

fellip: noun

Creature on Tarsis. Its nectar is used to make an alcoholic drink resembling beer.

fellip nectar: noun

Alcoholic drink made with the nectar of the *fellip*.

fennik: noun

Another form of currency in the Uncharted Territories.

festival of pregrar: noun

A Luxan festival, celebrated once each cycle.

filigran: noun

A flowering Delvian plant.

food cube: noun

Compact cubes (made from animal, vegetable, and mineral substances) which are sustaining, if not palatable, to many life forms.

frangle: noun

An engine part (possibly nonexistent) mentioned by Furlow.
—As in: 'Maybe an ionised frangle, as well—shouldn't be too tough to fix.'

frax: verb

Screw; bugger; colloquially, disregard; Sheyang term.
—As in: 'Frax your father.'

frell: noun, verb, interjection

The most well-known *Farscape* word, used as a replacement for the coarse Anglo-Saxon monosyllable indicating sexual intercourse, both directly and idiomatically.
—As in: 'Frell you,' or 'I want this miracle of life the frell out of me.'

frellwit: noun

Idiot; foolish or brainless person; shit-for-brains; Sebacean variant.

frelnik: noun

Something foul-smelling; the precise meaning of this word is uncertain but its Sebacean root *frell* leads to some spunky speculation about its meaning.

freslin: noun

An attractant drug; a powerful aphrodisiac known to affect several different races that occurs in at least two varieties. One variety, when ingested, makes others seem more attractive to the user. A second variety causes the user to emit pheromones and to appear differently to others; this effect is called an *aura morph*. Freslin is made using material extracted from the senil gland (found in most sentient species).

frodank: adjective

Wonky; stupid; ridiculous.
—As in: 'your frodank idea.'

froonium drive (or froon): noun

Nonexistent part (or substance) of a Prowler, mentioned by Chiana in an attempt to speak techno-babble intended to sound *Star Trek*-ish.

frotash: adjective or noun

Type of Luxan garden that D'Argo would like to plant.

frotein: noun

A refreshing beverage, probably alcoholic, perhaps a margarita.
—As in: 'Can I get you both some rations, some chilled frotein, perhaps?'—Aeryn

froth-mouth: noun

Someone who is frothing at the mouth; a lunatic.
—As in: 'Some froth-mouth with a metal eye shut off all the lights.'—Chiana

fweakin' insane: adjective

Crichton called Chiana this, which obviously means 'freaking insane.'

gah: interjection
Mild Nebari expletive.

garanta's brax: noun
Rat's ass; something worthless; possibly a Hyneirian term.

garbologist: noun
Staanz's profession; a connoisseur of things other people throw out; collector of things to make a profit.

garda: noun
Clansmen colloquialism for male (with a bit of attitude).

gavrok: noun
An aromatic medicinal herb, prized and used in dried form by Zhaan.

gelt sty: noun
Mess; although the meaning of *gelt* is uncertain, this parallels 'pig sty.'

geometric pregnancy: noun
A result of genetic modifications to the Sebacean physiology of soldiers bred into a battle unit. Pregnancy is accelerated so that Peacekeepers are not out of service long term.
—As in: 'It's a geometric pregnancy . . . We will be having it sooner than you think . . . Essentially we are going to be parents in a matter of solar days.'—Aeryn

glarian scale: noun
A temperature scale similar to Celsius or Fahrenheit.
—As in: 'We've taken him to 105 below the glarian frost point.'—Pilot to Aeryn

gleebo: noun
Fool; tyro; ninny; idiot; silly person; dipshit; Nebari word.
—As in: 'Why do I always get stuck with the gleebos that don't have any plan?'—Chiana

glendian pleasure vessel: noun
A ship on which passengers come and go at will and are treated well.
—As in: 'Has Moya turned into a glendian pleasure vessel now?'—Rygel

grandeer: noun
The title of the leader of the Aquarans.
As in: 'You know, this grandeer stuff is really quite comfortable!'—
Rygel

greebol: noun
Fool; tyro; ninny; idiot; silly person; dipshit; Nebari word; also *gleebo*.

grezz: noun
Engine part (possibly nonexistent).
—As in: 'A blown grezz conductor is my guess.'

grimmit: noun
Chicken; wimp; person lacking bravery; Raxil called Ka D'Argo a grimmit when he didn't want to use a hangi.

gris: noun
Crap; similar to *dren*; Nebari word.
—As in: 'we beat the gris out of him.'

grolack: noun
Some foodstuff.

grolash: noun
Moron; fool; idiot; a mild insult.

grot: noun
Drudge; military 'grunt'; dogsbody; with a touch of idiot/imbecile; pos-
sible Sebacean word.
—As in: 'This is grot's work.'—Aeryn

grotless: adjective
Witless; Nebari term.
—As in: 'I'm scared grotless.'

hammond side (or haman): noun
A direction used on space stations and ships. The 'starboard' or right
side.

hasmot: noun
Equivalent to bitch; probably a Luxan word.
—As in: 'You son of a hasmot.'—D'Argo

heat delirium: noun
A debilitating (but nonlethal) reaction that Sebaceans have to prolonged exposure to heat. It can quickly cause *living death* (a perpetual catatonic state) if left untreated. As the cells overheat, the nervous system shuts down, first the short-term memory is lost, then motor functions, and finally long-term memory.

hentas: noun
A small unit of linear distance; about an inch; Hyneirian word.

hepatian minced stew: noun
A feast item, prepared by Chiana as a favored dish of the crew.

hetch: adjective
Either a unit or a description of speed; perhaps, the equivalent of *Star Trek*'s 'warp speed.'
—As in: 'Leading to our current maximum speed which is barely hetch 2.'—Pilot

hezmana (or hez): noun
Hell, literally and idiomatically; Luxan word.
—As in: 'Where the hezmana in my orders did you find the phrase preemptive attack?' or 'Where the hezmana is that siren coming from?'

hierarch: noun
The title given to the head priest of the peacemaking Eidilons of Arnessk, as in Hierarch Yondalau.

hingemot: noun
Fool; Sebacean word.

horodalay: noun
The ability to encourage rationality and tranquility in others, it is an ability possessed by the Eidilons of Arnessk upon maturity; the capacity to influence others toward peace.

hurlian stone: noun

Ring-like object that Rygel uses for bartering on the first commerce planet to which the crew travels after escaping.
—As in: 'You only expose your ignorance if you don't concede knowledge of the Hurlian Stone.'—Rygel to trader

hygic system: noun

One of Moya's control systems.

Hyneirian cream soap: noun

A substance desired by Rygel after their original escape from Peacekeeper captivity.

hyper-rage: noun

A sometimes uncontrollable fit of super violent rage to which Luxans are susceptible. Hyper-rage is said to have an amnesia-like effect on the one raging.
—As in: 'It's Luxan hyper-rage. It doesn't just go away.'—Aeryn to John

identifile: noun

Identifying data files on many wanted and known criminals, from Peacekeeper information, such as those held by Moya in her data storage bank. Used to identify Staanz.

intellent virus: noun

A sophisticated virus that passes from one host to another or can produce spores to infect many hosts. The viral cells can carry limited memories from previous hosts. This virus can use the host's memory and brain to carry out complex actions.

inton: noun

Unit of linear measurement; this word may have a second definition as a Hyneirian panic attack or asthma.
—As in: 'every inton of conduit.'

iriscentent fluid: noun

A substance Moya uses as fuel, and necessary for her functioning.

janeray syrup: noun

A sweet food of which Rygel is fond, and which he desires after their first escape from Peacekeeper captivity.

jellifan fire paste: noun
A substance that can be used to make a bomb; used with *sevva crystals* and detonators.

jibber: verb
To talk in a nonsensical manner.
—As in: 'Must you jibber while I'm eating?'—Rygel to John

jick-tied: adjective
Tightly restrained; made helpless; Sebacean equivalent of hog-tied.

jikset or jixit root: noun
A medicinal herb commonly used by apothecaries and by Zhaan to treat illnesses.

jilnak: noun
A purgative; a cleansing restorative; a medicine that causes biological evacuation, especially of the bowels.

jinka poles: noun
A method of public display.
—As in: 'If you damage the captain's prize, he'll have your heads on jinka poles.'

juka: exclamation
Used like 'god' or 'heavens' in English, idiomatically indicating wonder.
—As in: 'My Juka'—Br'Nee, on learning that Zhaan is a Delvian

juxt: interjection
Mild Hyneirian expletive, probably 'heck.'

kal tanega chivorko: phrase
Crais' exclamation when examining Talyn. Aeryn's reply to him indicates this means a crowning glory.

Kay'me maia kosa Visha'meel maia kosa ah Khalaan ah Khalaan: religious prayer
A Delvian chant that Zhaan used on the Halosian ship, and heard repeatedly on the New Moon of Delvia.

kalvo: noun
Scarran unit for energy. At high levels, the energy can be harmful. For example, Kalvo 10 can kill a person.

kelvic crystals: noun
Small, green gems that can be used as currency in the Uncharted Territories. Rygel won some while playing *tadek*.

kelvoy levels: measurement
A system used to measuring levels of energy. The Kelvoy levels are used by Sebaceans and are similar to the Scarran *kalvo*.

Khalaan: noun
A Delvian god, goddess or religious figure.
— As in: 'Khalaan help me.' — Zhaan

khamsin/kampshan: adjective
A term describing some sort of mess or chaos.
— As in: 'We're in the middle of a massive khamsin.'

khan: interjection
A profanity Chiana acquired from the Clansmen; loosely translated, it means 'asshole'.
— As in: 'You frelling Khan!' — Chiana to Crichton, after he injected her with a knock-out shot

kijrot root: noun
A medicinal herb; Zhaan used it to try to heal the injuries D'Argo received when he was attacked by Br'Nee, in an effort to stop internal bleeding.

kinkoid: adjective
Crazy, weird or nuts.
— As in: 'Is everyone aboard this ship kinkoid?' — Chiana's reaction to having to lick Zhaan's bed sheet

kishmot root: noun
Used for medicinal purposes by Zhaan.

klances: measurement

The universal unit for temperature. For example, a budong's stomach is an inferno, it burns at 5,000 klances.

klendian flu: noun

A sniffling, sneezing disease similar to the common cold or flu. While not fatal, the illness is characterized by excessive phlegm and respiratory difficulty. When Rygel became infected with this, D'Argo brought him some *ointment of yuvok* to relieve the symptoms.

koldivara blinearian grain: noun

A lush plant which used to grow on Sykar before the harvest of the *tannot root* took over.

kordla: noun

A food prepared by Chiana.

korvinium: noun

Presumably an element or precious metal of some value, it comes in various purities; it is demanded by the Tavleks as a ransom for Rygel.
—As in: 'We want korvinium, purity 9, enough to fill your transport hanger.'

krastic: adjective

Messed up or strange.
—As in: 'Is that krastic ship still frelling with us?'

krawldar: noun

Hyneirian delicacy. One of the foods Chiana prepared for the crew's special supper in 'Family Ties' (1.22).

krell: adjective

Cool; awesome or excellent.

kretmas: noun

Another type of currency used in the Uncharted Territories; but unlike the *fennik* the kretmas are more widely used.

ku-mah: noun

An Acquarian male.

laka bug: noun

A bug found on the planet Arnessk. Its intestine contains a substance which 'if jammed up your nose, causes nothing to bother you for 500 microts.' Sniffing of the laka essence will cause a deadening of the emotions. Used by Crichton from 'Sacrifice' (4.02) until 'Twice Shy' (4.14).

lenarts: measurement

A unit of weight or volume; it is used to measure chromextin, a drug that was used to heal Talyn.

level risers: noun

Peacekeeper term for stairways.

life discs: noun

A pair of surgical implants that create a permanent link between the *life forces* of two beings. Each individual receives one disc which can emit powerful signals. As long as both remain alive, the life discs remain active. The range of the disc's emissions appears limitless and unrestrained by intervening physical obstacles. If one of the bonded entities dies, the life disc possessed by the other will go dark, signifying the other's passing. When the life disc embedded in Chiana's abdomen suddenly ceased functioning, she thought that her brother had died.

life force: noun

Used in connection with the *life disc*. It determines whether or not the person is still living.

life link: noun

The link between two people created by their *life discs*.

light of truth: noun

This test goes back to the root of Litigaran law, mentioned in *The Axiom*. A burning torch is held up to a person testifying. The light gets brighter if the person is not telling the truth.

living death: noun

The final stage of Sebacean *heat delirium*. Victims are left in a state of neural shutdown; a horrible, coma-like state from which death is the only end. Sebaceans lack the gland to regulate heat, so when subjected for too long to very high temperatures, they move from *heat delirium* into the living death.

loomas: noun
Breasts; boobs; female mammary glands.

lost people: noun
When a Clansman doesn't *take the stone* at twenty-two cycles, the *gardas* and *nixars* don't like seeing the resulting slow death by radiation poisoning. Thus, the dying Clansmen go off and make themselves 'lost'.

lurg: directional vector
The last part of a set of coordinates.
—As in: 'Delta 6, premno 9, lurg 8.'—Zhaan

lutra oil: noun
A substance that becomes highly explosive when mixed with *cronite*. It was an ingredient in the bomb that John and D'Argo used to set off the explosion that destroyed Scorpius' Gammak base. It is also used as a cooking fluid. Chiana claimed that the pot blew up while she and Jothee were making soccherins because she used too much lutra oil.

Luxan chase: noun
Luxan courtship ritual; little is known about this ritual, however it is well known amongst other species including Ilanics.

ly-jel: noun
One of the components, along with bet-tur, that are included in a salve that can inhibit the Delvian budding process.

magnetic crypt encoder: noun
A device to crack Peacekeeper door codes. Attempts at the code have to be made one at a time. Stark spent two cycles collecting metals to make his.

magra: adjective
To the extreme; often accompanied by another adjective; for example, *magra-fahrbot*.

magra-fahrbot: adjective
An especially emphasized form of *fahrbot*, probably meant to mean 'insane'.
—As in: 'you're not just fahrbot, you're magra-fahrbot!'

maldik: noun
A musical instrument native to Sykar.

malik: insult
No clear definition.
—As in: 'The little malik will eat anything that isn't maggot covered.'—Rygel, referring to Chiana stealing food

mallot: measurement
A unit of volume that may be close in size to a liter.

malsonic labor stockade: noun
A type of prison camp. Staanz spent nine cycles at one.

mank: noun
Gunk or dirt.
—As in 'You're getting mank everywhere.'—Jool admonishing Chiana

marjols: noun
A Hyneirian delicacy resembling escargot or snails; highly desired and sought after by Rygel.

masata: noun
The Acquarian word to mean prophesied savior and deity. They believed Rygel was the Masata; the Masata is to rise up and lead the Aquarans to the light, as it is written in the *Timbala*.

'May rah'nalan be with you': phrase
Zhaan uses it often as a farewell, analogous to 'May the Force be with you.'

Maxilian Pilayder Day Parade: event
A loud event.
—As in: 'My head is pounding like a Maxilian Pilayder Day Parade.'—D'Argo

mela nerve: noun
A nerve in a Nebari's back. Pressing on it can paralyze a Nebari from the neck down, either temporarily or permanently.

mellett: noun
An undesirable food (presumably like liver).
—As in: Rygel: 'What am I? chopped mellet?' Zhaan: 'I can stomach mellet.'

metra: measurement
Unit of length equivalent to a kilometer.

micropollen: noun
An allergen released by Delvian buds. If not contained, they can cause Zhaan's plant-life form to begin to flower and potentially die.

microt: measurement
Roughly equivalent to a second. Three microts are equal to four seconds; and 180 microts equals four minutes. Can also represent any short amount of time
—As in: 'I'll be there in a microt!'

midmeal: noun
Lunch.

milon: noun
Another large unit of length; it is about the equivalent to a mile.

Mippippippi: noun
D'Argo's version of 'Mississippi.'

mivonks: pronoun
A slang term for part of the male reproductive anatomy; literally, testicles. Often used in a derogatory sense, as in, 'being led around by his mivonks.'
—As in: 'Don't get your mivonks in a twist.' —Chiana to D'Argo

morna lobes: pronoun

A mushroom with hallucinogenic properties. It is found on the Royal Cemetery planet. Of the four caps on each mushroom, three will get you high and one will kill. There is no way to tell which lobe is fatal.

nano-moment: measurement

A millisecond.

narl: noun

A term used by the Clansmen, meaning a baby, birth or life.
— As in: 'A new narl emerges,' 'The narl is in your stomach?' or 'I can't birth a narl? I don't want a narl? I hate narls? I'm still a narl myself!' — Chiana

nashtin cleansing pills: noun

Yellow-colored gel capsules, they are an Uncharted Territories cure for the hangover. When giving them to Chiana, Rygel said, 'Take one immediately, one at the midmeal, and one if needed that night.' It should be noted that if one takes all the pills at once, they have the side effect of making the person hyperactive and very talkative.

nawnuk: noun

A belittling expression.
— As in: 'Tell the nawnuk he's clear to come over, but remind him we're in no mood for *yotz*.' — D'Argo

negnik: noun

A species of weak or helpless animal.
— As in: 'You couldn't kill a negnik.'

neural block: noun

A contrivance devised to block out memories. The Ancients possibly placed one in Crichton's mind to hide the wormhole technology information they gave him. Even the Aurora Chair could not penetrate beyond the block.

neural stroke: noun

A fighting technique used by Scorvians. Matala used the 'neural strike' to knock Aeryn out, which alerted her to the fact that Matala wasn't truly an Ilanic.

nixar: noun
A word used by the Clansmen on the Royal Cemetery planet meaning girl, gal, or babe.

nogelti crystals: noun
Valuable stones extracted from the body of the budong and used as currency.

nonk: noun
A male Tavlek.

nurfer: noun
Peacekeeper derogatory slang, roughly meaning 'dork,' 'geek,' or 'loser.' One of the Peacekeeper commandos, after being told Chiana was Crichton's non-reg server, decided Crichton was not as big a nurfer as he originally thought.

numdas: noun
Guts, *mivonks*.
— As in: 'You haven't got the numdas to put me in the chair!' — Crais to Scorpius

off-worlder: noun
Litigaran term for non-Litigarans.

ointment of yuvok: noun
A preparation of salve or ointment used to clear breathing passages. D'Argo slathered some on Rygel's nose to relieve the pressure when he was suffering from *klendian flu*. According to Rygel, it smells like 'trat.'

onlux: element
The Denean term for *clorium*.

onnyxi play partners: noun
Green dolls belonging to Staanz. She uses them for fuel. They particalize and they levitate. She has collected over nine million of them and expects to someday sell them for a small fortune.

orican: noun

A Luxan holy person who has acquired strong spiritual powers and is revered by Luxans as a 'seeker of truth.' The worthiness of potential 'attendants' is tested by the orican putting their hand into the individual's chest.

ossoh scent: noun

A potent perfume-like substance, available in varying levels of pheromones. According to Rygel, the stronger varieties can make just about anybody irresistible.

otec lamp: noun

A Luxan light fixture commonly used to ward off evil.

others: noun

Sykaran reference to the enslaving Peacekeepers, who return every half-cycle.

pantak jab: noun

A highly effective Peacekeeper hand-to-hand combat maneuver that can take someone down with one blow.

paralitic embalming agent: noun

A gas used by the Scarrans on prisoners that they want to dissect whilst they are still alive, it preserves living tissue without harming the brain. Combustible at a very high temperature; heavier than air, it sinks downward.

paraphoral nerve: noun

A part of Sebacean physiology. The nerve removes toxins from a Sebacean's body. If damaged, it does not regenerate and toxins will build up until death. A tissue graft from a genetically compatible donor is the only way to repair it.

pa'u: noun

The word for a Delvian priest, or priestess, as in Pa'u Zotoh Zhaan.

pellish venker: insult

A personal slur.
—As in: 'A hiccup is involuntary, you pellish venker!'

pewnkah: adjective

A derogatory term meaning 'low-life.' Kcrackic asked Rygel and Zhaan if they'd seen a ship, 'run by a pewnkah named Staanz.'

photo-gasm: noun

A reaction that occurs in Delvian females when exposed to ionic radiation, such as that accompanying solar flares. Stimulating the photosynthetic reaction and causing a rush of an endorphin-like compound, photo-gasms can last for several hours. Zhaan explained this light-induced orgasmic sensation was one of the gifts of the Delvian Seek.

pleeb: verb

Damn, *frell*.
—As in: 'Don't tell me . . . you're not a pleebing ocular physician.'— Aeryn

pleek: verb

Term meaning 'mess with' or sneak.
—As in: 'Stop pleeking around!'—Chiana when the Clansmen were playing a bit of cat and mouse with her

plock: noun

A Tavlek term meaning crap or *dren*.
—As in: 'Sick of hearing your plock.'

postral: noun

Similar to a pustule except it is filled with acid. Postrals are found on dead *budong* flesh.

premno: directional vector

The middle part of a set of coordinates.
—As in: 'Delta 6, premno 9, lurg 8.'—Zhaan

priestan: noun

Acquarian religious figure.

probakto: noun

An expletive meaning 's.o.b.' or bastard. Normally used in a positive sense.
—As in: 'Go, you lucky probakto.'—Rygel's farewell to John

prowt: adjective

An unpleasant odor.
— As in: 'Smells like prowt.'

prowser fruit: noun

A fruit, possibly Luxan or Hyneirian in origin.
— As in: 'Rygel's invited us to Hyneiria? Thought I could do some work with my hands ... plant some prowser fruit, make some wine.' — D'Argo

quadra helix: noun

A form of the DNA double helix that can pinpoint a species' origin using a genetic map. Extracted from the eye by Namtar.

rha: noun

Delvian god, goddess, or prophet.

raslak: noun

An alcoholic drink that can be served warm. Chiana drank this on the Gammak base.

rauliss buds: noun

A species of flower.
— As in: 'What have you guys been thinking all this time? What? She was out picking rauliss buds while all the other mean Peacekeepers did all the really nasty stuff?' — Chiana

regenerative fascia membranes: noun

Part of Zhaan's physiology.

ribbonhole: noun

Denean for a wormhole.

ritual of passing: noun

Utilizing the spiritual link between an Orican and her attendant to allow the Orican to pass on into the next life.

ritual of renewal: noun

Utilizing the spiritual link between an Orican and her attendant to allow the Orican to become young again. When Nilaam realized the strength of D'Argo, she performed the ritual of renewal instead of the *ritual of passing*.

samat: measurement
Unit of length, equivalent to a foot.

sanctity root: noun
A twisted root whose tree forms the heart of the Delvian temples. It is toxic to everyone but Delvians. It represents the purity in thought and intent of the spiritual teachings of the Delvian missionaries. Those grown on the new moon of Delvia are stunted and twisted because of the toxic atmosphere.

scope: verb
A Clansman term meaning 'to realize' or 'to decide.'

sentra chords: noun
Sounds made by D'Argo's *shilquen* that were heard when he was tuning it up in 'DNA Mad Scientist' (1.09).

servicers: pronoun
A derogatory term meaning 'non-combatant.' D'Argo used this term for Pilot and the DRDs.

sevva crystals: pronoun
A crystalline substance used in the creation of high-explosives. A reasonably high proportion of sevva crystals is required for a strong blast. These crystals, combined with other ingredients (including *jelifan fire paste*), made up the bomb Rygel used in his attempt to kill Captain Durka.

shadow depository: noun
A secure bank that asks no questions of its patrons. It is heavily guarded and defended. The one visited by the crew was run by Natira.

shai: interjection
An Acquarian admonition meaning 'enough' or 'go away'.

shalton: adjective
A slang term.
—As in: 'I've been screaming my shalton head off!'—Rygel to Pilot

shakit sonnet: noun
Luxan songs or poetry often written about great Luxan warrior heroes.

shilquen: noun
A Luxan four-stringed instrument. D'Argo handcrafted the one that he played for Pilot in an unspoken apology for chopping off one of his arms.

shivvies: noun
Underwear.

shlock: verb
To take a *dren*.

'single infection stage': noun
Early stage in the development of an *intellent virus* during which the virus can only infect one host at a time. During this stage, it can move from one host to another, preferring to kill its previous host, if possible.

sisil's ass: noun
Cultural equivalent of 'rat's ass.'
—As in: 'I don't give a sisil's ass.'

slim duck: noun
D'Argo's mishearing of 'slam dunk.'

smoked prongo sinew: noun
A cooked animal preferred by Nebaris.

snarking dellot: insult
A disparaging insult.
—As in: 'Let us out of here, you snarking dellot!'

snurch: verb
To steal or borrow without permission.

solar reflective flare wrap: noun
A wrap that protects the wearer from intense light.

sonic cowl: noun

A subterranean pit on the Royal Cemetery planet involved in a rite of passage. Chiana managed to remain in the cowl for more than fifteen microts to beat the previous record.

sonic howl: noun

A device used in one of the Clansmen's rites of passage. The person is suspended upside down between two cement blocks and vibrations are created by humming.

sonic net: noun

A net sustained by the humming sound of a being's voice used to cushion their fall. Used by the Clansmen when dropping into the *sonic cowl*. Also used by Peacekeepers during aerial combat training.

spirit painting: noun

A type of artwork created by Delvians for recreation. The painting captures the true spirit of a being. Zhaan painted Rygel'sportrait which, according to Rygel, resembled his most honored ancestor, Rygel the Great.

squag: noun

An intensely hot substance or location. A slang term used in reference to hell.
— As in: 'It's hotter than squag!' — Rygel

stiv: verb

To urinate.
— As in: 'Peacekeeper officer can't even stiv without his troops.' — Sikozu; Scorpius replies that he can stiv on his own.

stomata

The yellow tinting on Zhaan's skin, used for the transportation of water.

tadek: noun

A part-strategy, part-gambling game played on an illuminated board, by moving crystals around with Y-shaped clear rod and building holographic columns. Holograms appear above the game upon completion of certain moves. The object seems to be to make piles of the crystals. A keen sense of bluffing is involved. Rygel claims to be a master player of the game and this appears not to be an idle boast. He played against the Zenetan pirates and intentionally lost to Kcrackic to misdirect the pirate crew.

'take the stone': phrase

On the Royal Cemetery planet, when the Clansmen reach the age of twenty-two cycles, rather than grow old and deformed by radiation, they deliberately cease the *sonic howl* part way into the leap into the *sonic cowl* which disinigrates the *sonic net* and causes them to hit this rocks below resulting in instantaneous death. This is called 'taking the stone.'

tankas: noun

The tentacles on D'Argo's face.

tannot root: noun

A plant grown and harvested on the planet Sykar. Tannot root is edible, although chemicals within the root generally cause the individual to become submissive and unquestioningly compliant. This effect can be averted by the insertion of the rare Skykarian worm into the anatomy, which consumes the toxins. A small percentage of individuals are naturally immune to the effect of the root. The root also has an interesting effect on Hyneirian physiology. Certain chemicals present within the Hyneirian digestive system combine with the root to produce an explosive effect—most bodily excretions, sweat, urine and so on, become explosive. It is this latter property of the root that makes it of interest to the Peacekeepers. The root can be processed to create *chakan oil*, which powers Peacekeeper weaponry.

telemissions: noun

Litigaran term for electronic messages.

temporal dislocation: noun

The result of being exposed to a black hole. It causes the individual to shift back and forth in time.

terleum mollusks: noun

One of the delicacies Rygel enjoyed on the Command carrier.

thoddo: noun

A careless unintelligent person.
— As in: 'John, you thoddo!'—Aeryn to John when he sits on the control panel causing Moya to yaw violently, while he is trying to have a heart-to-heart chat with Aeryn.

Timbala: noun

The holy book of the colonists of Acquara. It was written in ancient Hyneirian and chronicled how the people of Acquara came to be left on that planet. Over time, it was embellished upon by the priestans of Acquara in a selfish attempt to raise their own importance and gain power over the tribe. It also contains star charts and the story of the *masata*.

tinked: adjective

Slang term used in an expression of disbelief.
— As in: 'Are you tinked?' —Chiana

toeska: noun

Derogatory term.
— As in: 'If those toeskas have left us, after all I've done for them.'

topographic bioprint: noun

A map depicting concentrations of different life forms on a planet. Pilot made one of Acquara to pin down Crichton, D'Argo and Rygel's location.

trad: measurement

The universal unit for power. 200 trads is the equivalent to 80% of a transport pod's power capacity.

tralk: noun/adjective

A disparaging slang term, which seems to be slightly versatile in use, but mainly to mean, trollop, slut, or amoral individual.
— As in: 'That little tralk!' — Aeryn on discovering that Chiana had taken her Prowler, and on the Royal Cemetery Planet, Chiana says to Crichton that she is his tralk (kneels in front of Crichton) only in his dreams.

trankass: noun

A derogatory noun
— As in: 'You've killed us all, you trankass.'

transit madness: noun

A possible result of unprotected exposure to space. Aeryn was concerned that Crichton's odd behavior in was due to this because of his experience while at the breakaway Sebacean colony planet.

trasnik: noun

Analogous to 'jerk' or 'idiot.'

—As in: 'I know I've been a trasnik.'—D'Argo, when apologizing to Chiana

trat: noun

A foul, unpleasant smelling substance. After being slathered with *ointment of yuvok*, Rygel remarks 'smells like trat'.

'Tre bawk ru fishalto chenias prami bukeko': phrase

D'Argo growled this to Rygel, and Chiana said it meant, '. . . something about his corpse . . . and a bodily function.'

treblin side: noun

Refers to one side of a ship, the opposite of hammond side. Crais told Talyn to turn to his treblin side to get away from solar flares.

trelkez: noun

A small, bird-like creature with multiple heads. Their brains are considered to be extremely tasty, so there is a direct relationship between the number of heads and the value of the trelkez in question. Trelkez should be eaten raw.

trellon oil: noun

A sensual stimulant, used to enhance the conjugal experience. Sold by Liko.

triple quadra hent: noun

A game move in *tadek*. Difficult to set up and implement.

tronkan shrill singer: noun

Rygel refers to a two-headed one of these, and compares it to the noise of the Paddac Beacon.

tuperadinous cellulose tissue: noun

Part of Zhaan's physiology.

twinning: noun

A technology developed by Kaarvok. It replicates beings down to the exact DNA level.

union tattoo: noun
Luxan symbol of courage, honour and loyalty.

ucuz: noun
An extremely hot alien fruit, which looks much like an apple, found on
  many of the planets in Tormented Space.

valtek: noun
Sebacean equivalent of 'Freeze!' or 'Don't move!'

veen: noun
Nebari expletive.

vector gappa: noun
A vector on a spatial grid, defined as by longitude and latitude.

vigilar: noun
Traitor, deviant or double-dealer.

voojo: noun
Akin to 'mojo.'
—As in: 'Bad voojo.'

votch: verb
To vomit.
—As in: 'Votched up all my second lunch.'

wakket hole: noun
Sebacean slang for mouth.

walteran fountain: noun
Spectacular, pluming water source.

wanta chant: noun
Delvian chant to assist work efficiency.

welnitz: noun
Expletive utilized by Furlow.

yave of the yuvo: noun
Equivalent of 'state of the art.'

yotz: noun
Hyneirian expletive.

yotzah: exclamation
Hyneirian pleased exclamation.

y'tal cavity: noun
A Leviathan's very first neural cell, the y'tal cavity is a particularly rich source of high quality toubray tissue. Once the y'tal cavity has been severed, the Leviathan's Pilot and all its functions will cease to operate

zacron: noun
Unit of measurement used by the Zenetan pirates.

zannet: noun
Personal insult indicating treachery, possibly Sebacean in origin.

zelka: noun
Red alert, an emergency indicator.

zangblats: noun
Curse word, equivalent of 'dammit', 'phooey.'

zy-limbron: noun
Banik term for limbo or purgatory.

Notes

Introduction

1   Also its most expensive to produce, weighing in, by Season 4, at approx. $1.2 million per episode (www.watchfarscape.com).
2   Noah Porter made the point—in email correspondence—that *Farscape* fans aren't actually looking for closure. They are, in fact, looking for further openings and expansions of the story itself. So, rather than complete closure, I am referring here merely to the closure of one story arc (the Crichton/wormhole story).
3   We should establish that wormholes and black holes are not the same thing, although they emerge from similar traditions of cosmological theorizing. An astronaut traveling through a black hole, as Stephen Hawking explains in *A Brief History of Time* (1988), would be turned into 'spaghetti' due to the tremendous opposing gravitational forces on both her head and her feet (effectively pulling her apart); an astronaut traveling through a wormhole could theoretically survive, although we can't predict exactly what the physical conditions would be inside of a wormhole, given that we can only postulate their existence within either 'phase space' (many-dimensional space used by mathematicians, especially chaos theorists) or 'imaginary time' (multi-axis time used by mathematicians for complex equations).
4   WatchFarscape.com, 'Project Docu.Dot', interview, 2004 (http://docu.watchfarscape.com/).
5   Ibid.
6   *Farscape* fits within the 'space opera' genre because much of its action takes place on board a spaceship, Moya; it breaks with the conventions of that genre because its 'ship' is actually a living being, and its conflicts often stem from personal rather than technological causes. As David Pringle points out in his essay 'What Is This Thing Called Space Opera?', the label is probably a modification of 'horse opera,' a denigrating term used to describe the rash

of Western films that emerged during the 1930s, many starring a young John Wayne (Pringle 2000).

7   This pairing is made less controversial by the fact that Sebaceans are genetic relatives of Humans, and thus appear exactly alike. Sebaceans do have some physiological differences; they are extremely sensitive to heat, and their bodies have different apparatuses for filtering out toxins. They also experience pregnancy differently (which I will discuss further in the chapter that focuses on Aeryn Sun).

8   Colonel Wilma Deering, Buck's aggressive, no-nonsense, female counterpart (who also happens to be a blonde knockout)—and eventual love interest—is perhaps an interesting proto-version of Aeryn Sun.

9   This is an interesting modification of *Star Trek*'s 'universal translator' idea; rather than a device that aurally translates alien languages into English, the translator microbes 'colonize at the base of the brain' ('Premiere,' 1.01), triggering some manner of Chomskyan language acquisition that allows the recipient to decode multiple languages. Crichton's dadaist reply when he learns of this—'colonize . . . brain?'—alludes to a sense of colonial discomfort that *Star Trek*'s universal translator does not produce.

Chapter I

1   My emphasis.

2   It is significant that Crichton calls D'Argo, Rygel, and Zhaan *people* here rather than *aliens*. Even from the show's beginning, Crichton appears sensitive to alternative conceptualizations of 'human.' Thanks to my colleague, Matt Rohweder, for reminding me of this.

3   These 'multiple reality' theorems draw upon several different discussions within theoretical cosmology, including Richard Feynman's 'sum over history' debates, which argue that particles have an infinite number of histories—that is, directions—within various kinds of space: primarily *not* within the three-dimensional space that we perceive. Stephen Hawking also suggests in his work (1993) that, within a singularity (i.e., the center of a black hole), it would be possible to reverse time's direction—as well as the direction of entropy—and therefore 'remember' the future rather than the past. However, it would be impossible to report what this experience might be like, given that the gravitational forces of the black hole would tear you apart. At any rate, *Farscape*'s wormhole thesis depends upon quantum theory, which Einstein rejected (saying,

famously, 'God does not play dice'), and its claims that the laws of physics break down within singularities (like the kinds found in black holes and, perhaps, wormholes).

4   Leviathans are bred by the Peacekeepers in captivity, and Leviathan Pilots are fitted with a device, called a control collar, that places them firmly under the manipulation of the Peacekeepers.

5   Viewers should note that these credits are replete with ideological codes: the phrase 'United States of America' flashes across the screen several times, both as disembodied text (in Seasons 3–4), as a label inscribed on Crichton's module (Seasons 1–2), and in synechdochal form as the fictional IASA (International Aeronautics and Space Association) patch on Crichton's astronaut uniform.

6   No translation is ever given for this term. Perhaps 'Gamma,' as in the fourth such version of this base (or the fourth base of its kind in Peacekeeper space?).

7   Most of these definitions come from the superb online resource, 'The Farscape Encyclopedia' (www.farscape-1.com), created by Adam Garcia and Tom Wilkerson.

8   Carlen Lavigne notes that Crichton's 'relationship' with this gun is actually a fairly complex one: 'Forced by circumstance to perform cold acts, Crichton displaces emotions and becomes attached to his weapon, becoming distinctly agitated when it is missing or taken' (Lavigne: 2005).

9   Extra-Vehicular Activity, which includes space walks and lunar walks.

10 This competency is undermined by the show's constant deployment of Crichton as an evolutionarily inferior being. D'Argo is much stronger than him; Zhaan has both psychic and merely psychological abilities that Crichton doesn't; Aeryn has extensive military training that he can never match; and Rygel can breathe underwater (as well as digest three stomachs' worth of food). This 'de-skilling' (I think the labor studies term works here, given the capitalist overtones that influence SF as a genre) of Crichton is meant to compensate for his physical attractiveness and cultural mobility—with audiences—as a heterosexual white male.

11 As a queer male spectator, I find many of the masculine interactions on *Farscape* intriguing. The show often places male characters in situations of intense physical and emotional vulnerability, and it also—often playfully—presents affection between male characters. Playful versions of this include the sexually loaded quips between D'Argo and Crichton, although their relationship also exhibits a much deeper level of intimacy. Generally, it is Crichton who is placed in positions where his masculinity becomes refractory or deconstructable—such as the scene in 'The Hidden Memory' (1.20)

where Crichton lies vulnerably in Stark's lap, or multiple episodes in which Crichton visibly cries (although it is always, of course, just a single, manly tear).

12 *Farscape*'s use of puppetry provides all sorts of interesting opportunities for theoretical discussion around bodies, prostheses, alienation, and the like—discussion that this book will gesture towards, but not engage in substantively due to space (pardon the pun) constraints.

13 The Sebaceans' obsession with 'contamination' and genetic purity is a bit of a clumsy nod towards Nazi concerns around miscegenation during the Second World War. Clearly, the Sebaceans in general, and Peacekeepers specifically, are being strained through the recognizable ideological marker of Nazism in order to establish them as uncritically evil. Like stereotypical tropes of Russian communism, the Nazi mythos has been repeatedly and unselfconsciously mined by SF literature as a benchmark for intergalactic villainy.

14 My emphasis.

15 'The Farscape Encyclopedia' reports that one cycle is equal to 0.96 solar years.

16 I apologize for the repetition, but I thought that Zhaan's individual 'citation' of each character in this episode—just before her death—provided an ideal framework for introducing the qualities that make each character engaging and coherent.

Chapter 2

1 In her essay 'Cyborgs to Companion Species' (2004), Haraway uses dogs as an example of a companion-species existing in a 'co-constitutive relationship' with humans. Tracing their probable evolution from wolves, she notes that a beneficial human/wolf relationship emerged as a result of mutual cooperation and sensitivity. If the wolves were calm enough, they 'could get a good meal near human habitations' (Haraway 2004: 305), and if the humans were equally tolerant of the wolves, they could utilize the wolves' protective capabilities. Domestic dogs now depend upon humans to help raise their pups, while wolves have no problem raising their own pups in the wild.

2 We should note that Pilot and Moya are among the most nurturing and sensitive aliens within the show, and yet they are also the least sexually embodied.

3   Anne Balsamo, in *Technologies of the Gendered Body* (1996), discusses the ways in which popular media such as women's magazines transform celebrity pregnancies into spectacular events. Generally, these events are seen as 'life-changing' for the new mothers involved, and celebrity women offer testimonials about the magic of childbirth (and how their bodies 'magically' bounce back, via an expensive personal trainer, only a few months later). Such celebratory narratives deliberately ignore the fact that these women are receiving some of the world's best prenatal care, and that this care somehow emerges free of race or class issues. Balsamo notes that 'while more than 82 percent of white women receive early pregnancy care, only 61 percent of Hispanic women and 60 percent of Black women [do]' (1996: 103), not to mention the fact that low-income mothers are often used in potentially dangerous medical drug trials. The fact of the matter is that expensive NRT tend to work *for* certain women (like celebrities), and work *upon* other women (such as poor mothers).

4   Although all of the characters are worried about Talyn's weapons, they seem remarkably unconcerned by the pulse pistols that they carry around (and fire) on a daily basis. In this way, the show gets to defer anxiety around destructive weaponry onto an alien being (Talyn) who is then destroyed, while their own use of deadly arms gets rationalized away.

5   Creed also notes that 'in outer space, birth is a well-controlled, clean, painless affair. There is no blood, trauma, or terror' (1990: 129). This sterility seems to act as a containment of the deliberate materiality of childbirth, the organic chaos of it, which patriarchally inflected visions of the future see as an obsolescence related to the mother's body (and so eliminate the body altogether).

6   Moya's choice to let Talyn destroy himself comes to be seen, by the show's characters, as an example of superior reasoning. She is able to view the situation from a utilitarian perspective, and she understands that Talyn's death is 'the best thing' for everyone. In this sense, Moya's protective maternal instincts are only useful when they apply to her crew.

7   I feel as if my own subjectivity as a queer male writer has been conspicuously absent during this discussion of women's reproductive issues. It is not my intent to hijack what is a very specific and politically charged series of debates in order to provide some interesting metaphorical contrast to my discussion of SF narratives. I do believe that media depictions of pregnancy affect public thinking about reproductive issues, and that problematic depictions of pregnancy—as seen in many SF programs—often place women's autonomy in jeopardy by suggesting that, in the future, we will

either a) not need the mother's body at all, or b) that her body will be even more strictly regulated by technological interventions. As someone who is most often judged by what I 'do' (or what people think I 'do') with my body (as opposed to what I would be 'doing' if I were straight), I do perhaps have some understanding of what it means to be divested of bodily ownership and reduced to one's own biological functions.

8   It is perhaps telling that Crichton, ever the curious ethnographer, never bothers to ask Pilot if he has a name other than 'Pilot,' and never gives him a nickname

9   The Relgarians appear to be another technologically advanced race whose talents have been conscripted by the Peacekeepers. The militarization of science in *Farscape* continually suggests that there is no such thing as 'pure scientific' knowledge—that all empirical productions of knowledge can be utilized by a much larger war machine in the services of colonization and destruction. When Crichton finally admits to being afraid of what his wormhole knowledge could do in the wrong hands, Einstein tells him that 'fear is the correct response.' *Farscape* thus has no ostensibly peaceful blanket organization like the United Federation of Planets to regulate technology on a galactic scale. All technical knowledge within the show is potentially deadly.

10 Both Butler and Haraway have become known for 'inaugural' concepts: Butler for her discussions of gender performativity in the early 1990s, and Haraway for her conceptualizations of the cyborg in the mid-1980s. Both have also spent the last ten to fifteen years trying to expand upon and complicate these concepts, and have done much crucial work outside of these 'celebrity' areas, but they continue to be discussed, cited, lauded, and criticized for ideas that they will never adequately be able to explain.

11 Academia has a way of 'sexing up' concepts by apparently politicizing them, while actually divesting them of much of their *specific* political value in order to make them universally attractive and cross-disciplinary. An example of this is the discipline/debate of Postcolonial Studies, which academics will merrily continue deconstructing for the next few decades, while third world feminists and writers in exile actually engage in human rights struggles. It has become quite normal to hear of generous federal grants being awarded to doctoral research that focuses on postcolonial political issues, writing, and other cultural production. But it is a lot less common to hear about third world labor unions, women's organizations, smaller NGOs, and other vital social programming being funded by universities. Clearly, we need to complicate these 'big name' academic disciplines by dividing them into their specific

political investments, and remember that an academic's 'postcolonial studies' is often an activist's 'third world studies.'

12 In this sense, we have to understand that the violence depicted by televisual SF narratives can be even more upsetting than the intra-human violence that we might watch on *NYPD Blue* or *CSI*, because spectators are being made to believe that alien deaths aren't supposed to matter. We don't have to grieve these deaths. This is the type of western philosophical detachment, the rationalization of graphic murder, that has framed and contributed to unnecessary military interventions throughout the world, as well as genocidal practices 'somewhere else' that could not have persisted without the cooperation of powerful western nations. It isn't just about puppets and fake aliens — it's about the ghostly erasure and 'fakening' of people, of ungrieveable lives.

Chapter 3

1 We can easily think of them as a trinity as well, with Scorpius representing the paternal principal (who must educate Crichton), John himself representing the son, whose most profound lessons are also the most painful, and D'Argo standing in as a kind of Luxan holy spirit who balances John's innocence with Scorpius' selfishness. I don't make any detailed eschatological readings of *Farscape* in this book, but the show could definitely support such readings.

2 Interestingly, neither D'Argo nor Scorpius professes to believe in any unifying concept of God, or even a deity of any sort. The difference between them is that D'Argo translates this nihilism into compassion, locating the spiritual within his friends, while Scorpius chooses to embrace negation for its own sake, choosing to do whatever he wishes since the universe — as he sees it — has no guiding moral framework.

3 My use of 'subaltern' here is cautious and qualified. I am working alongside Gayatri Spivak's definition of the term, which she in turn borrows from Gramsci — he originally used it loosely to refer to the proletariat. In interview, Spivak admits that '[the] word, used under duress, has been transformed into the description of everything that doesn't fall under a strict class analysis. I like that, because it has no theoretical rigor' (1990: 141). She elaborates on her use of the term in *A Critique of Postcolonial Reason* (1999), linking it more concretely with third world women, and by using it here I am certainly recontextualizing it. I will further recontextualize it in the next chapter when I discuss Chiana and Aeryn.

4 An exception to this occurs in the episode 'Won't Get Fooled Again' (2.15), when Crichton encounters a dream-version of his ill mother—who died of cancer six years earlier. 'This is cruel . . . it's cruel,' John whispers, to no one in particular. Ironically enough, the only person who hears him—other than the ruthless Scarran interrogator—is the neural clone of Scorpius, who has become his constant companion. Like Stark, Scorpius acts here as a confessor figure.

5 From Leslie Fenberg, *Stone Butch Blues* (1st edn), San Francisco: Firebrand Books, 1993.

6 'Non-white' as a term is imprecise and insufficient, but it's difficult to find a simpler and less ambiguous one for the purposes of this discussion.

7 Because this is *Farscape*, we have to follow a tragic moment with a comic one. After D'Argo resolves to use his last remaining moments to assault the Scarrans in a hail of pulse rifle fire, Crichton says: 'Show 'em who daddy is.' This of course refers back to an Abbott and Costello exchange between Crichton and D'Argo in the episode 'Thanks for Sharing' (3.07), when Crichton says 'D'Argo, tell him who his daddy is,' and D'Argo replies—with perfect intonation—'I'm your daddy.' In D'Argo's final scene, as he relentlessly opens fire on the Scarran infantry, we hear his epic and wonderfully appropriate last words: '*I'm your daddy!*'

8 Deleuze clarifies this point in *Nietzsche and Philosophy* when he says that 'according to Nietzsche, it has never been understood that the tragic = the joyful. This is another way of putting the great equation: to will = to create. We have not understood that the tragic is pure and multiple positivity, dynamic gaiety' (1983: 36).

9. I'm not sure if 'Banik' has any grammatical connection with 'bannock,' which is a kind of bread that is central to many aboriginal traditions, and which perhaps represents something along the lines of a colonial signifier. If this is the connection that the show is trying to make, then it does so rather clumsily, and at the cost of eliding the specific histories of Native American/First Nations communities.

10 I am not trying to deride Hegel here, and understand perfectly well that he was probably the most comprehensive of all western philosophers, demonstrating a truly astounding breadth of knowledge and talent for philosophical synthesis. Just as Marx didn't simply *invert* Hegel's dialectic in order to create a Marxist-materialist view of history, but rather incorporated and recombined Hegelian thought, I'm certainly not advocating that we should forget Hegel. I trust that, like Nietzsche, he has an expansive sense of humor.

11 In this instance as well, Crichton #1 (or perhaps it's Crichton #2) has a moment of physical intimacy with Stark. In 'Icarus Abides' (3.15), when Stark is easing John's pain, he gently places his hand on John's forehead. As he starts to move his hand, John actually clasps it, holding it there. Stark simply nods. Once again, their communication is silent and secretive, something that not even Aeryn gets to overhear.

12 Scorpius admits that he's willing to die in order to cripple the Scarran empire ('We're So Screwed III,' 4.21), and does die symbolically when Grayza shoots him ('Sacrifice,' 4.02).

13 We learn in this episode that Scorpius was part of a Scarran breeding program, the first infant to survive a Scarran/Sebacean sexual pairing, although his birth ends up killing his mother. It is no wonder that Scorpius constantly entwines creation with destruction, since he emerged from such traumatic circumstances, and was effectively born from a murder.

14 Robinson also points to the figure of the wounded white male, whose 'male power is actually consolidated through cycles of crisis and revolution, whereby men ultimately deal with the threat of female power by incorporating it' (2000: 9). Crichton provides an excellent example of the wounded white male, whose body is constantly being assaulted even as it gains sympathy and cultural currency with every blow.

15 Here I am referring to Derrida's evolving notion of iterability, which 'alters, contaminating parasitically what it identifies and enables to repeat 'itself'; it leaves us no choice but to mean (to say) something that is (already, always, also) other than what we mean (to say), to say something other than what we say *and* would have wanted to say, to understand something other' (1988: 62). For Derrida, this is actually a pretty clear definition. Iterability is the original contamination of the self/other boundary, the spectral predecessor behind every claim to an 'origin,' and the ghost of the un-uttered statements that construct everything that we say.

16 I'm not trying to market a theory here, although, if I was, I would call it 'Alien Theory' and pitch it to Routledge right away.

Chapter 4

1 Given the Peacekeepers' predilection for racist models of 'evolution,' I am using this term quite critically.

2 See such examples as *Star Trek: Voyager*'s Seven-of-Nine (the ideal cyborg female), *Star Wars*' Princess Leia (seemingly competent, but

still in need of fairly regular rescue), Talia of *Babylon 5* (psychically powerful, but rarely placed in any sort of combat situation, and usually given a 'mystical' role as counselor), and *Star Trek: The Next Generation*'s Beverly Crusher (the doctor, valued more for her gentle bedside manner than for her biomedical advice).

3   Interestingly, Velorek's character is inflected here with traditionally feminine characteristics (much like John, who seems 'feminine' when his own fairly complicated gender is diffracted by Aeryn's female masculinity). Velorek is nurturing to Pilot, he protests (and seems emotionally affected by) the death of Moya's original Pilot, and he pushes Aeryn towards physical intimacy rather than simple 'recreation.'

4   The 'proper' Freudian term for the psychoanalytic interviewee. Like Deleuze and Guattari, I prefer this to 'patient.'

5   Freud and Lacan (less so) also try to encapsulate all of human behavior through the mythical frame of the Oedipus complex—a frame whose efficacy is quite severely criticized by Deleuze and Guattari in both *Anti-Oedipus* (1983) and *A Thousand Plateaus* (1987).

6   This triptych also resembles the proto-Celtic tripartite goddess, appearing throughout several different mythological cycles, who encompassed the archetypal personalities of Maiden, Mother, and Hag (or Crone).

7   Aeryn both rejects and refashions the Sebacean god Djancaz-bru in this moment, vowing that ' I will now make a deal with anyone . . . to save this baby' ('Prayer,' 4.18).

8   Aeryn is offered an overdose of sleeping pills by another patient, who turns out to be a Scarran spy. Given that they are primarily a conquering and competitive race, having evolved from massive reptiles into reptilian bipeds, the Scarrans demonstrate a remarkably sophisticated model of psychological torture here. On a simplified historical spectrum, the Scarrans seem to fit into a model of Italian fascism—complete with brownshirt brute squads—while the Peacekeepers have a military-autocratic society that, as mentioned earlier resembles the 'height' of Nazi Germany.

9   Aeryn first claims that the baby belongs to Velorek, and then switches tactics, saying that s/he belongs to a secret operative that she met while she was an assassin. The interrogator, however, is relentless, and keeps digging until she admits that 'it was Crichton. It was always Crichton.'

10 In *The Phenomenology of Spirit*, Hegel outlines the master/slave relationship as a play between production and differential consciousness (1998). The master owns the slave, and hence owns the slave's labor (or 'labor power,' in Marxian terms)—but the mas-

ter can't own the generative power of the slave. The slave's consciousness, which allows her to create a material reality—a product—belongs to her, and only her. The master owns, but the slave creates; hence, the slave is actually conscious, while the master is effectively enslaved to the logic of capital. Eventually, the slave's developing consciousness will reach a nadir point, and the slave will revolt. Although Marx is often said to 'invert' Hegelian principles, this is really the functional core of his proletarian theory.

11 Kierkegaard also takes up this problem, claiming that Christianity is at heart a tragic worldview because it is based upon an unendurable contradiction—that Christ is both (hu)man and God, that he dies and is then resurrected, and that the disciples who sealed his doom are the same people who transmit his theological message.

12 Two other inter-sexed characters, the male/female Rygel and the male/female D'Argo who live aboard the alternate-reality Moya, are also killed (by Scorpius and Crichton, significantly) in 'Prayer' (4.18). Unlike Hubero, whose death can be grieved because s/he is 'real,' these characters are presented within a matrix of gender schizophrenia. Their bodies are almost psychotic in their admixture of masculine and feminine 'parts.' Crichton does seem to genuinely regret killing them, but there is still the disturbing and palliative notion that, somewhere, this gender-dysphoric reality exists, and that killing these aliens isn't the same as killing the authentic D'Argo or Rygel.

13 Even Crichton, at times, seems to take a certain amount of covert sexual pleasure in his proximity to Chiana. Her physical advances please him, flatter him, even as he attempts to ignore and disavow them.

14 When Zhaan chooses to share 'unity' with Crichton, the experience seems more mystical then erotic—but when she is under the influence of powerful sunlight (as in the pulsar light in 'Crackers Don't Matter' (2.04), she is definitely in the throes of orgasmic pleasure. Her erotic life seems to be very evenly divided between sensual fulfillment and sexual desire.

Chapter 5

1 In 'Won't Get Fooled Again' (2.15), Zhaan appears as a psychotherapist intent on analyzing John. When he points out that 'you're blue,' she asks him: 'Do you have a problem with people of color?' I use 'schizoanalysis' here in the sense that Deleuze and Guattari

'define' it (do they ever define anything?) in *Anti-Oedipus*, as a process of psychoanalysis that goes beyond the Oedipal formulation by acknowledging the 'schizophrenic' nature of our bodies and their relationship to production (Deleuze and Guattari 1983). Could Zhaan have any connection to Prof. Theodor Zaahn, the German philosopher and professor of theology, who offered revisionist critiques of the New Testament? Hmm . . ..

2   Judith Butler reiterates this when she says, in *Bodies that Matter*, that 'it is important to resist that theoretical gesture of pathos in which exclusions are simply affirmed as sad necessities of signification' (1993: 53).

3   In Lacan's terminology, the *objet-a* or *petit-objet-a* is the object of lack, the signifier (a person, place, thing) that stands in for the primordial lack caused by separation from the mother.

4   A fluid vital to Moya's inner workings.

5   'All production is at once desiring-production and social production. We therefore reproach psychoanalysis for having stifled this order of production, for having shunted it into *representation*' (Deleuze and Guattari 1983: 296).

6   'Crime is nought but the means Nature employs to attain her ends in regard to us and to preserve the equilibrium so indispensable to the maintenance of her workings . . . it is not for man to punish crime, because crime belongs to the Nature that possesses every right over us' (Sade 1968: 734).

7   Sade's many lurid and imaginative worlds, as well as his unerring focus on the body and its rootedness in sexuality and violence, are doubly ironic when we consider that he wished fervently to be buried in an unmarked grave.

8   At the end of the episode, Aeryn proves that turnabout is fair play when she tells John that she also did some exploring of her own. 'You were in my shoes, I was in your pants,' she tells him teasingly.

9   S/M scenarios and costumes are a recurring theme within *Farscape*. Scorpius is the original dominatrix (or penetratrix). Later, in the episode 'Won't Get Fooled Again' (2.15) both Rygel and Zhaan appear in Crichton's fever-hallucination as leather-wearing power tops. Rygel even has a cat-o'-nine-tails whip. Zhaan offers to teach Crichton the 'left handed Latvian Rodeo torture,' and Rygel proclaims: 'All of you bitches out now! Crichton is mine!'

10 Part of Aeryn's impetus for fleeing to Valdon is her refusal to be a sexual object, either for Crais or for Stark. When Stark tries to comfort her, she recoils, telling him: 'I swear that I will spear the last eye you have left. Do you know what makes you so much worse . . . is the fact that you think you're so much better than him. Always pressing . . . against me. Stealing looks. Get out of here.'

11　At the end of the episode, after Crichton has died, Aeryn wraps a blanket around his body and holds him. 'The Choice' (3.17) reverses this position, with Crichton using his body as a blanket, wrapping his arms around Aeryn, and holding her.

12　Up until now, we have understood '*dren*' to be the signifier for shit. But this episodes prevents us with a new word—'*shlock*.'

13　Food and 'dietetics,' that is, a regimen for eating and living, have long been the concern of western philosophy. In both *The Use of Pleasure* and *Care of the Self*, parts two and three of his trilogy on sexuality and morals, Foucault points out that the ancient Greeks had wildly complex and comprehensive methods for eating and exercising. Plato, Hippocrates, and Galen all mention strict regimens for eating, and sex is often seen as something that interferes with the alimentary process (Foucault 1990).

Chapter 6

1　Gwyneth Jones points out that these explanations are often structured as 'accidents' within SF narratives, when in fact they are calculated events. 'Characters complaining about the new zoning system or about their tiresome family relationships 'accidentally let slip' vital clues about the way the future or distant world is run' (1999: 10).

2　As an example of this: Chiana mentions her brother, Nerri, in passing (in Season 1), and he is then revealed in Season 2 to be the leader of the Nebari resistance.

3　Linguists are still arguing over exactly what Saussure meant by his cryptic terms *langue, langage,* and *parole*. He describes *langue* as 'a storehouse filled by members of a given community through their active use of speaking (*parole*), a grammatical system that has potential existence in each brain, or more specifically in the brains of a group of individuals. For language is not complete in any speaker; it exists perfectly only within a collectivity' (Saussure 1983: 13). In the simplest sense, then, *langage* is the 'language faculty' in general, *langue* is the specific language through which speech-acts are interpreted, and *parole* is the speech-act itself, as well as the context(s) around it.

4　This echoes Derrida's point in *Limited Inc.* that 'the limit of the frame or border of the context always entails a clause of nonclosure. The outside penetrates and thus determines the inside' (1988: 152). Like Althusserian ideology, which also has a permeable inside/outside (or can be seen as nothing *but* outside), language and outer space within *Farscape* share a 'nonclosure,' a violability where the laws of physics seem to break down (as in a naked singularity).

5 There are certain words in the show, such as *frell*, *dren*, *mivonks* (a personal favorite of mine, as in, 'D'Argo was being led around by his *mivonks'*), *fahrbot*, *hezmana* ('hell'), *yotz* (seemingly a combination of *frell* and *dren*) and *tralk*, which the translator microbes don't seem to work on. In spite of that fact, various speech communities all seem to know what these words mean, which suggests that they're a part of some common intergalactic trading language. Alternately, they could be derivations of a language that was relatively far-reaching within the Uncharted Territories, such as Sebacean or Scarran. I doubt this, though—when we hear Aeryn speaking in her own language in the episode 'A Human Reaction' (1.16), Sebacean appears to be composed mostly of vowels; and the Scarrans have their own unique curse-words.

6 Several characters have visible difficulty in understanding English. Aeryn struggles with pronunciation, sounding out crucial words like '*worm-hole*' (it sounds more like *wourrm-huoll* when she says it ['Unrealized Reality,' 4.11]). When Sikozu first meets Crichton (in 'Crichton Kicks,' 4.01), she asks him to recite the English alphabet because her 'brain cannot tolerate translator microbes.'

7 Austin's many rules for ensuring the 'felicity' of performatives—that is, for outlining the proper contexts that help to create truth value—are also, we must remember, rules for producing a specific politico-ethical environment. Miller states that 'the ultimate goal of Austin's work is to secure the conditions whereby law and order may be kept' (Miller 2001: 57).

8 Lévinas uses this term in *Totality and Infinity* (1969) to describe the one who 'witnesses' the encounter between Self and Other, although this witnessing in itself produces a paradox—which Paul Célan summarizes in his aphorism: 'Nobody bears witness for the witness' (Célan 2006: 'Ashglory,' 178).

9 Variations on this verb (and noun) include: *frelnik* (which translates roughly as 'idiot'), *frell you* (explanatory), *got frelled, frelled up*, and the imperative *frell*! Interestingly, although Crichton frequently uses this verb, he often resorts to 'screwed' when he is under physical duress. As an example, in the episode 'Lambs to the Slaughter' (3.20), after Scorpius threatens to kill him if he doesn't cooperate, John replies (only half-jokingly): 'Oh grasshopper, you are so screwed.' Grasshopper is Crichton's nickname for the 'real' Scorpius; Harvey is his nickname for Scorpius' 'neural clone,' who lives inside Crichton's unconscious.

10 In *Limited Inc* (1988), Derrida admits that *différance* is not an explan-
    atory term in itself, but only one of several incomplete terms (like
    trace, impurity, iterability) that point, catachrestically, to a cultural-
    linguistic phenomenon that has no proper name.

11 This phrase spawned the name of a popular chat board within
    Farscape's fan community, which served as an instrumental forum
    for discussion when the Save Farscape movement was at its height.
    The board is still operational, and encompasses multiple conversa-
    tional threads—everything from continuing strategies for getting
    the show resurrected, to discussions about the *Peacekeeper Wars*
    miniseries.

12 Austin linked the performative value of the speech-act with its
    'truth value,' meaning both the honest intent of the speaker and the
    facticity of the statement itself. When language was, on the con-
    trary, *not* 'used seriously, but [rather] in ways *parasitic* upon its
    normal use'—such as through modalizing registers like sarcasm
    and irony, or within alienating climates like poetry—then the
    resulting speech acts became '*etiolations* of language' (Austin 1980:
    22).

13 Aeryn reverses this interpellation in 'The Hidden Memory' (1.20),
    when Crais is trapped in the Aurora Chair. Leaning close to him,
    she asks 'does this contaminate you, Crais?'

14 Later in this episode, we discover that Aeryn had a romantic rela-
    tionship with Velorek—although she ultimately turned him in to
    the Peacekeeper authorities so that she could regain her old mili-
    tary position as a Prowler pilot.

15 Like many other actors on *Farscape*, both Gigi Edgley and Paul
    Goddard, who play Chiana and Stark, have conspicuous Austral-
    ian accents. The cast of the show is primarily Australian, which is
    yet another thing that makes *Farscape* unique. Although 'imported'
    shows filmed in Australia are fairly common on American prime-
    time television, Australian shows with Australian actors are not
    common at all. In some sense, Ben Browder's (Crichton's) Ameri-
    can accent sounds 'alien' in comparison to the Australian accents
    all around him. This is never more apparent than when Browder
    attempts to affect the Sebacean 'pan-British' accent, which sounds
    either playfully mimetic and self-conscious, or painfully incorrect,
    depending upon how you listen to it.

16 In the episode 'Scratch 'n' Sniff' (3.13), Chiana is subjected to a bio-
    chemical process (meant to drain a particular hormone from her
    body) which inadvertently imbues her with precognitive powers.
    She is able, for a few seconds, to 'slow down' an event as it hap-
    pens—realistically, this must mean that she perceives the event
    happen much faster than normal, which is why it appears to occur,

for her, in slow motion. Either way, it seems to be a violation of general relativity, unless we determine that her *reactions* are simply much faster than those of an ordinary Nebari (or human). Immediately after one of these 'slow downs,' Chiana loses her eyesight temporarily, and these periods of blindness grow longer each time she 'uses' the ability (although the power seems, most often, to use her instead).

17   Chiana generally wears a form-fitting outfit, something like a cross between a leather bodice and body armor, which resembles the standard 'alien female' outfit within most SF genres. The character Jool wears quite a similar one, which leads us to believe that either a) only Delvians wear loose-fitting clothing, or b) we are meant, very much, to notice these women's exposed bodies, since that exposure metaphorically suggests a deeper psychological 'nakedness' and vulnerability.

18   Crichton is surprisingly forceful with Chiana, on several different occasions. Given that both Aeryn and D'Argo are physically superior to him, and Zhaan possesses as-yet-undefined psychic powers of defense (she is also trained in some combat techniques), it seems clear that Chiana is the only character whom Crichton has a chance of physically overpowering.

19   John remains, to my knowledge, the only character who doesn't, at least once, call Chiana a *tralk*. In fact, John has endearing nicknames for everyone on board Moya: Chiana is *Pip*; Zhaan is *Blue*; D'Argo is *Bro*; Jool is *Princess*; Sikozu is (my favorite) *Sputnik* (also a clear gesture towards the 'communist threat' within most American SF traditions, and a nod towards her stereotypical and inevitable betrayal of the crew); Rygel is *Buckwheat* or *Sparky*. These names have, as well, an organizing principle behind them, in that John is using his own language to rename the characters, to re-interpellate them within a human context that he understands.

20   In 'The Ugly Truth' (2.17), Crais calls Stark 'the Banik slave' upon meeting him again; Stark corrects him by saying 'my name is Stark.' For Crais, Stark has no subjectivity other than his status as an indentured servant. For Stark, exceeding the limits of this interpellation remains a painful struggle.

21   One example that I don't have room to discuss is the act of 'translation' that occurs during the title credits from Seasons 2–4. Ideographic alien characters first appear on the screen, and then are stylistically translated into the actors' names. It is a minor representation, but one of many occurring simultaneously during the visually complex credit sequence, which encodes a great deal of ideological data about the show.

Chapter 7

1 Grayza's transition to motherhood is interesting, and I'm not sure why it isn't given any more attention within *The Peacekeeper Wars*. The audience is startled to see a pregnant Grayza aboard the Peacekeeper Command carrier, and, as with all expectant mothers on television, the camera fetishizes her growing stomach—but we learn very little about the father of Grayza's baby (whom she assassinates) or her personal motivations for having a child in the first place. In the end, Grayza agrees to make peace with the Scarrans 'for the sake of our children,' with little D'Argo Crichton serving as a living metaphor for children across the galaxy—but we learn almost nothing about her own unborn child.

2 The Ancients test John in order to see if he is worthy of holding the wormhole-technology information, which will be implanted directly into his subconscious. This is the first invasion of John's mind; the second will be perpetrated by Scorpius.

3 Nestor Garcia Canclini also notes, in *Hybrid Cultures*, that the ability to 'cross space' within North America is closely connected to capital—perhaps even more so than racial/ethnic background. 'There is no identity document in the United States; it is replaced by the driver's license and the credit card, that is, by the capacity to cross space and by participation in a game of fiduciary contracts between North American citizens' (Canclini 1995: 233).

4 In her article 'Closing Ranks: Racism and Sexism in Canada's Immigration Policy,' Sunera Thobani notes that racist immigration policy in Canada is currently moving towards a point where almost all people of color are forced to justify their existence within the paternalistic boundaries of the (white) country. 'By tying immigrants to 'cultural' and 'social' diversity, all people of color become constructed as immigrants. This racialized use of the category 'immigrant' identifies all people of color as part of the same problem which immigrants of the future ... are said to represent' (Thobani 2000).

5 In *Capital, Vol. I*, Marx states that, in the industrial factory, 'every organ of sense is injured to an equal degree by artificial elevation of the temperature, by the dust-laden atmosphere, by the deafening noise, not to mention the danger to life and limb among the thickly crowded machinery, which, with the regularity of seasons, issues its list of killed and wounded in the battle of industry' (1995: 262).

6 Crichton corrects himself by saying that 'missing family' was the worst part, but one has to admit that lack of toilet paper would be equally upsetting.

7 This phrase, 'more human than human,' also recalls the slogan of the Tyrell Corporation in *Blade Runner*—a company that builds robots, called 'replicants,' who are invested with a storehouse of memories pilfered from real human subjects.

8 It seems only fitting that John should lose his virginity to Chiana, since she they have always had such a playfully erotic relationship, a slightly incestuous brother/sister connection that is nevertheless traced with the hint of desire. In some sense, Chiana's inauguration of Crichton's manhood, the way in which she ushers him into masculinity, queers him just a bit.

9 This gives a whole new cast to the term 'the local is global.' What happens when the global is recast as the galactic? Is SF, then, the very embodiment of globalization literature, with the galactic appearing as the new global?

10 Like Marx's characterization of the German paper mill as 'a mechanical monster whose body fills whole factories, and whose demon power, at first veiled under the slow and measured motions of his giant limbs, at length breaks out into the fast and furious whirl of his countless working organs' (1995: 235).

11 John's insistence that 'wormhole weapons don't make peace, they don't even make war,' recapitulates arguments around nuclear deterrence, wherein 'nuclear' countries possess a negative rather than a positive power in nuclear weaponry—the ability to destroy each other ultimately, which they must then agree to never use.

12 We should remember that gays and lesbians who stage political protests, or even simply those who flout the visual parameters of conventional gender difference, are also often placed within the realm of extremism. On the contrary, Ellen DeGeneres, who has an award-winning talk show, has won the hearts of millions precisely because she *doesn't* draw attention to her lesbian sexuality in any way.

13 Belize also observes that the longest, highest note in the American national anthem, always fetishized and rendered within the operatic, is also impossible for the majority of the population to reproduce—like a living wage, or social assistance, or even basic 'human rights' (read: white rights), it is consummately beyond their reach.

Bibliography

Acker, Kathy. *Bodies of Work*. London: Serpent's Tail, 1997.
——. *In Memoriam to Identity*. New York: Grove Press, 1990.
——. *Empire of the Senseless*. New York: Grove Press, 1988.
——. *Blood and Guts and High School*. New York: Grove Press, 1978.
Alkon, Paul K. *Science Fiction Before 1900: Imagination Discovers Technology*. New York: Twayne, 1994.
Althusser, Louis. 'Ideology and Ideological State Apparatuses', in Ben Brewster, ed. and trans. *Lenin and Philosophy, and Other Essays*. London: New Left Books, 1971.
Armitt, Lucie. *Contemporary Women's Fiction and the Fantastic*. London: Macmillan, 1999.
——. *Theorising the Fantastic*. London: Arnold Press, 1996.
——. *Where No Man Has Gone Before: Women and Science Fiction*. London: Routledge, 1990.
Attebery, Brian. *Decoding Gender in Science Fiction*. New York: Routledge, 2002.
Austin, J.L. *How to Do Things With Words* (2nd edn). Oxford: Oxford University Press, 1980.
Bacon-Smith, Camille. *Science Fiction Culture*. Philadelphia: University of Pennsylvania, 2000.
Bakhtin, Mikhail. *Speech Genres and Other Late Essays*, Caryl Emerson and Michael Holquist, eds. Austin, TX: University of Texas Press, 1986.
——. *Rabelais and his World*, Helen Iswolsky, trans. Bloomington, IN: Indiana University Press, 1984.
——. 'Discourse in Life and Discourse in Poetry: Questions of Sociological Poetics', in Ann Shukman, ed. *Bakhtin School Papers*. Oxford: RPT Publications, 1983: 5–30.
——. *The Dialogic Imagination: Four Essays*, Michael Holquist and Caryl Emerson, eds. Austin, TX: University of Texas Press, 1981.
Balsamo, Anne. *Technologies of the Gendered Body: Reading Cyborg Women*. Durham, NC: Duke University Press, 1996.
Baudrillard, Jean. *Simulacra and Simulation*, Sheila Glaser, trans. Ann Arbor, MI: Michigan University Press, 1994.
Ben-Tov, Sharona. *The Artificial Paradise: Science Fiction and American Reality*. Ann Arbor, MI: Michigan University Press, 1995.

Bhabha, Homi. *Nation and Narration*. New York: Routledge, 1993 [1990].

Booker, Keith. *Monsters, Mushroom Clouds, and the Cold War: American Science Fiction and the Roots of Postmodernism, 1946–1964*. Westport, CN: Greenwood, 2001.

Bourdieu, Pierre. *Distinction: A Social Critique of the Judgement of Taste*, Richard Nice, trans. London: Routledge, 1984.

Brossard, Nicole. *Mauve Desert*, Suzanne Harwood, trans. Toronto: McClelland and Stewart, 1998.

Butler, Judith. *Precarious Life*. New York: Verso Books, 2004.

——. 'Doing Justice to Someone', *GLQ*, vol. 7, no. 4, 2001: 553–91.

——, John Guillory and Kendall Thomas, eds. *What's Left of Theory?: New Work on the Politics of Literary Theory*. New York: Routledge, 2000.

——. *Excitable Speech*. New York: Routledge, 1997.

——. *Bodies that Matter: On the Discursive Limits of* Sex. New York: Routledge, 1993.

Byers, Michele. 'Gender/Sexuality/Desire: Subversion of Difference in Construction of Loss in the Adolescent Drama *My So Called Life*', *Signs*, vol. 23, no. 3, 1998: 711–34.

Canclini, Nestor Garcia. *Consumers and Citizens: Globalization and Multicultural Conflicts*, George Yudice, trans. Minneapolis: University of Minnesota Press, 2001.

——. *Hybrid Cultures*. Minneapolis: University of Minnesota Press, 1995.

Carlberg, John. '*Farscape* Post-Mortem', unpublished conference paper, 2005.

Célan, Paul. *Breathturn*, Pierre Jorris, trans. Los Angeles, CA: Integer Press, 2006.

Cixous, Helene. 'The Laugh of the Medusa', in Robyn Warhol and Diane Price Herndl, eds. *Feminisms: An Anthology* (2nd edn). New Brunswick, NJ: Rutgers University Press, 1997.

Cobley, Paul, ed. *The Routledge Companion to Semiotics and Linguistics*. New York: Routledge, 2001.

Creed, Barbara. '*Alien* and the Monstrous Feminine', in Annette Kuhn, ed. *Alien Zone: Cultural Theory and Contemporary Science Fiction Cinema*. London: Verso, 1990: 128–44.

Croucher, Sheila. *Globalization and Belonging*. Lanham, MD: Rowman and Littlefield, 2004.

Davis-Floyd, Robbie and Joseph Dumit. *Cyborg Babies: From Techno-Sex to Techno-Tots*. New York: Routledge, 1998.

Deleuze, Gilles. *Nietzsche and Philosophy*, Hugh Tomlinson, trans. New York: Columbia University, 1983 [1962].

—— and Felix Guattari. *A Thousand Plateaus*. Minneapolis: University of Minnesota Press, 1987.

——, ——. *Anti-Oedipus*. Minneapolis: University if Minnesota Press, 1983 [1977].

Derrida, Jacques. *Of Grammatology*, Gayatri Spivak, ed. and trans. Baltimore: Johns Hopkins University Press, 1997.

——. *Limited Inc.* Evanston, IL: Northwestern University Press, 1988.

Fallon, Kathleen Mary. *Running Hot.* Melbourne: Sybylla, 1989.

Fiske, John. *Reading Television.* London: Methuen, 1978.

Fitzgerald, F. Scott. *The Great Gatsby.* New York: Scribner, 2004.

Foucault, Michel. *Discipline and Punish: The Birth of the Prison.* New York: Vintage, 1995 [1977].

——. *The History of Sexuality Vol I.* New York: Vintage, 1990 [1978].

——. *Vol 2: The Use of Pleasure*, Robert Hurley, trans. New York: Vintage, 1990 [1983].

——. *Vol 3: The Care of the Self*, Robert Hurley, trans. London: Penguin, 1990 [1984].

Franklin, Sarah. 'Fetal Fascinations: New Dimensions to the Medical-Scientific Construction of Fetal Personhood' in Sarah Franklin et al., eds. *Off-Center: Feminism and Cultural Studies*, London: HarperCollins Academic, 1991: 190–205.

Freedman, Carl. *Critical Theory and Science Fiction.* Hanover, NH: Wesleyan University Press, 2000.

Gramsci, Antonio. *Selections from Prison Notebooks*, Derek Boothman, trans. London: Lawrence and Wishart, 1995.

Grosz, Elizabeth. *Space, Time, and Perversion.* New York: Routledge, 1995.

——. *Volatile Bodies.* Bloomington: Indiana University Press, 1994.

——. *Jacques Lacan: A Feminist Introduction.* New York: Routledge, 1990.

——. and Elspeth Probyn, eds. *Sexy Bodies: The Strange Carnalities of Feminism.* New York: Routledge, 1995.

Halberstam, Judith. *Female Masculinity.* London: Duke University Press, 1998.

Haraway, Donna. *The Haraway Reader.* New York: Routledge, 2004, especially 'The Cyborg Manifesto': 7–46 and 'Cyborgs to Companion Species: Reconfiguring Kinship in Technoscience': 295–318.

——. 'The Promises of Monsters: A Regenerative Politics for Inappropriate/d Others', in Jenny Wolmark, ed. *Cybersexualities: A Reader on Feminist Theory, Cyborgs, and Cyberspace.* Edinburgh: Edinburgh University Press, 1999: 314–67.

Harvey, David. *Spaces of Hope.* Edinburgh: Edinburgh University Press, 2000.

Hawking, Stephen. *Black Holes and Baby Universes.* New York: Bantam, 1993.

——. *A Brief History of Time: From the Big Bang to Black Holes.* New York: Bantam, 1988.

Hayles, Katherine N. *How We Became Posthuman.* Chicago: University of Chicago Press, 1999.

Hegel, G.W.F. *The Hegel Reader*, Stephen Houlgate, ed. Oxford: Blackwell Publishers, 1998.

Helford, Elyce Rae. '(E)raced Visions: Women of Color and Science Fiction in theUnited States,' in Gary Slusser and George Westfahl, eds. *Science Fiction, Canonization, Marginalization, and the Academy*. Westport, CN: Greenwood, 2002: 127–38.

Hill, Walter E. *Genetic Engineering: A Primer*. Amsterdam: Harwood, 2000.

Hippocrates. *Hippocratic Writings*,W.H.S. Jones, ed. and trans. London: Penguin Classics, 1983.

Holdcroft, David. *Saussure: Signs, Systems, and Arbitrariness*. Cambridge: Cambridge University Press, 1991.

Holquist, Michael. *Dialogism: Bakhtin and His World*. London: Routledge, 2002 [1990].

Irigaray, Luce. *This Sex Which Is Not One*, Catherine Porter, trans. New York: Cornell University Press, 1985 [1977].

Jackson, Rosemary. *Fantasy: The Literature of Subversion*. London: Methuen, 1981.

Jones, Gwyneth. *Deconstructing the Starships: Science, Fiction, and Reality*. Liverpool: Liverpool University Press, 1999.

Kristeva, Julia. *Interviews*, Ross Mitchell Guberman, ed. New York: Columbia University, 1996.

——. *Language—the Unknown: An Initiation into Linguistics*. New York: Columbia University Press, 1989.

——. 'Revolution in Poetic Language', [1974] in Toril Moi, ed. *The Kristeva Reader*. New York: Columbia University, 1986.

——. *Desire in Language*, Leon Roudiez, trans. New York: Columbia University Press, 1980.

Kuhn, Annette, ed. *Alien Zone: Cultural Theory and Contemporary Science Fiction Cinema*. London: Verso, 1990.

Kushner, Tony. *Angels in America, I and II*. New York: Theater Communications Group, 2003.

Lacan, Jacques. *Écrits*, Bruce Fink, trans. New York: W.W. Norton, 2002.

——. *Four Fundamental Concepts of Psychoanalysis*, A. Sheridan, trans. New York: W.W. Norton, 1977.

Landon, Brooks. *Science Fiction After 1900: From the Steam Man to the Stars*. New York: Twayne, 1997.

Lavigne, Carlen. 'Space Opera: Melodrama, Feminism, and the Women of *Farscape*', *Femspec*, vol. 6, no. 2, 2005.

Lay, Mary, et al., eds. *Body Talk: Rhetoric, Technology, Reproduction*. Madison WI: University of Wisconsin Press, 2000.

Lefanu, Sarah. 'Sex, Sub-Atomic Particles, and Sociology' in Lucie Armit, ed. *Where No Man Has Gone Before: Women and Science Fiction*. New York: Routledge, 1991: 178–85.

Le Guin, Ursula K., ed. *The Norton Book of Science Fiction*. New York: W.W. Norton, 1993.

L'Engle, Madeline. *A Wind in the Door*. New York: Farrar, Strauss, Giroux, 1973.

——. *A Wrinkle in Time*. New York: Bantam Doubleday, 1962.

Lévinas, Emmanuel. *Totality and Infinity*, Alphonso Lingis, trans. Pittsburgh, PA: Duquesne University Press, 1969.

Lingis, Alphonso. 'Deadly Pleasures', in Deepak Sawhney, ed. *Must We Burn Sade?* New York: Prometheus, 1999: 31–50.

Malmgren, Carl. *Worlds Apart: Narratology of Science Fiction*. Bloomington, IN: Indiana University Press, 1991.

Martin, Emily. 'The Fetus as Intruder: Mother's Bodies and Medical Metaphors', in Robbie Davis-Floyd and Joseph Dumit. *Cyborg Babies: From Techno-Sex to Techno-Tots*. New York: Routledge, 1998: 125–42.

Martin, Ed. 'Fresh Sc-Fi Fare Delivers the Fix', *Advertising Age*, April 12, 1999: 20ff.

Marx, Karl. *Capital Vol 1*. London: Oxford Classics, 1995.

Mendlesohn, Farah. 'Science Fiction in the Academies of History and Literature', in George Slusser and Gary Westfahl, eds. *Science Fiction: Canonization, Marginalization, and the Academy*. Westport, CN: Greenwood, 2002: 119–26.

Miller, J. Hillis. *Speech Acts in Literature*. Stanford, CA: Stanford University Press, 2001.

Minh-ha, Trinh T. *Woman, Native, Other*. Bloomington, IN: Indiana University Press, 1989.

Mitchell, John Cameron, dir. *Hedwig and the Angry Inch*. New Line Cinema, 2001.

Morley, David and Kuan-Hsing Chen, eds. *Stuart Hall: Critical Dialogues in Cultural Studies*. New York: Routledge, 1996.

Nietzsche, Friedrich. *Genealogy of Morals*, Horace Samuels, trans. London: T.N. Foulis, 1919.

——. *Thus Spake Zarathustra*, Thomas Common, trans. New York: Heritage Press, 1962.

Pinsky, Michael. *Future Present: Ethics and/as Science Fiction*. Danvers, MA: Rosemont, 2003.

Plato. 'The Timaeus', in Benjamin Jowett, trans. *The Essential Plato*. New York: Book Club, 1999.

pleasureandpain. 'Happy and Gay.' Crichton/D'Argo fanfic. http://www.fanfiction.net, accessed December 31, 2005.

Porter, Noah. '*Farscape*: Gendered Viewer Interpretations in Virtual Community', *Journal of Virtual Environments*, forthcoming 2006.

——. 'The Save Farscape Movement: Emotional Sustenance in an Internet Fan Movement', unpublished conference paper, 2005.

Pringle, David. 'What Is This Thing Called Space Opera?', in Gary West-fahl, ed. *Space and Beyond: The Frontier Theme in Science Fiction*. Westport, CN: Greenwood, 2000: 35–47.

Probyn, Elspeth. *Carnal Appetites: FoodSexIdentities*. New York: Routledge, 2000.

Roberts, Robin. *A New Species: Gender and Science in Science Fiction*. Chicago: University of Illinois Press, 1993.

Robinson, Sally. *Marked Men: White Masculinity in Crisis*. New York: Columbia University Press, 2000.

Rockmore, Tom. *Marx After Marxism*. Oxford: Blackwell Publishers, 2002.

Rose, Nikolas S. *Powers of Freedom: Reframing Political Thought*. Cambridge: Cambridge University Press, 1999.

Roy, Arundhati. *Power Politics*. Cambridge, MA: South End Press, 2001.

Sade, Marquis de. *Juliette*, A. Wainhouse, trans. New York: Grove Press, 1968.

——. *Justine, Philosophy in the Bedroom, and Other Writings*, A. Wainhouse, trans. New York: Grove Press, 1966.

——. *The 120 Days of Sodom*, A. Michelson, trans. New York: Grove Press, 1966.

Said, Edward W. *Culture and Imperialism*. New York: Vintage Books, 1993.

Sainsbury, Clare. 'Who Killed Farscape?', *StrangeHorizons.Com*. http://www.strangehorizons.com/2002/20021014/farscape.shtml.

Sandoval, Chela. 'New Sciences: Cyborg Feminism and the Methodology of the Oppressed', in Jenny Wolmark, ed. *Cybersexualities: A Reader on Feminist Theory, Cyborgs, and Cyberspace*. Edinburgh: Edinburgh University Press, 1999: 247–63.

Sarup, Madan. *Jacques Lacan*. New York: Harvester Wheatsheaf, 1992.

Sassen, Saskia. *Globalization and its Discontents*. New York: New Press, 1999a.

——. *Guests and Aliens*. New York: New Press, 1999b.

Saussure, Ferdinand. *Course In General Linguistics*, Roy Harris, trans. London: Duckworth, 1983.

Sawhney, Deepak, ed. *Must We Burn Sade?* New York: Prometheus, 1999.

Sedgwick, Eve K. *The Epistemology of the Closet*. Berkeley: University of California Press, 1990.

Slusser, George and Gary Westfahl, eds. *Science Fiction, Canonization, Marginalization, and the Academy*. Westport, CN: Greenwood, 2002.

Sobchack, Vivian. 'The Virginity of Astronauts: Sex and Science Fiction Film', in Annette Kuhn, ed. *Alien Zone: Cultural Theory and Contemporary Science Fiction Cinema*. London: Verso, 1990: 103–15.

Spivak, Gayatri C. 'From Haverstock Hill Flat to the U.S. Classroom, What's Left of Theory?', in Judith Butler, John Guillory and Kendall Thomas, eds. *What's Left of Theory?: New Work on the Politics of Literary Theory*. New York: Routledge, 2000: 1–39.

——. *A Critique of Postcolonial Reason*. Cambridge, MA: Harvard University Press, 1999.

——. 'Interview. Negotiating the Structures of Violence', in Sarah Harasym, ed. *The Post-Colonial Critic*. New York: Routledge, 1990: 138–51.

Suvin, Darko. *Metamorphoses of Science Fiction*. London: Yale, 1979.

Thobani, Sunera. 'Closing Ranks: Racism and Sexism in Canada's Immigration Policy', *Race and Class*, vol. 42, no. 1 (July 2000): 35–55.

Tucker, Robert C. *The Marxian Revolutionary Idea*. New York: W.W. Norton, 1969.

Westfahl, Gary, ed. *Space and Beyond: The Frontier Theme in Science Fiction*. Westport, CN: Greenwood, 2000.

Williams, Linda. *Porn Studies: A Reader*. Durham, NC: Duke University Press, 2004.

Zipes, Jack. *Fairy Tales and the Art of Subversion*. New York: Routledge, 1991 [1983].

Žižek, Slavoj. *Welcome to the Desert of the Real!: Five Essays on 11 September and Related Dates*. London: Verso, 2002.

Index